Philosophy as
Stranger Wisdom

SUNY series in the Thought and Legacy of Leo Strauss

Kenneth Hart Green, editor

Philosophy as Stranger Wisdom

A Leo Strauss Intellectual Biography

Carlo Altini

SUNY
PRESS

Cover: Thomas Fearnley, *Old Birch Tree at the Sognefjord* (1839), National Museum of Art, Architecture and Design, Oslo.

Published by State University of New York Press, Albany

© 2022 State University of New York

All rights reserved

Printed in the United States of America

No part of this book may be used or reproduced in any manner whatsoever without written permission. No part of this book may be stored in a retrieval system or transmitted in any form or by any means including electronic, electrostatic, magnetic tape, mechanical, photocopying, recording, or otherwise without the prior permission in writing of the publisher.

For information, contact State University of New York Press, Albany, NY
www.sunypress.edu

Library of Congress Cataloging-in-Publication Data

Name: Altini, Carlo, author.
Title: Philosophy as stranger wisdom : a Leo Strauss intellectual biography / Carlo Altini.
Description: Albany : State University of New York Press, [2022] | Series: SUNY series in the thought and legacy of Leo Strauss | Includes bibliographical references and index.
Identifiers: LCCN 2022005760 | ISBN 9781438490052 (hardcover : alk. paper) | ISBN 9781438490076 (ebook) | ISBN 9781438490069 (pbk. : alk. paper)
Subjects: LCSH: Strauss, Leo. | Philosophers—United States—Biography. | Philosophy, American—20th century.
Classification: LCC B945.S84 A66 2022 | DDC 109.2—dc23/eng/20220608
LC record available at https://lccn.loc.gov/2022005760

10 9 8 7 6 5 4 3 2 1

Contents

Acknowledgments		vii
Introduction		1
Chapter One	Marburg and Freiburg (1899–1924)	11
Chapter Two	Berlin (1925–1932)	37
Chapter Three	Paris (1932–1933)	65
Chapter Four	London and Cambridge (1934–1937)	85
Chapter Five	New York (1937–1948)	113
Chapter Six	Chicago (1949–1967)	147
Chapter Seven	Claremont and Annapolis (1968–1973)	195
Notes		215
Bibliography		225
Leo Strauss's Writings		225
Correspondences		232
Critical Literature		232
Index		239

Acknowledgments

This book would not have been possible without the generous support of the SUNY Press, especially of Michael Rinella, and without the kind attention of Kenneth Hart Green, director of the "SUNY Series in the Thought and Legacy of Leo Strauss." I am also pleased to thank the two anonymous readers who expressed a positive opinion on this research, and who suggested some very useful questions on which I could improve my work. I am also very pleased to thank those who have carefully followed the editorial work: Ryan Morris, Susan Geraghty, and Céline Parent. A decisive help in the editing of the book was also provided to me from some friends in Italy: Giovanni Cerro (Fondazione San Carlo, Modena), Marco Menon (University of Pisa), and Stefano Suozzi (Fondazione San Carlo, Modena). To Giacomo Mariani (University of Modena and Reggio Emilia) I owe a very important contribution for the English version of my text.

Even a book of philosophy, like any other book, shares the destiny of being "here and now," in an endless dialectic between the historical background and the search for truth, between being and becoming. Like our actions and thoughts, like our hopes and fears, even the books we write are conditioned by the relationships we have with the world, and above all with the people who live there with us. In some respects, all books (even those written by a single author) are "collective" works, because we are all, either consciously or not, the result of the manifold encounters between singularity and plurality, between the individual and the collective.

This consideration is true also for this book, which is in fact the outcome of a series of reflections and discussions that I have had the pleasure of experiencing over the years during many occasions, either academic or not. It is always difficult to make a list of the people to whom we are grateful for the generosity and the intelligence they shared with us on such occasions, but I would try to do it. For the challenging conversations and discussions, I am grateful to Dario Antiseri, Giulio Busi, Giuseppe Cambiano, Saverio Campanini, Michele Ciliberto, Raimondo Cubeddu, Vincent Delecroix, Costantino Esposito, Kurt Flasch, Luc Foisneau, Ute Heidmann, Philippe Hoffmann, Alfonso M. Iacono, Bruno Karsenti, Antonio Lastra, Josep Monserrat Molas, Michel-Yves Perrin, Stefano Poggi, Philippe Portier, Pier Paolo Portinaro, Wolfgang Reinhard, Jörg Rüpke, Francesco Tuccari. Most of all, I discussed Strauss's thought, with great pleasure, also with friends who unfortunately left us: here I wish to remember with gratitude Martin Bertman, Aldo G. Gargani, Stéphane Mosès, Elena Pulcini, Paolo Rossi, Salvatore Veca, Mario Vegetti, Franco Volpi.

I have discussed the contents of this volume in seminars and lectures with Antonella Besussi, Mauro Bonazzi, Dominique Bourel, Pierre Bouretz, Rémi Brague, Riccardo Caporali, Furio Cerutti, Pierpaolo Ciccarelli, Cristina D'Ancona, Giuseppe Duso, Adriano Fabris, Mauro Farnesi, Giovanni Fiaschi, Giovanni Filoramo, Francesco Fistetti, Simona Forti, Gian Franco Frigo, Alessandra Fussi, Carlo Galli, Marco Geuna, Alberto Ghibellini, Giovanni Giorgini, David Janssens, Irene Kajon, Heinrich Meier, Paul Mendes-Flohr, Davide Monaco, Francesco Mora, Michele Nicoletti, Corine Pelluchon, Stefano Perfetti, Mario Piccinini, Sergio Sánchez, Maria Michela Sassi, Emanuela Scribano, Eugene Sheppard, Daniel Tanguay, Nathan Tarcov.

However, I cannot fail to recall that my first steps about the thought of Leo Strauss, and more generally about the philosophical and political *modernity*, took place many years ago in the Department of Philosophy at the University of Florence, thanks to the suggestions made by Bruno Accarino and Carmelo D'Amato. Without that *incipit*, this book would not exist. Nor would it have been possible to delineate the purpose of this intellectual biography, which is the attempt to read the meaning of *philosophy* and some *philosophical questions* through the Straussian works, in order to understand more about the human condition in the modernity.

Introduction

> I have sworn faithfulness to a flag, with an oath that recites: *moriatur anima mea mortem philosophorum.*
>
> —Leo Strauss

It is never easy to classify a philosopher in an unambiguous way by using the labels—idealism/realism, right/left, laity/religion, theory/praxis—by means of which we commonly order complexity in the world. Philosophers, just like all human beings, have shades; they change ideas, shift perspectives, provoke, and are subject to events that reproduce the complexity of the world, even though inside the limits of their specific microcosm. Leo Strauss made no exception to this rule, although in recent decades some—friends and foes, disciples, and detractors—have attempted to build a compact and monolithic image of him. Strauss has been defined a skeptical philosopher, a reactionary in politics, a radical thinker, a nostalgic traditionalist, an ultramodern visionary, a fierce critic of modernity, a disciple of Machiavelli, a follower of Plato, an orthodox Jew, a Jewish philosopher, a right-wing atheist, and a left-wing atheist. Probably Strauss would have smiled in front of such classifying fury, which would have tickled his vanity and increased his irony. Nevertheless, he would not have been surprised. After all, he asserted that George Lichtheim was right when he defined him a hopeless reactionary and a victim of the indoctrination operated by his *Gymnasium* studies ("which I actually am," Strauss wrote to his friend Gershom Scholem on 6 September 1972: Strauss and Scholem 2001, 770). He also claimed, in numerous public conferences delivered in Chicago in the 1950s and 1960s, to be a Jew who had Judaism at heart. Meanwhile, in many letters he defined himself as a skeptical philosopher, who looked at religion from a rational point of view, as an object of study of political philosophy and as a useful, even necessary, foundation for the stability of social order ("I can not believe in God," Strauss writes to Gerhard Krüger on 7 January 1930: Strauss and Krüger 2001, 380. Cf. also Strauss and Scholem 2001, 742ff., 770–71).

These examples do not only concern ironical affectation, reticence, or the vanity of a thinker who, having reached fame, meant to surprise his interlocutors through the studied presentation of different facets of the same prism. Rather they reflect the complexity of his actual intellectual biography, entirely developed on a *frontier line*, to the point that it could be described as a permanent *exile*, a continuous peregrination of a stranger in a land that he knows but that does not belong to him. Always straddling across philosophy and politics—and split between Athens and Jerusalem—Strauss's exile did not consist so much in a concrete condition of life, but rather in a spiritual and existential category, in an interior space between expectation and experience, origin and destiny, possibility and necessity, desire and fulfillment. Indeed, we can speak about *exile* not in respect to a biological or cultural origin, but in respect to three different places of mind and heart—Berlin (modernity), Athens (philosophy), Jerusalem (Judaism)—the essence of which appears elusive and boundless. Politically and philosophically exiled from Berlin (due to his anti-historicism and anti-modernism) and interiorly exiled from Jerusalem (due to his skepticism), Strauss could not find a home in Athens either. Undoubtedly, for Strauss Athens represented both a *model of knowledge* and a *style of life*. However, besides being intrinsically impossible in modernity, the classical philosophical life still represented an existence on the brink of solitude and at the borders of the city. Indeed, due to his nature, the philosopher is a stranger at home; he belongs to the city without however completely identifying in the citizen, he is in exile when he is at home, in his own city.

Throughout his career—as a young researcher and as an established professor—Strauss never found a permanent home in any philosophical trend, political party, or academic context. He always sided with "criticism," especially of modernity, faced with which he elaborated a strategy of "return." In his youth, this took the form of a return to Judaism, in the 1930s a return to Maimonides, from the 1940s a return to Plato and classical philosophy. Strauss was against an eclectic or relativist perspective—two philosophical inclinations very far from his vision—but in favor of the awareness that there exists a difference between theory and praxis, or between philosophy and politics. He believed that knowledge is provisional, that the foundations of human life are a mystery, that the complexity of the world is irreducible, that philosophy is *search* for, not control of, truth. Moreover, throughout his life, Strauss always stood on the verge between different worlds: both German humanism and Zionist movements simultaneously attracted him, philosophy and Judaism, Plato and Nietzsche, Maimonides and Hobbes, Machiavelli and Lessing, Xenophon and Al-Farabi. Alone and exiled, Strauss experienced the twentieth century and its tragedies testifying to the "a-topical" and "timeless" character of philosophy. The question "what is philosophy?" is always present without any surrendering to trends and academic conveniences: indeed, philosophy moves between Scylla and Charybdis, between the here and now of human condition and the eternal dimension of the quest for truth. In its desire of truth, philosophy is a *stranger wisdom* that, in respect to the city's opinion, is always *atopos*. The philosopher is always a stranger interpreting the *thaumazein* as *search* of knowledge, even when this entails a critical eye towards shared opinions, consolidated by the social, political, and religious tradition to which one belongs. However, precisely for this reason, philosophy has an *intrinsically* edifying character, showing the primacy of contemplative life over practical life, of comprehension over engagement.

The concrete events of Strauss's life display his disconnection from the contexts he experienced, effectively showing his constant "exile" in respect to any given situation. In the 1920s, he studied philosophy in German universities while taking part in Zionist congresses. In Germany, he taught to grown-up Jews in small peripheral towns while—at the *Akademie für die Wissenschaft des Judentums* in Berlin—he engaged in specialized research on Spinoza, Hobbes, Mendelssohn, and medieval Islamic and Jewish philosophy. A Jew devoted to the Jewish cause, in Weimar Germany he gravitated towards reactionary modernism, due to his juvenile inclination for the connection between *political radicalism* and *philosophical conservatism*, which, from the late 1920s, became the connection between *philosophical radicalism* and *political conservatism* that accompanied him henceforth. He lived as an *émigré* in Paris and England—in miserable hotel rooms or small rented flats, poor and hassled by a constant uncertainty on his own and his family's future—without being able to have any real contact with local academic institutions, notwithstanding the praise he received for his works on Spinoza, Maimonides, and Hobbes. In England, he lived in total isolation, but he worked in solitude in

New York too, having few personal contacts as well as the obstacle of pertaining—he, a conservative opposed to any model of philosophy of history—to an institution such as the New School that waved cultural and political progressivism as its flag. In Chicago, he—a philosopher of classical inspiration—taught in the Department of Political Science, because the Departments of Philosophy and Classics did not want him among their faculty. A fierce critic of social positivism, he found himself teaching political science in the US, where a scientific inclination with an empirical and behaviorist perspective dominated social sciences. At the end of his career, he preferred leaving Chicago, where his colleagues ostracized him, to find refuge among friends in small academic venues such as Claremont and Annapolis. The list of such personal, professional, and intellectual situations lived by Strauss as a *stranger* could go on, but we may stop here. His internal solitude and his disconnection from the world were partly due to his hard character: discrete and introverted, timid and irritable, suspicious and clumsy, pedantic and obsessive, often coarse and aggressive in debates, haughty in criticism and academic relations. However, for the most part, they were due to the originality and independence of his philosophical position.

This intellectual biography has no apologetic intentions. The historian of philosophy has the duty to recover past thought, highlighting the historical aspect, concerning the concrete context of its origin, as well as the philosophical one, regarding its theoretical dimension. Indeed, the historian of philosophy has to consider the philosophical value of past doctrines, but, in the meantime, he cannot attribute to any of these doctrines an absolute degree of truth; otherwise, he abdicates his duty as a historian. It is a contradictory and infinite task—just like contradictory and infinite is the relationship between philosophy and history of philosophy—but not a useless one, despite it is today forgotten or believed obsolete among philosophical disciplines, the identity of which, in Western universities, is increasingly uncertain, indefinite, and hardly comprehensible. Well aware of the complexity of this theoretical issue, the present intellectual biography aims at offering a contribution to the knowledge on one of the greatest philosophers of the twentieth century. It is not about proving Strauss's arguments right, nor about defending his *oeuvre* from critics, nor about building a linear, coherent or polished image of his intellectual work. It is about trying to understand the questions that have guided his research and the contexts that he crossed, analyzing the most noteworthy points of his life as well as the main philosophical contents of his writings.

The purpose of this book is therefore twofold. On the one hand, it is to provide a contribution to historical knowledge on Strauss's intellectual biography; on the other hand, it is to understand the nature of philosophical and political questions by presenting his theoretical position. After all, the importance of Strauss's figure does not lie in his writing alone, but also in his being a witness to a plurality of issues and events that have accompanied philosophy and politics throughout the twentieth century and that surface in his work also when it treats Xenophon, Maimonides, Plato, or Al-Farabi. He lived and experienced German Judaism, Weimar and Nazi Germany, the crisis of philosophical and political modernity, the heritage of Enlightenment, the battle on scientific rationalism, the two World Wars, the Shoah, the establishment of liberal democracy, the diffusion of social positivism.

Aiming at historical and philosophical knowledge, this monograph does not give up on providing a key—as objective as possible—to interpret Strauss's work, which has undergone often unbearable forcing. Indeed, an unexperienced reader confronted with academic writing on Strauss would immediately ask who Leo Strauss really was. Was he possibly Felix Davarr, Abe Ravelstein's teacher, the *dandy* professor well connected inside the US administration described in *Ravelstein* by Saul Bellow, who concealed the figures of Strauss and Allan Bloom behind these pseudonyms? Was he perhaps the enemy of liberal democracy and modernity, against whom a number of American constitutionalists and social scientists have written some spiteful pages? Was he maybe a nostalgic lover of traditionalism, even a reactionary, who longed for Zion or for the return of an anti-egalitarian society like in Athens? Was he maybe the esoteric teacher accused by the *New York Times*? Or was he the teacher of American neo-conservatives? It is not necessary to be Strauss's loyal disciple to see how all the accusations fall apart and how they lift a fog that makes it almost impossible to distinguish the true outline of the issue. Some basic assertions can help us understand the fundamental outline of Strauss's figure. His hermeneutical equipment—far from being elitist or aristocratic, mystic or hermetic—relied on a *rational* conception of philosophical activity. Reticence in philosophical writing is a direct consequence of two distinct and converging phenomena in the history of political societies: persecution and education. This also confirms how his appeal to Greek classics did not have a traditionalist character, but rather sent back to an *anti-traditionalist* and *anti-conformist* conception of philosophy. Moreover, reticent writing favors the scholar's relationship with the great thinkers, represented as a path in the sand, covering which one leaves traces that others will follow, moving in his footsteps. This summarizes one of the great merits of Strauss's philosophical work: the ability to bring texts of the past back to life, giving them a new and in the meantime ancient voice, using history of philosophy as a means to recover forgotten philosophical questions. Thus, it becomes clear how Strauss's anti-modernism—grown out of his contempt for mass culture and bourgeois consumerism—did not imply any nostalgic shortcuts towards the past (and not even any theory on history's necessary decadence) because it concerned the recovery of classical philosophical categories (virtue, good, liberality, etc.), not of pre-modern illiberal and anti-egalitarian styles of life.

Of course, this does not mean that it is impossible to come across aporia, contradictions, and incoherence in Strauss's thought, nor that his philosophical and political positions stand above criticism. All the opposite. In this sense, for instance, we might consider the numerological theories that feature inside his reading of Machiavelli's *Prince* or the *Discourses* contained in the volume *Thoughts on Machiavelli* (1958), as they also feature in his introduction to the American edition (1963) of Maimonides's *Guide of the Perplexed*. We might also consider his inability to interpret concrete political pictures—not a minor problem for a political philosopher!—that we can trace throughout his life and especially in the Weimar years (during which he underestimated the danger represented by Hitler). Another issue that would deserve discussion is his category of "historicism," too indefinite. However, in this book, dedicated to Strauss's intellectual biography, it is fundamental to show in an organic and reasoned way, as objective as possible, whence his thought, his education, his research, his contacts, his discussions, his questions, his solutions, and his outcomes originated. This perspective, which may appear minimal, is not such. Instead, it implies the reading of a trajectory as articulated as Strauss's life through a precise interpretative key, by means of which it is possible to comprehend the complex theoretical, philosophical, and political kaleidoscope produced by his thought: *philosophy as stranger wisdom*. Of course, other interpretative keys would be relevant, interesting, and legitimate, but others, as well as the present book's author, have already undertaken them.

Strauss was a political philosopher, a historian of philosophy, and a theoretical philosopher with a Platonic orientation, but he was not a moral philosopher. In his vision of philosophy, moral virtue—self-discipline or self-control—was a relevant element to philosophize, but it was neither necessary nor sufficient by itself. The definition of philosophy as a style of life does not concern the philosopher's moral conduct, but the way he considers the hierarchy of goods, at the peak of which is knowledge. Indeed, the perfection of the human being consists in the *knowledge of the essences of all beings*, which is in the degree of theoretical knowledge represented by philosophy. It does not consist in the *knowledge of the styles of life*, imaginative knowledge, of lower degree, represented by politics. Thus intended, philosophy requires a conversion of the soul and consists in the search of the truth on being, animated by the conviction that only such search makes life worth being lived. Therefore, only philosophy is necessary and sufficient to lead to *perfection* and *happiness*. However, this is not the conviction that stands at the foundation of cities and political societies, which live in the reign of *belief* and *opinion* and have, at the peak of their hierarchy of goods, richness and honor, recognition and piety, luxury and pleasure, certainly not knowledge. The specific nature of philosophy lies in this *difference*, in its being *stranger wisdom* due to its *critical* character in respect to any established authority, any normative habit, any political myth, any social custom, and any religious tradition. The philosopher is and, at the same time, is not part of the city, because—to the opposite of the ruler—his *eros* is not directed towards the *demos*, but towards the search for knowledge, which is a disruptive factor for the shared opinions on which the city is based. Politics is characterized by principles of *prudence* in relation to tradition, myths, city's gods, social consent, and public and private interests. Facing these factors, philosophy remains, and must remain, indifferent: all this equates to recognizing and justifying the radicalism of philosophical thought in opposition to the moderate character of what we can ask of political life. From this point of view, in Strauss's thought, political conservatism is the other face of the coin of philosophical radicalism. Political philosophy cannot be conservative, given the fact that its ground is the awareness of the superiority of good and noble over traditional and ancient. After all, philosophy is aware that any political society is a peculiar society founded on a myth, which is belief, not knowledge. The *eros* for *sophia* guides the philosopher, but he is well aware of the necessities of material life, which he cannot simply disregard as low opinions. Instead, he must consider these necessities, since they constitute the "first" (in a chronological, not logical, sense) and necessary foundation of a political society. The "first" good, however, is not "supreme" good. Indeed, "logical" and "chronological" primacy do not coincide: philosophy, not politics, is the supreme good;

but politics, not philosophy, is the "first" good, because human beings can only live in society. Strauss asserted the primacy of theoretical life, but what has "logical" primacy (philosophy) does not have "chronological" primacy (which pertains to political life). Or even better: the assertion of the "chronological" primacy of political life does not erase the assertion of the "logical" superiority of theoretical life, precisely because theoretical life, in its being *virtue* and *happiness*, is the supreme good, although it is not the "first" good. In as much as he is a Platonic philosopher, Strauss is able to keep together, without contradiction, wisdom and moderation, utopia and conservatism, precisely because politics is not the realm in which it is possible to unconditionally achieve the truths of philosophy. Moderation is not a virtue of thought, since thought has to be radical. However, its public expression has to be moderate, due to the problems posed by persecution, social responsibility, and the necessities of material life. Therefore, there is an unavoidable difference between philosophy and politics, between philosophers and non-philosophers, as it appears clearly from the story of the pious ascetic narrated by Al-Farabi, which represents the way in which the Platonic philosopher presents the truths of philosophy to the rulers and citizens:

> Once upon a time there was a pious ascetic—a man who withdraws and abstains for the sake of mortification and abasement, or who habitually and knowingly prefers the painful to the pleasant. He was known as a man of probity, propriety, abstinence, and devotion to divine worship. In spite of this, or because of this, he aroused the hostility of the oppressive ruler of his city. Seized with fear of the ruler, he desired to flee. The ruler ordered his arrest and, lest he escape, caused all the gates of the city to be carefully watched. The pious ascetic obtained clothes which would be suitable for his purpose and put them on . . . Then taking a cymbal in his hand, pretending to be drunk, and singing to the tune of the cymbal, he approached one of the gates of the city at the beginning of the night. When the guard asked him "who are you?" he replied in a mocking vein, "I am that pious ascetic you are looking for." The guard thought that he was making fun of him and let him go. Thus the pious ascetic escaped safely without having lied in his speech. (Strauss 1957a, 320)

For these reasons, it is still worth reading Strauss's writings. Perhaps, precisely today—in the age of technoscience and globalization, of international commerce and artificial intelligence, of computer science and social networks—it is even more urgent to regain contact with an author who invites us to look at the most human aspects of our existence and of our history. Naturally, demonic and divine, selfish and altruistic elements coexist in this "human" character of our existence, because—and here Machiavelli and Shakespeare were right—our individual and social life always unfolds between the opposite extremities of good and bad, love and hate, nobility and misery, often without finding a solution. But human experience is not void of traits of greatness and care, responsibility, and beauty. The current planetary tyranny, governed by technology, anesthetizes and trivializes these traits, but it does not depoliticize them. Recovering this dimension of greatness and nobility, of responsibility and care is what is most urgent today, in order for what is human to survive, in an age in which humanism and philosophy at this point appear to have come to an end. An infinite endeavor, so it seems, even if we should not underestimate the fact that, despite the blinding brightness of technological innovation, there will always be groups of humanistic resistance, unsatisfied with the colorful beads passed off by global society as opportunities for happiness.

Chapter One

Marburg and Freiburg (1899–1924)

Childhood and Adolescence

Leo Strauss was born on 20 September 1899 in Kirchhain, a small rural village near Marburg. The family of his father Hugo Strauss (1869–1942) had been living in Kirchhain since the mid-nineteenth century, when Leo's grandfather Meyer Strauss (1835–1919) opened a wholesale shop of groceries and agricultural tools. This enterprise provided the family with a moderate economic welfare and made of Meyer, for about fifty years, one of the main members of the local Jewish community (then made up of around 150 families), which he regularly financed for the maintenance of the synagogue, also taking care of its administrative and political interests. In the family shop founded by Meyer—to whose memory Leo dedicated his second monograph, *Philosophie und Gesetz* (1935)—both his sons found employment: Hugo, the elder, and David. Leo's mother Jennie David (1873–1919) was also a native of Kirchhain. Like her husband Hugo, she made a lukewarm and customary practice of traditional Jewish religion, far from any reformed or liberal vision. Therefore, Leo was born in a middle-class Jewish family, culturally and politically conservative, socially recognized from the local community (Hugo was even nominated city councillor in 1902). Attention to the respect of religious observances and rituals was present in his family, but without a true knowledge of Jewish history or the meaning of those rituals: "I was brought up in a conservative, even orthodox Jewish home somewhere in a rural district of Germany. The 'ceremonial' laws were rather strictly observed but there was very little Jewish knowledge" (Strauss 1970d, 2).

Although the region of Marburg was crossed by significant phenomena of antisemitism, two factors contributed to maintaining a certain atmosphere of peace and serenity: on the one hand, the Kaiserreich placed public order at the center of its political thoughts; on the other hand, the traditionalist and nationalist character of the Jewish community of Kirchhain, generally adverse to any form of modernization, favors the development of good relations between non-Jewish and Jewish citizens. This fortunate situation appears even more evident when, around 1905, Strauss witnessed a remarkable episode (Strauss 1994, 44): for a few days, in his family home, were hosted some Russian Jews escaped from the Chisinau pogroms. Their testimonies, in which they told of brutal violence and persecution, shocked little Leo.

From March 1912, Strauss attended the *Königlichen Gymnasium Philippinum* in Marburg, where he met Carl Joachim Friedrich. To attend school, the young Leo had to move to Marburg, where he was entrusted to the care of a tutor, Abraham Strauss (not related to Leo's family), known teacher and acknowledged by the Jewish community for his efforts against antisemitism and for his relationships with figures such as Hermann Cohen and Kurt Eisner. In his first school years, Strauss became passionate about reading classics of Greek and German philosophy, namely Plato, Schiller, Schopenhauer, and Nietzsche: "In the *Gymnasium* I became exposed to the message of German humanism. Furtively I read Schopenhauer and Nietzsche. When I was sixteen and we read the *Laches* in school, I formed the plan, or the wish, to spend my life reading Plato and breeding rabbits while earning my livelihood as a rural postmaster. Without being aware of it, I had moved rather far away from my Jewish home, without any rebellion" (Strauss 1970d, 2). However, while the separation from his family in the first years of school was due to his *intellectual* encounter with Greek philosophy and German humanism, a more radical *political* inclination (the desire to overcome the bourgeois model of life) determined this separation in the last years of school, leading the young Strauss to encounter Zionism.

The abandonment of his family's traditionalism in favor of political radicalism, due to the need to *belong* to a living community, is a trait that characterized the young Strauss up until the end of the 1920s. At that time, a "change of orientation" occurred in his philosophical and political perspective, bringing him to believe in the possibility to overcome modern rationalism by recovering pre-modern philosophy.[1] Up to that point, the distinctive trait of Strauss's thought was *anti-modern political radicalism* (with a right-wing orientation, since socialism appeared to him as a radicalization of liberal democracy), developed by endorsing political Zionism, by criticizing modern thought and by abandoning the bourgeois education (*Bildung*). The philosophical expression of this radically anti-modern and anti-bourgeois inclination is visible in the young Strauss's fascination for Nietzsche. It is also retrospectively testified in the letter he addressed to his friend Karl Löwith on 23 June 1935: "As old Nietzschean that I was, . . . I am very obliged to you for making comprehensible to me the decisively important connection between nihilism and eternal return . . . I am by no means a Nietzsche specialist; I can only say that Nietzsche so dominated and bewitched me between my 22nd and 30th years, that I literally believed everything that I understood of him" (Strauss and Löwith 1988, 182–83).

Before reaching this radical inclination oriented to political mobilization, which characterized his thought between 1916 and 1928, Strauss began to attend a school in which the curriculum was traditionally oriented to the humanistic *Bildungsideal*. His studies contemplated mathematics, natural science, Latin and Greek literature, philosophy, history, French and English poetry, German literature, as well as a weekly course of religious studies. Among the authors he studied, there were Homer, Herodotus, Thucydides, Plato, Xenophon, Livy, Cicero, Virgil, Tacitus, Horace, Luther, Lessing, Goethe, Schiller, and Kleist. He gave his final exam in February 1917 on Sophocles (cf. Strauss 2002a), namely with a four-page essay dedicated to verses 332 and subsequent of *Antigone*. The final mark attributed to Strauss's work was positive—especially for his interpretation of Kant's idealism and of Schiller—but not exceptional: good (+). The essay discusses the ambivalence of human nature, the most prodigious being on earth, but also showing its frailty and caducity in respect to fate and divinities. The beginning of the essay is significant. Indeed, the first word is *thaumazein*, intended not only as the essence of philosophy, but also as the fundamental trait of the human being's existence in the world. The human being is born and lives in danger, exposed to natural events and death. However, in this precarious and miserable condition, the human being is able to lift itself as a moral agent, since it is provided with freedom and responsibility and since it can realize progress through the union of reason and will, force and conscience. The lesson of German humanism and idealism, especially Schiller, Kant, and Hegel, stands to indicate the truth of this positive path, which implicates that the human being voluntarily *chooses* to fulfill its own *duty*. The human being is the only living being able to overcome its condition of necessity providing itself with moral rules, creating art, building social relations, and planning a common life inside the State. Despite these explicit assertions, the impression gained from reading the essay is that the young Strauss diligently exposed the philosophical contents of German humanism's classical readings, typical of German education between nineteenth and twentieth century (which is the bourgeois model of *Bildung*), without however endorsing them.

After the end of school, in the late spring of 1917 Strauss enrolled at the Philipps-Universität-Marburg, with the intention to study law and political science. However—despite his clumsy attempt to avoid military conscription by faking health problems, namely an appendicitis, which was immediately uncovered (cf. Banfield 1991, 493)—in July that year he was enrolled in the German army and sent to the Belgian front, at first as an interpreter, then as a medical assistant. The beginning of his academic career was delayed to the end of the war, in November 1918, when he decided to change academic subject and undertake philosophical studies. Meanwhile, from 1916, the young Strauss decided to endorse the movement of political Zionism. Sentiment and passion motivated this endorsement, not intellectual or religious reasons. As for many young German Jews of his generation, also for Strauss World War I represented a fracture, certifying the end of the old liberal and bourgeois world preconized by Nietzsche and anticipating the birth of a new world, with an uncertain and indefinite outline, in which mobilization prevailed against modern rationalism. Moreover, the failure of the project to assimilate German Jews, transforming them into German citizens of Jewish faith, became clear. Return to orthodoxy, however, did not represent the alternative to this failure. Rather, the solution appeared in a heroic and affirmative stance, in an existential decision that committed the self to become part of a group. Inside the group, the single could find meaning for his own life and resolve his individual aspirations, dissolving them into the belonging to a political and religious organization. Political Zionism thus became the community mission that canalized the energies and passions of the young Strauss, by then convinced that the ideals of German humanism, which he had loved during his school years, were part of a glorious past, now dead and incapable of providing nourishment. Despite his passionate endorsement of political Zionism, however, Strauss did not completely break off with German philosophical culture: his life in the 1920s unfolded between two worlds, philosophy and Judaism.

University Studies

As contemplated in the academic customs of the time, Strauss's university studies did not take place in Marburg alone. Here, in 1920, he met Jacob Klein, with whom he remained bonded by a fraternal friendship for the rest of his life (cf. Strauss 1970d, 1–2). For his studies, Strauss also attended other universities, namely in Frankfurt, Berlin, and Hamburg. In Marburg, Strauss attended classes taught by Paul Natorp, Nicolai Hartmann, Karl Reinhardt and Eduard Fraenkel, respectively dedicated to the Platonic theory of ideas, to Kant's epistemology, to ancient philosophy, and to classical philology. Strauss graduated in Hamburg on 17 December 1921 with a dissertation on the theory of knowledge in Friedrich H. Jacobi, supervised by Ernst Cassirer, one of the main members of the neo-Kantian school founded by Hermann Cohen in Marburg. However, despite his deference for Cohen, Strauss progressively took distance from his teaching: "Cohen attracted me because he was a passionate philosopher and a Jew passionately devoted to Judaism . . . His school was in a state of disintegration. The disintegration was chiefly due to the emergence and ever-increasing power of phenomenology . . . But also, Cohen belonged definitely to the pre-World War I world" (Strauss 1970d, 2). With his cosmopolitan liberalism and his "religion of reason," Cohen incarnated the aspiration of modern democracy and safeguarded the German Jews' process of emancipation primed with the Enlightenment in the eighteenth century and represented by the figure of Moses Mendelssohn. This process experienced the vanishing of many hopes in the early twentieth century, due both to the crisis of modernity and to persisting antisemitism. This situation determined, among the young German Jews, the surfacing of different forms of "return" to Judaism, separated from rabbinic orthodoxy as much as from liberal assimilation and thought with the intention to overcome the enlightened position of the *Wissenschaft des Judentums*.

Strauss was not alone in stepping away from Cohen's teaching, since disillusion fell suddenly upon all German Jews. However, he took his own path, solitary and independent, in a frontier course between *Deutschtum* and *Judentum*, between philosophy and politics, between Athens and Jerusalem, which distinguished him from Rosenzweig and Scholem, from Buber and Löwith, from Benjamin and Jonas. During his university years, Strauss's education branched into two apparently incompatible programs: a theological and political one and another of philosophical and theoretical kind. On one side, he undertook a proselytizing activity in favor of political Zionism that also entailed a reflection on the religious dimension of Judaism. On the other, he pursued in his distinctly theoretical philosophical studies that aimed at discussing issues of metaphysics and theory of knowledge through the lens of neo-Kantianism and phenomenology. A common trait between these two programs, however, exists and we can find it in the *radically anti-modern* perspective with which the young Strauss confronted philosophical, theological, and political issues of his time, either circumscribed to the Jewish world or connected to the world of German culture.

Strauss's intellectually restless character appears not only from his moving between different questions and contexts, but also from his dissertation on Jacobi. The title—*Das Erkenntnisproblem in der philosophischen Lehre Fr. H. Jacobis*—has a neo-Kantian imprint. Its contents, however, are different and they show the distance that separated—and would always separate—Strauss from Cassirer (cf. Strauss 1924d). Despite its still uncertain and contradictory theoretical frame, influenced by recent readings from Max Scheler, Ernst Troeltsch, Max Weber, and Rudolf Otto, the dissertation expresses the depth of Strauss's dissatisfaction with modern philosophy and science through the analysis of Jacobi, who had been a proud opponent of Enlightenment. The research object is well delimited, given that Strauss excluded any historical reconstruction on *Pantheismusstreit*, while he exclusively focused on the theoretical contents of Jacobi's epistemology, used to identify the limits of modern rationalism. Hence the young Strauss's interest to investigate the possibility of the immediate experience of the transcendental and "irrational" God, beyond any idealistic or rationalistic interpretation of religion, which allowed Jacobi to avoid the traps of subjectivism while admitting to the subjective character of knowledge. Indeed, despite known objects determining our sensitive knowledge of the external world, they are outside the range of action of our mind, since this has a purely formal character. For this reason, Jacobi dedicated particular attention to an aspect of perception that assures the reality of the external object, identified by Strauss in faith, intended as the immediate certainty of natural reality's transcendence.

The dissertation on Jacobi is important to understand the young Strauss's anti-modern orientation, as well as to identify an aspect that appeared in a generic form in the dissertation, but that played an important role inside his intellectual biography: the distinction between theology and religion (or Law). In 1921, this distinction—although present—had yet to receive a clear elaboration. However, as soon as 1923, in an essay on Rudolf Otto (cf. Strauss 1923c), in which Strauss underlined the importance of the work *Das Heilige* (1917) inside the criticism of modern reason, theology became the discipline that deals with God in the context of modern rationalism (producing *philosophy of religion*, as well as the ideas of *religious experience* and *religious conscience*). Conversely, religion expressed the *fact* of revelation, the excess of transcendence, which cannot be led back neither to experience nor to idea. God, religion, Law, and transcendence therefore represent an obstacle for modern rationalism and, in this sense, Strauss employed them from a *theoretical*, not a confessional perspective. Notwithstanding his appreciation for Otto's proposal, Strauss did not miss out on detecting a critical aspect, according to which not all religions can be exclusively founded in the "numinous," since Jewish religion represents the surfacing of a "rational" religion—certainly not "rational" in a modern sense—that resists to all that is "myth."

Inside this anti-modern frame, the most important readings for Strauss were Franz Rosenzweig's *Der Stern der Erlösung* (1921) and Karl Barth's *Römerbrief* (1919, 1922[2]), the most vivid testimonies of a renewed interest for religion as a ground for the discussion of modern culture's crisis. Max Weber was also a figure of central reference: "Up to [1922] I had been particularly impressed, as many of my contemporaries in Germany, by Max Weber, by Weber's intransigent devotion to intellectual honesty, by his passionate devotion to the idea of science, a devotion that was combined with a profound uneasiness regarding the meaning of science" (Strauss 1995a, 304). The young Strauss's philosophical interests—though accompanied by his engagement in favor of the Zionist movement—did not show signs of decreasing. After obtaining his degree, Strauss continued his academic studies, beginning a specialization at the University of Freiburg in 1922, to attend Edmund Husserl's courses on the theory of knowledge, which contributed to his final abandoning of neo-Kantianism:

> Husserl explained to me who at that time was a doubting and dubious adherent of the Marburg school of neo-Kantianism, the characteristic of his own work in about these terms: "the Marburg school begins with the roof, while I begin with the foundation." This meant that for the school of Marburg the sole task of the fundamental part of philosophy was the theory of scientific experience, the analysis of scientific thought. Husserl however had realized more profoundly than anybody else that

> the scientific understanding of the world, far from being the perfection of our natural understanding, is derivative from the latter in such a way as to make us oblivious of the very foundations of the scientific understanding: all philosophic understanding must start from our common understanding of the world, from our understanding of the world as sensibly perceived prior to all theorizing. (Strauss 1971, 3)

However, Strauss did not grow an attraction for Husserl, completely disinterested towards the theological issues that instead Strauss deeply felt: "When I once asked Husserl about the subject, he replied, 'If there is a *datum* God we shall describe it'" (Strauss 1970d, 2). In Freiburg, Strauss attended, with interest, Julius Ebbinghaus's and Martin Heidegger's seminars, where he met Karl Löwith and Hans-Georg Gadamer. In Ebbinghaus's seminar, on social and political doctrines from the Reformation to the Enlightenment, Strauss discovered the anti-traditional image of Hobbes that accompanied him until the mid-1930s and that fostered his studies on the English philosopher. However, Heidegger's lessons on Aristotle's *Metaphysics* in particular fascinated Strauss. He referred their theoretical strength and philosophical content to Rosenzweig when the two met at the *Freies Jüdisches Lehrhaus* in Frankfurt:

> I said to him: in comparison with Heidegger, Weber appeared to me as an orphan child in regard to precision, and probing, and competence. I had never seen before such seriousness, profundity, and concentration in the interpretation of philosophic texts. I had heard Heidegger's interpretation of certain sections in Aristotle. Sometime later I heard Werner Jaeger in Berlin interpret the same texts. Charity compels me to limit the comparison to the remark that there was no comparison. (Strauss 1995a, 304)

Strauss considered Heidegger's theoretical work a revolution in respect even to Husserl's position, whom, at this point, he listed as a representative of pre-war philosophy. Indeed, Strauss was convinced that, in reference to the relationship between scientific and pre-scientific knowledge, Heidegger was able to radicalize the criticism to neo-Kantianism much more than Husserl did with the concept of "perception of sense":

> According to Heidegger, Husserl *himself* began with the roof: the merely sensibly perceived thing is itself derivative; there are not first sensibly perceived things and thereafter the same things in a state of being valued or in a state of affecting us. Our primary understanding of the world is not an understanding of things as objects but of what the Greeks indicated by *pragmata*, things which we handle and use. (Strauss 1995a, 305)

Strauss's restlessness continued unabated, and he took numerous trips across Germany to develop his philosophical interests. At the University of Berlin, he attended Werner Jaeger's classes on Aristotle and Classical Greek philosophy in 1923. However, always central in these years remained his interest for Jewish issues, dealt both on a political level, through his interpretation of Zionism, and on a historical and philosophical level, through his studies on the classics of medieval Judaism. Indeed, still in Berlin, at the *Hochschule für die Wissenschaft des Judentums*, between 1924 and 1925 he attended Julius Guttmann's lectures on Maimonides and Joseph Albo, also beginning his study of the writings of Saadia Gaon and Abravanel. In 1924 and 1925 he took part in the work of the *Freies Jüdisches Lehrhaus* in Frankfurt, where he came in personal contact with Gershom Scholem, whom he had met at several Zionist congresses of the *Kartell Jüdischer Verbindungen*. In this institution he held some lectures (for a public of adult Jews) on Cohen's *Religion der Vernunft aus den Quellen des Judentums* (May–July 1924) and on Spinoza's *Tractatus Theologico-Politicus* (October–December 1924), as well as on the theory of political Zionism (January 1925). Moreover, from 1925 Strauss obtained a long-serving research appointment at the *Akademie für die Wissenschaft des Judentums* in Berlin. Between philosophy and Judaism, the path towards the *theological-political problem*—which accompanied Strauss for his whole life—had already begun.

Endorsing Political Zionism

Strauss completed his intellectual education in Germany, where Zionism was a consolidated cultural and political reality and where the phenomenon of the "return" (*teshuvah*) to Judaism characterized most of the German Jewish youth, unsatisfied of the Jewish *status* in modernity offered by either religious liberalism or orthodoxy. Indeed, it is not necessary to wait until 1933 to verify the young German Jews' annoyance for the *impasse* experienced by the assimilationist strategy (even due to increasing antisemitism). The impact of the Zionist movement founded by Theodor Herzl is notable since the first years of the twentieth century. It deeply influenced Strauss's juvenile education, awakening his passion for the cultural identity, the socio-historical dignity, and the political responsibility of the Jewish people, in a perspective radically opposed to everything that represented the Old World (liberalism, bourgeoisie, and capitalism), which by then had reached its end. The perspective that appeared to the young Strauss and to many other young Germans—not only of Jewish origin—was not reassuring. Even without dwelling on the more purely socio-political issues visible in the tensions that tragically accompanied the Weimar Republic, it is sufficient to mention the name of Oswald Spengler to perceive the spirit of "decline of the West" that dominated the intellectual circles of the 1920s. It is thus in such times of crisis, in regard to *Deutschtum* as much as *Judentum*, that Strauss's intellectual biography unfolded, unsatisfied with *Haskalah* as well as *Wissenschaft des Judentums*, with Jewish orthodoxy as well as the philosophical and political outcomes of modern Enlightenment.

The attempt to spiritualize Judaism made by reformed movements from the end of the eighteenth century was challenged as much as the traditional endorsement of an idea of Judaism condensed in the binding character of the Law. Both these perspectives excluded from the horizon of Jewish history the expressions of vitality that did not conform to a humanistic and rational image of the world or to a traditional image of piety and obedience. Both liberal and orthodox Judaism lacked a key element of Jewish identity, on which the young Strauss pointed his attention: the claim of the Jewish people's dignity and responsibility awaiting its historical fulfillment. An element strongly felt by political Zionism, the movement which the young Strauss endorsed: "When I was seventeen, I was converted to Zionism—to simple, straightforward political Zionism" (Strauss 1970d, 2). Strauss initially endorsed the youth movement *Jüdischer Wanderbund Blau-Weiss*, oriented to the creation of an experience of common life in the nature, in a romantic and anti-modern perspective, in order to rebuild the feeling of being part of a community of Jewish tradition. However, the endorsement of the *Blau-Weiss* did not last long,[2] since from 1917 his interests consolidated on a strictly *political* interpretation of Zionism, hardly pursuable inside the *Blau-Weiss* confraternity.

Nevertheless, Strauss's endorsement of political Zionism was complex, since theoretical interests and philosophical passions acting deep inside push him to elaborate a series of sophisticated conceptual distinctions in analyzing the political questions dealt by Zionism. Such intellectual quality lured the attention of the youth movements' directors, who invited him to take part in assemblies of Zionist associations with speeches, in which Strauss connected the crisis of modernity with the political discussion on the Balfour Declaration and with the destiny of religion in the age of post-Enlightenment. Strauss greatly praised Herzl's political realism while expressing notable criticism of Max Nordau's spiritualist and neo-orthodox view. Moreover, he was firmly critical of Asher Ginzberg's and Martin Buber's cultural Zionism, as well as of the *Mizrahi* organization's religious Zionism, since both movements attempted an unsuccessful conciliation of Herzl's political secularism and traditional Judaism. Thus, for the young Strauss, Jews had just one true alternative between orthodoxy and political Zionism (cf. Strauss and Klein 2001, 517). Strauss was politically active since 1919 in the Zionist student movements gathered around the *Kartell Jüdischer Verbindungen* (among which the *Saronia* group in Frankfurt that he contributed to the creation of, becoming a member of its board for a brief period in 1924). Between 1923 and 1925, he actively contributed to the journals *Jüdische Rundschau* (the official publication of the *Zionistische Vereinigung für Deutschland*, directed by Robert Weltsch) and *Der Jude* (directed by Martin Buber). He had been friends with the managing editor of this latter journal, Ernst Simon, since 1919, given also their common participation in the *Kartell*. Moreover, between 1925 and 1929, he wrote some articles for the journal *Der jüdische Student*, official publication of the *Kartell* (cf. Zank 2002).

The articles that the young Strauss wrote for the Zionist journals offer the image of a politically radical and, at the same time, culturally conservative and theoretically rigorous thinker, with a contradictory effect. His participation in Zionist movements did not implicate the abandonment of German culture nor of his philosophical studies, which remained vivid, though not visible. Moreover, Strauss did not miss any occasion to highlight the necessity to distinguish between biblical religion and the immanent and nationalist interpretations of Jewish religion that characterized Zionist movements. Indeed, on the one hand, Strauss admired political Zionism. He did so for its radical rebellion against the decay of German Jews, on their way to secular assimilation and against the orthodox Jews' void observance of ceremonials. He also admired political Zionism for the proud claim of a Jewish identity able to give sense and meaning to a young Jew's existence in a post-Nietzschean and post-war Germany, in complete moral, social, and political decline. However, Strauss could not avoid detecting political Zionism's many limits, keeping faith to his own intellectual honesty (a *Redlichkeit* inspired by Nietzsche) that imposed the clear identification, since 1923, of Zionism's unsolved contradictions. Firstly, Strauss noted a considerable lack in Zionism's cultural awareness and intellectual depth, since its Jewish contents were often merely formal. Even among his Zionist companions, he noted a deep enthusiasm for political action, accompanied, however, by the same amount of indifference for Jewish history and culture. An episode from his biography clearly illustrates the peculiarity of Strauss's approach to Zionist movements. During a meeting with Vladimir Jabotinsky, the founder of the revisionist movement inside Zionism, Strauss brought the conversation on the Bible, on Jewish history, and on the theory of political Zionism, but, after just a few minutes spent on these topics, Jabotinsky abruptly interrupted him asking him about his ability with guns . . . (cf. Strauss 1994, 51). Secondly, in his juvenile articles, Strauss created an original mix of *cultural conservatism* and *political radicalism*, of anti-liberalism and anti-messianism that made him hardly classifiable in the already complex galaxy of Jewish movements. To the point that his articles resulted unusable for the socio-political debates connected to the construction of the Jewish State, while they amplified the philosophical and theological antinomies connected to the problematic nature of Jewish existence.

In his "Zionist" essays,[3] Strauss did not show any interest for the practical and organizational aspect of Zionist policies and focused on the philosophical and theological issues. These demonstrate, on the one hand, his uncommon theoretical ability and, on the other hand, his being present, but actually marginal, in the Zionist organizations of the time. Without asking Jabotinsky's crude question, it is clear that Strauss's philosophical arguments often appeared inappropriate within Zionist assemblies, in which the central question is, "What do we do?" and not the critical reflection on the philosophical or religious nature of Zionism. Therefore, already from 1923, Strauss's *radicalism* began to shift from the political to the theoretical level, from practical revolt against liberal and bourgeois society to philosophical criticism of modernity. This was a slow but decisive shift in Strauss's intellectual biography. He progressively abandoned his juvenile *political radicalism*, accompanied by *cultural conservatism*, to approach—from the end of the 1920s—the *philosophical radicalism* accompanied by *political conservatism* that characterized his maturity.

The main target of Strauss's criticism in the early 1920s was Martin Buber's[4] and Asher Ginzberg's cultural Zionism, which tried to find a compromise between political Zionism and tradition. Since according to Buber, religious experience precedes God (cf. Strauss 1923a), his immanent interpretation of religion leads to the absolutization of the human being[5]: cultural Zionism understood Jewish religion as a *product* of the Jewish people's spirit, thus appearing as a romantic variation of modern Enlightenment, of secularization and atheism (cf. Strauss 1925b). Thus, cultural Zionism represented a dishonest form of atheism, since it did not recover, but pretended to recover the contents and forms of traditional Jewish faith, offering an unbearable neo-orthodox variation of tradition, justified with a void ideology of return to Judaism. Moreover, the endorsement of tradition could not derive from a moral preference, since this meant remaining inside the modern and individualistic *Weltanschauung*. Jewish tradition *is*, but it cannot be "chosen" as any ideology (cf. Strauss 1925c).

The atheistic perspective was also present in political Zionism, but at least, in this case, it was honest. Indeed, it did not mean to reinterpret the foundations of biblical religion and it aimed at confronting and solving the Jewish issue in purely secular terms. Political Zionism aimed at providing concrete tools to defend the dignity of the Jewish people (for instance, safeguarding them from the spiritual colonization operated by modern Europe) and at seeking a solution for the issue of exile, of the diaspora (*Galuth*). Soon, however, deep doubts surfaced, which led the young Strauss to take a distance from political Zionism. Indeed, he realized that, far from being fully opposed to liberal assimilation, the Zionist political proposal was a continuation of it, in the opposite direction (since it was founded on the nationalistic element and not on the individualistic one). Precisely by asserting that the *Galuth* had no significance for the political struggle, it strengthened the de-Judaizing tendencies of emancipation (cf. Strauss 1923d, 660). Without leaving any room for utopia—and even less for secularization—Strauss confirmed the importance of transcendence in Jewish faith. Jewish faith cannot exclude the call to revelation, or else the Jewish people lose their uniqueness and their tradition. Naturally, the young Strauss was aware of the Jewish paradox implied in the *Galuth*. Thanks to their faith in God's omnipotence and in the covenant, the Jewish people, in theory, live in the maximum of existence's possibilities; however, in practice, they live in a condition with the smallest possibility of action, since they are dispersed on Earth and governed by others. Political Zionism attempted to find a solution to this secular aspect, but could not intervene in any way on the relationship with transcendence, which, in the meantime, the Zionist solution contribute to further aggravate, since it could not provide remedies to the spiritual situation of Judaism in modernity, being *modern* itself.

Therefore, Strauss's "Zionist" articles represent his ambivalence towards political Zionism. On the one hand, we read his admiration for the claim of a Jewish national and cultural identity against any moral and cultural threat coming from the German world, as for instance from the juvenile movement *Wandervogel* or from Paul de Lagarde (cf. Strauss 1924a), as well as from the more general antisemitism[6] and right-wing parties (cf. Strauss 1925c). On the other hand, however, we read his awareness of the limits of such a position, which substantially modified Judaism's historical and religious legacy, only worrying about the political issue: the belief that the Jews' state of emergency could only find a solution in the creation of a Jewish State characterized political Zionism. This perspective in favor of autonomy and responsibility necessarily implied the abandonment of Jewish messianism: political Zionism acknowledged the existence of a Jewish issue; however, it only dealt with what the Jewish people could achieve with their own efforts and actions (cf. Strauss 1923b). Yet is reclaiming the values of Jewish tradition without returning to Judaism possible? Is a Jewish secular nationalism alongside Jewish religion possible? Indeed, Jewish traditional faith is *non-political* and does not contemplate politics' active intervention to achieve salvation and the Jewish destiny: this non-political character of Jewish tradition is nonexclusively a result of exile, since it is originally assumed by the faith in the God of Israel (cf. Strauss 1924e). For Zionism, instead, the perspective of a nationalist "normalization" of the Jewish people—in order for them to become a people like all others—had nothing to do with the messianic expectations, nor with Jewish religion. To the point that, according to Strauss, the only intellectually honest perspective would consist in presenting political Zionism as a *radically atheistic movement inside Judaism*, aimed at organizing the Jewish people by means of atheism and not Jewish religion!

Formulating such critical position concerning political Zionism did not prevent Strauss from continuing to attend the *Kartell* even after 1923, given that his participation continued until the end of the 1920s, although—especially from 1925—it grew fainter, as also his importance inside Zionist congresses grew fainter. Indeed, the deduction he made around 1923—political Zionism as a radically atheist movement—could not be seriously considered by any of the movement's leaders, both in principle and for pragmatic reasons. After all, the original philosophical, political, and theological position held by the young Strauss—who, also when a Zionist, remained a *philosopher*—could not go unheard inside Zionist organizations. Despite the undoubtable fascination worked by the width of his cultural references and by the lucidity of his theoretical distinction, a certain intolerance began to develop towards his radical criticism of religious Zionism, cultural Zionism, and the neo-orthodox trends of political Zionism. Such criticism was in fact considered politically inappropriate in a phase in which it was necessary to strengthen alliances between different Zionist movements with the aim of an effective political action. The fierce and salacious ways in which Strauss expressed himself both in speech and in writing contributed to incrementing intolerance towards him: always prone to fierce criticism, when he intervened, Strauss went through the positions and writings he examined with a sarcastic and aggressive tone, scorning his interlocutors. Such manners provoked irritation in his interlocutors, who consequently grew a strong aversion towards him (this is an attitude that, though partly mitigated, characterized Strauss also in his mature years and often caused his academic isolation).

An episode effectively illustrates the fundamental distance between Strauss and the Zionist movements. In the days between 29 July and 1 August 1924, the *Kartell* organized a summer camp in Forchtenberg, in the Stuttgart region. In light of his long participation in the Zionist movement and in light of his academic titles, Strauss was a member of the leading board and was considered an *alter Herr*, that is a prominent member among the "confreres." He therefore had the honor to pronounce the event's opening lecture, entitled "Das jüdische Kulturproblem in unserem Erziehungsprogramm" ("The Problem of Jewish Culture in Our Educational Program"), as well as that of speaking in memory of Herzl at the end of the meeting. In the pages 196–200 of the issue number 8–9, dated October–November 1924, the journal *Der jüdische Student* published a long editorial report of the Forchtenberg summer camp, including a summary of Strauss's opening lecture, held in front of about eighty people (among whom Scholem). The lecture focused on the relationship between political Zionism and Jewish tradition, starting with a radical criticism of cultural Zionism. In February 1925 an article by Hans Weinberg,[7] who had taken part in the summer camp, appeared on the same journal, expressing a radical criticism of Strauss's position. Weinberg wrote that, despite Strauss's opposition to modern nationalism and Jewish religion, he declared himself unable to solve the dualism and therefore decided in favor of orthodoxy and against political Zionism. Weinberg undoubtedly misunderstood Strauss—who had no inclination for orthodoxy ("I am *not* an orthodox Jew!," Strauss wrote to Löwith on 23 June 1935: cf. Strauss and Löwith 1988, 185)—however, what matters here are the two relevant elements that emerge from Weinberg's criticism, useful to understand Strauss's problematic situation inside the *Kartell*. First, the misunderstanding itself of Strauss's arguments, which had a theoretical nature that could not be used inside Zionist congresses, since such nature led interlocutors to misinterpret his arguments and to consider him an orthodox Jew. Second, the fact that, despite how well argued his considerations on the problematic relationship between Zionism and Jewish religion were, it was anyway necessary for Zionist movements to decide "what to do" in action, to choose, for instance, between right-wing or left-wing policies: the theoretical questions are not important for Zionist movements.

Despite Strauss's difficulty to relate to most young Zionists, as this significant episode shows, he continued to propose his *atheistic* interpretation of political Zionism, not just in Zionist congresses, but also in articles published during the second half of the 1920s on the pages of that same journal *Der jüdische Student* (cf. Strauss 1928; 1929a), with catastrophic consequences. His articles were exposed to deep criticism, published on the same journal, in which Strauss was accused of proselytizing in favor of atheism and of wanting to exclude any sincere religious sensibility from political Zionism.[8] His participation in the Zionist movements—already superficial in the previous years—ended towards the end of the 1920s. The reasons lay both in Strauss's turn towards philosophical and theoretical interests of other nature—namely the *querelle des anciens et des modernes*—and in the fact that not even the pluralism typical of juvenile Zionist organizations could accept deleterious political positions like the ones supported by Strauss. In his 1928 and 1929 "Zionist" writings, Strauss reaffirmed that, if political Zionism intended to prosecute in its aim to "normalize" the existence of the Jewish people through the construction of a Jewish State that may turn the Jewish nation into a nation like all others, then it was necessary to deny the *Galuth*. It was necessary to acknowledge that, in the age of atheism, the Law no longer has a foundational role for the existence of the Jewish people, who have to provide alone to their existence and to their salvation. Therefore, atheism was the only possible foundation for political Zionism.

Abandoning Political Zionism

Strauss's participation in the Zionist movement is problematic and complex: it was active in the first half of the 1920s and continued (although fading) between 1925 and 1930, but it was also marked by criticism and doubts, which led him, since 1923, to elaborate a critical eye on any attempt to finding a *secular* solution to the Jewish issue. In his mature age, Strauss in person rebuilt this juvenile path of endorsement to political Zionism and then of estrangement from it. He did so in his 1962 *Preface* to the American edition of his 1930 monograph on Spinoza, which represents an autobiographical writing dedicated to his personal *Bildung* in 1920s' Germany. In retrospect, the analysis of the Weimar Republic is very severe (cf. Strauss 1965, 1ff.). Strauss recalled the weakness of German democracy and liberalism, the German people's dissatisfaction with the modern world (determined by the English and the French) and their romantic nostalgia for the Middle Age. He also recalled the ambiguous legacies of Goethe, Bismarck, and Nietzsche, the cultural opposition between East and West and, most of all, the precarious situation of German Jews, also due to the political situation of Weimar Germany, which provided arguments for the Zionist cause:

> Prior to Hitler's rise to power most German Jews believed that their problem had been solved in principle by liberalism: German Jews were Germans of the Jewish faith, i.e., they were no less German than the Germans of the Christian faith or of no faith. They assumed that the German state was or ought to be neutral to the difference between Christians and Jews or between non-Jews and Jews. This assumption was not accepted by the strongest part of Germany and hence by Germany. In the words of Herzl: "Who belongs and who does not belong, is decided by the majority: it is a question of power." At any rate it could seem that in the absence of a superior recognized equally by both parties the natural judge on the German-ness of German Jews was the non-Jewish Germans. As a consequence, a small minority of German Jews, but a considerable minority of German-Jewish youth studying at the universities, had turned to Zionism. (Strauss 1965, 4)

Strauss himself was part of this considerable minority of German Jewish university students. He soon manifested his separation from the Zionist solution to the Jewish issue, which only represented another face of the assimilationist and liberal solution (cf. Strauss 1925c): Zionism considered emancipation at a community level, liberalism considered it at the level of the single citizen's rights. However, the substance remained the same. Liberalism as much as Zionism considered the Jewish issue at a purely human and social issue, neglecting the essential aspect of Jewish tradition: faith. There was, of course, a difference between the Zionist perspective and the assimilationist one. Liberal Judaism meant to deny the existence of a Jewish issue (indeed, the problem became that of *single* Jews), whereas Zionism proudly asserted its persistence (thus the problem regarded the entire Jewish nation)[9]. Such difference between the individual and collective level does not seem to be decisive, given that in both cases the premise lies in the *fracture* with the Jewish tradition, with the entry into the age of atheism. Just as one cannot be both an orthodox and an assimilated Jew, one cannot be an orthodox Jew and a political Zionist, because it is impossible to appease biblical faith and humanism or nationalism, both atheistic. Therefore, Zionism is a modern ideological and political movement, characterized by an enlightened theoretical system typical of the eighteenth century and by a nationalist political perspective, typical of the nineteenth century (cf. Strauss 1965, 4–6).

Political Zionism presupposes *cultural* Zionism: if it does not want to remain inside the liberal political model, if it does not simply want to be a State *of* Jews, the Jewish State will have to be the specific fruit of Jewish culture. Cultural Zionism, however, in turn constitutes a fracture with Jewish tradition, because it interprets the Jewish legacy as a human and national culture. Judaism, instead, is not any national culture, but a divine gift and revelation, the meaning of which ends up being completely distorted once it is interpreted in the sense of "culture": "When cultural Zionism understands itself, it turns into religious Zionism. But when religious Zionism understands itself, it is in the first place Jewish faith and only secondarily Zionism. It must regard as blasphemous the notion of a human solution to the Jewish problem" (Strauss 1965, 6). The Jewish problem cannot even be solved by founding the State of Israel. Zionism can consider the founding of the State of Israel as the most important event in Jewish history after the fulfillment of the Talmud, but it cannot consider it as the realization of the Messianic age: "The founding of the State of Israel is the most profound modification of the Galuth that has occurred, but it is not the end of the Galuth; . . . the State of Israel is only a part of Galuth" (Strauss 1965, 6). Faced with the affinities between liberalism and Zionism, Strauss came to the conclusion that the Jewish issue was unsolvable, given that the available solutions, individualistic emancipation in legal terms (liberal) and social emancipation in nationalist and cultural terms (Zionist), were both purely secular solutions. The failure of the enlightened ideals did not only mean the German Jews' profound social and political disappointment, visible in the persistence of antisemitic forces, but it also demonstrated the obstacles that the modern project crossed in its entirety. Moreover, the Jewish issue became more generally the symbol of the human issue. Human beings can only solve finite problems, not infinite ones, and, for this reason, they will never be able to create a society void of contradictions, as Strauss asserted during a lecture held at the Hillel House in Chicago on 4 February 1962, which is in the same period he worked on the *Preface*:

> Judaism is not a misfortune but, let us say, a "heroic delusion." In what does this delusion consist? The one thing needful is righteousness or charity; in Judaism these are the same. This notion of the one thing needful is not defensible if the world is not the creation of the just and loving God, the holy God. The root of injustice and uncharitableness, which abounds, is not in God, but in the free acts of His creatures—in sin. The Jewish people and their fate are the living witness for the absence of redemption. This, one could say, is the meaning of the chosen people; the Jews are chosen to prove the absence of redemption. (Strauss 1994, 60)

Strauss was not satisfied with the typically *modern* solutions to the Jewish issue offered by political Zionism and enlightened and liberal assimilation. However, the different forms of "return" to Judaism elaborated at the beginning of the twentieth century did not satisfy him either. Certainly, he was not satisfied with the proposal contained in Cohen's *Religion der Vernunft aus den Quellen des Judentums* (1919) or in Buber's *Die Geschichten des Rabbi Nachman* (1906). But Strauss was not even satisfied with the proposal formulated in *Der Stern der Erlösung* (1921) by Rosenzweig, the most charismatic and representative figure of the "movement of return" to Judaism in the 1920s' Germany.

The Critique of the "New Thinking"

The impossibility of solving the Jewish issue understood as a *social and political issue* does not imply the impossibility of solving the issue of *single* Jews who have abandoned the Jewish community with the aim of becoming equal members of the liberal society. A goal they cannot reach due to the contradictions embedded inside the liberal project (contradictions that emerge with the opposite antisemitic and Zionist instances). The solution to this obstacle is the "return" to Judaism. Such a return, however, is only possible if Jewish faith demonstrates that the modern enlightened project has not confuted it. Especially thanks to the example offered by Rosenzweig's "new thinking," according to the young Strauss such a confutation is illusory. Rosenzweig, with his *Der Stern der Erlösung* showed the limits of any philosophical system in general and of Hegel's in particular, frustrating the claims of any radical objection to revelation and providing a renewed dignity for the biblical God. In the first half of the 1920s, Rosenzweig was the most relevant philosophical reference for the young Strauss, interested in theology from a philosophical and political perspective. Several factors testify to his importance for Strauss. Firstly, Strauss's active participation, between 1924 and 1925, in the activities of the *Freies Jüdisches Lehrhaus*, founded in Frankfurt by Rosenzweig. Secondly, Strauss's enrollment in 1925 at the *Akademie für die Wissenschaft des Judentums* in Berlin, favored, among others, by Rosenzweig. Thirdly, the dedication that Strauss placed on his first monograph (*Die Religionskritik Spinozas*, 1930) in memory of his late friend. Finally, the brief but significant necrology Strauss published on 13 December 1929 on the *Jüdische Wochenzeitung für Kassel, Hessen und Waldeck*. Inside it, Strauss recalled Rosenzweig's central role in the didactic and editorial activity of the *Akademie*, with special attention to Cohen. He also highlighted Rosenzweig's theoretical position, based on a *political* inclination, which appeared in his philosophical studies and in the scientific attention for historical studies, as well as in his attitude of *responsibility* towards Judaism and Jews: Rosenzweig vigorously affirmed responsibility for Jewish identity (Strauss 1929b). However, notwithstanding the great admiration for Rosenzweig's philosophical teaching and his Jewish identity, in his mature age Strauss remembered how his solution to the issue of "return" to Judaism was insufficient:

> Considerations of this kind seemed to decide the issue in favor of Rosenzweig's understanding of the new thinking, or in favor

of the unqualified return to Biblical revelation. As a matter of fact, Rosenzweig's return was not unqualified. The Judaism to which he returned was not identical with the Judaism of the age prior to Moses Mendelssohn . . . Whereas the classic work of what is called Jewish medieval philosophy, the *Guide of the Perplexed*, is primarily not a philosophic book but a Jewish book, Rosenzweig's *Star of Redemption* is primarily not a Jewish book but "a system of philosophy." The new thinking is "experiencing philosophy." (Strauss 1965, 13)

The traditional Jewish term *teshuvah* could not define Rosenzweig's "return" to Judaism, because such return was not absolute. He did not believe that his own return to the biblical faith could be a return to the way such a faith was intended in the past. He was the representative of the philosophy of existence in its Jewish form and was, as Cohen and Buber, a radically modern philosopher. Indeed, whereas the Jewish tradition understands the historical experience of the Jewish people in the primary and authoritative light of the Torah, which is presupposed to Jewish conscience, Rosenzweig, instead, moved in an opposite way, "sociologically," considering as a condition of possibility of Jewish experience not the Torah, but the concrete, or "natural," existence of the Jewish nation. Moreover, almost like in the tradition of religious liberalism, he operated an individual, personal, distinction between the various traditional beliefs, independently from their statute and their role inside traditional Judaism. According to Strauss, Rosenzweig "historicized" and "individualized" the Torah. In maintaining the centrality and primacy of the Jewish people in respect to the Torah, Rosenzweig obtained the same result—secularized and individualistic—as political Zionism and religious liberalism:

Rosenzweig agrees with religious liberalism as to the necessity of making a selection from among the traditional beliefs and rules. Yet his principle of selection differs radically from the liberal principle . . . Rosenzweig's principle is not a principle strictly speaking but "a force": the whole "reality of Jewish life," even those parts of it which never acquired formal authority (like "mere" stories and "mere" customs) must be approached as the "matter" out of which only a part can be transformed into "force"; . . . the selection cannot but be "wholly individual." (Strauss 1965, 14)

All this confirmed, according to Strauss, that Rosenzweig remained inside the horizon determined by modern philosophy, which, as such, is incompatible with Jewish traditional faith. Faced with such an individualistic faith as Rosenzweig was, an orthodox Jew would reprimand himself for his doubts.

Which solution, then, did the modern Jew have? Which "return" to Judaism was possible? Obviously, a return that was not the result of an "unfounded decision," but that could lean upon arguments able to confront rationalistic criticism, in order for Judaism to survive—not simply as a fossil—in the modern world. Having identified the secular limits of liberalism and Zionism, having verified the permanence of Rosenzweig's "return" to Judaism inside the modern individualistic scope, all that the young Strauss was left with was orthodoxy, the sole legitimate representative of Jewish traditional faith. Indeed, the other forms of "return" (from Cohen to Buber) were not returns, but rather "progressions." Still, an eminent obstacle weighted on orthodoxy: Spinoza. Strauss's question was at the same time simple and audacious: did the *Tractatus Theologico-Politicus*—that is modern Enlightenment—really refute Jewish orthodoxy? Inspired by the debate initiated by Cohen against Spinoza's *Tractatus*, Strauss engaged in his personal confrontation with Spinoza. His intention was to verify, on the one hand the arguments of the *Tractatus* and, on the other hand, the current state of Jewish traditional faith intended as a solution for the current Jew, lost inside the modern world (cf. Strauss 1965, 15ff.).

Spinoza, Cohen, and the Emancipation of German Jews

In the early twentieth century, Spinoza was at the center of the interests of the German Jewish community. Instead of seeing Spinoza as the apostate of Judaism and the quintessential example of atheism, German Jews considered him the emblem of their emancipation:

> Spinoza . . . showed the way toward a new religion or religiousness, which was to inspire a wholly new kind of society, a new kind of Church . . . It was of the utmost importance to that Church that its father was not a Christian but a Jew who had informally embraced a Christianity without dogmas and sacraments. The millennial antagonism between Judaism and Christianity was about to disappear. The new Church would

transform Jews and Christians into human beings . . . The new society emancipated the Jews in Germany. Spinoza became the symbol of that emancipation which was to be more than emancipation but secular redemption. (Strauss 1965, 17)

An authoritative and strong voice had raised to contrast the praises of Spinoza, reaffirming the condemnation the Dutch philosopher had received from the Amsterdam synagogue. Between 1910 and 1915, Hermann Cohen expressed a relentless accusation, together human and scientific, against Spinoza.[10] On a human level, the Dutch philosopher was condemned as the accuser of Judaism in front of Christians, a traitor to his people, whom he contributed to persecuting out of the spite and spirit of revenge that took hold of him following the condemnation he received from the Amsterdam Jewish community. He was not the philosopher who showed Jews the path for emancipation, but rather the one that, possessed by an unfaithful and evil frame of mind and heart, accomplished a humanly unconceivable betrayal. Indeed, Cohen observed that Spinoza, while denigrating Judaism, "idealized" Christianity: the whole *Tractatus* was directed against Moses's particularistic teaching in faith and politics, whereas it exalted in several places the spirituality and universality of the Christian message. On a scientific level, besides observing with Kant how Spinoza's pantheism was untenable, Cohen pointed his attention to biblical science. Spinoza persisted in trying to demonstrate the historical particularism of the Jewish theocratic State as well as Judaism's character of national religion, in which rituals are adapted to the State's authority and law. Such demonstrations, if accomplished, would crumble the idea, supported by Cohen, of Judaism as a universal monotheistic and messianic religion. To refute Spinoza's theory, Cohen turned his exegetical analysis on the figure of the *stranger*, with the aim of tracing the idea of the messianic unity of humankind inside the Bible. Based on his philological analysis, Cohen held that Judaism found the biblical *neighbor*, i.e., *humankind*, in the stranger and on this the biblical commandments of justice, piety, charity, and love were conceived, in defense of the ethical concept of equity as a source for all justice. Therefore, Judaism offered itself, fully justified, as the universal messianic humanism that acknowledges the ethical concept of equality. Jewish prophetical universalism and messianic and socialist universalism derived from Kant—i.e., *Deutschtum* and *Judentum*—find reciprocal composition in the *idea* of God and in the corresponding idea of "moral duty."

The young Strauss immediately noted the shortcomings of the neo-Kantian philosopher's reading of Spinoza. In 1924, he published an article on the Cohen-Spinoza case in the journal *Der Jude*, raising serious doubts on the plausibility and accuracy of Cohen's work, filled with psychological conjectures and historical and philosophical misinterpretations (cf. Strauss 1924c). Strauss ascribed Cohen's wrong reading of the *Tractatus* primarily to the misunderstanding of the text's spirit and style; secondly to Cohen's specific philosophical and political position. In the seventeenth century, the connection between biblical criticism and theory of knowledge, as well as a politicized interpretation of the Bible, were sufficiently justified by the aims Spinoza pursued, namely philosophical freedom, the State's freedom from ecclesiastical pretensions, and the constitution of a liberal democracy. In Spinoza's historical context, the connection between political philosophy and biblical criticism is extensively motivated by the necessity to affirm the legitimacy of a political authority independent from the ecclesiastical hierarchy (be it Jewish, Catholic, or Calvinist). Arguments of reason are not sufficient to support the lack of such legitimacy—common to all natural right thinkers of the seventeenth century. Arguments deriving from the interpretation of the Scriptures are also necessary. It is necessary to guarantee the freedom of research, rendering it independent from both temporal and ecclesiastical powers, and it is necessary to show that the Scriptures cannot be an authority able to limit freedom of research (cf. Strauss 1924c, 36–37).

Therefore, it did not seem necessary to postulate, as Cohen did, an evil and anti-Jewish frame of mind and heart to understand Spinoza's reasons. The seventeenth-century spiritual condition offered a simple and direct interpretative key to understand the method, purpose, structure, and results of the *Tractatus*, which is a Christian-European book, not a Jewish one, aimed at contesting ecclesiastical authorities' and the Scriptures' claims of religious, political, philosophical, and scientific primacy. Even Spinoza's critical and exegetical method and the dislocation of the relationship between Judaism and Christianity typical of the *Tractatus* become completely understandable if one keeps in mind that Judaism in the seventeenth century was Law and not "religion of reason." Since the foundation of liberal democracy necessarily needed the refusal of any religion intended as Law, Spinoza could not avoid stepping outside the only Judaism present at his time, orthodox Judaism. For this reason, Strauss accused Cohen of having little historical awareness in attacking a theory, Spinoza's, from which the neo-Kantian philosopher instead derives. He also asserted this in the 1962 *Preface*:

> Cohen does not discuss at all the issue between Spinoza and Jewish orthodoxy, i.e., the only issue with which Spinoza could have been concerned, since there was no modern or liberal Judaism in his time . . . Cohen commits the typical mistake of the conservative, which consists in concealing the fact that the continuous and changing tradition which he cherishes so greatly would never have come into being through conservatism. (Strauss 1965, 27)

In Strauss's interpretation, one may agree more or less with Spinoza's assertions; however, they are historically motivated and, most importantly, they do not require personal psychological explanations. In his fury against Spinoza, Cohen forgot that Spinoza had been the founder of liberal democracy, of the political and cultural condition that allowed the emancipation of Jews. The foundation of the liberal State requires the abrogation of the limiting character of the Mosaic Law. Therefore, the *Tractatus* aimed at the liberation of the Jewish people, although by means of a Machiavellian method. Cohen did not understand that Spinoza had the same critical objective as the Enlightenment. Therefore, the enlightened Cohen did not understand Spinoza's enlightened program. Spinoza may well have hated Judaism, but he did not hate Jews. Indeed, the *Tractatus* bears elements that allow both an assimilationist solution (in a secular and atheistic perspective, not by means of the conversion to Christianity) and a Zionist solution to the Jewish issue. After all, Spinoza did not speak against Jewish monotheism, nor against the prophets' social ethics, but against revealed religion *in all forms*, including Christianity.

However, Strauss did not limit his criticism to uncovering the hermeneutical inability that Cohen demonstrated in his reading of the *Tractatus*. He even offered proof of the profound contradictions that characterized Cohen's reading of Spinoza also concerning the possibilities of biblical criticism (cf. Strauss 1965, 25ff.). Strauss found numerous contradictions in the humanitarian and messianic socialism proposed by the neo-Kantian philosopher, who was also wrong in trying to demonstrate the theoretical difference that separates Spinoza's *Ethics* from his *Tractatus* (regarding, for instance, the interpretation of will). Simplifying, we can say that Cohen opposed Spinoza's "cruelty" to mildness of spirit but did not build for this reason a coherent political theory. According to Strauss, the reason for the violent accusation Cohen made against Spinoza was not difficult to understand. The *Tractatus* contributed to mining the foundations of the integration between *Deutschtum* and *Judentum*. Cohen's desire was to make it possible for German Jews to become German citizens of Jewish faith as quickly as possible. Cohen hoped that German Jews, *together* with German Christians, could propel a movement of reciprocal integration, destined to clash, on a practical level, with antisemitic and Zionist trends, while precisely Spinoza, the denier of Jewish universalism, represented the most prominent obstacle on the theoretical level. In Strauss's interpretation, the weakness of Cohen's reading of Spinoza was due to the clear implicit difficulty of trying to hold together a plurality of theoretical options and political motivations, from humanistic and messianic socialism to neo-Kantianism, from anti-Zionism to biblical science, which undermine the theoretical analysis, due to the presence of unjustified moral preferences (close to socialist humanitarianism). The Cohen-Spinoza case ended in favor of the Dutch philosopher. Strauss had to deal precisely with Spinoza, in order to verify if he had truly confuted religious orthodoxy. A return to Judaism was only possible after having completed a confutation of Spinoza, i.e., of modern rationalism.

Chapter Two

Berlin (1925–1932)

Jewish Issues and German Problems

Despite Strauss taking a distance from political Zionism, he continued to maintain his interest for the relationship between Judaism and modernity. The perspective of such research, however, became primarily philosophical and acquired historical depth. Even in the second half of the 1920s, he continued to contribute to a number of Zionist organizations and to some Jewish journals, but his interests progressively acquired philosophical breadth. Anyway, his connection to Jewish institutions remained steady. In 1925, appointed by Rosenzweig's *Freies Jüdisches Lehrhaus* Strauss became Hebrew language teacher for the Jewish community in Kassel, where he resided on several occasions. From 1925, however, Strauss lived in Berlin, even if his trips to Kirchhain, Kassel, Marburg, and Frankfurt did not cease. Through Scholem, in Berlin Strauss met Walter Benjamin, who immediately appreciated his philosophical-political and theological interests. Moreover, in the years he spent in Berlin he consolidated his friendship with Klein. Especially from 1926, the two friends studied together at the *Staatsbibliothek*. A recurring topic in the discussions between the two was Heidegger's philosophy. Strauss owes to Klein his understanding of the epochal scope of the activity of the author of *Sein und Zeit* (1927), which focused on the issue of the preconditions of Western thought (cf. Strauss 1970d, 3). According to Strauss, Klein understood that Heidegger's work allowed a return to classical Greek philosophy and especially the possibility to make a *radical* distinction between ancient and modern. Klein's intuition provided a decisive element of thought for the young

Strauss, which he used in the years to come, when, looking for a way to overcome the crisis of modernity, he found a way to return to Plato. The solution offered by Heidegger, however, did not convince him. Heidegger's return to Greek classics did not appear to him as a true return, but rather as a radicalization of modernity that abandoned the level of philosophical rationality, as he wrote to Krüger on 12 December 1931: "In the meantime I read something from *Sein und Zeit* again . . . This work expresses the essence of modernity in the purest way, that is, the modern reserve against the Greeks, Jews and Christians" (Strauss and Krüger 2001, 398). Indeed, Strauss was distant from Heidegger's insistence on the themes of angst (*Angst*), resolution (*Entschlossenheit*), and authenticity (*Eigentlichkeit*), which do not answer philosophical questions elaborated in a *rational* form. After Nietzsche, also Heidegger put an end to modern rationalism, by unveiling its uncertain foundations. However, he did not give way to a new rationalism, but to the analytics of *Existenz*, meaning an existentialism based on a decision (*Entscheidung*) that justifies relativism and definitively abandons the idea of truth. Heidegger did not renounce posing the question on being in the form in which Plato and Aristotle had asked that same question, but, while for the classics "being" meant "being always," for Heidegger "being" meant "existing." Therefore "existential" is the opposite of "theoretical," because, while it necessitates a radical criticism of contemplative life, it sensibly approaches the re-evaluation of a "practice" that becomes "existence." Since existence precedes essence, truth and its meanings are uniquely based on human freedom, while, from a metaphysical point of view, there is only *nihil* (cf. Strauss 1995a, 311ff.): the human being is a finite being incapable of absolute knowledge.

However, the theoretical revolution represented by Heidegger was not the sole reference to German philosophy that crossed Strauss in the 1920s. Indeed, confronting German culture during the Weimar Republic meant confronting the modern crisis, which implied not only a loss of faith in progress, but also a radical and general disorientation, represented in an exemplary way in Oswald Spengler's *Der Untergang des Abendlandes* (1918–1922) and in Robert Musil's *Der Mann ohne Eigenschaften* (1930–1943). Facing such disorientation even the existential and rational answers, provided by Max Weber with his 1919 lectures *Wissenschaft als Beruf* and *Politik als Beruf*, were insufficient. Rationalization and massification, mechanization and reification, modernization, leveling, and displacement constituted a radical obstacle for the search for sense and meaning that followed the collapse of the "old world." No "new world" was visible beyond it, to the point that one feared to be living in a desolate and desolating landscape of petrification and indifference, without directions or goals. The determinism of mechanical philosophy does not respond to the human need for stillness, sense, and comfort, because man and his world are only the last and subtle result of mechanical concatenations in their cold indifference. The connection between science, rationalism, and liberalism did not answer the promises of progress and happiness. Instead, it appeared unable even to govern the present, given the chaos that characterized the Weimar years. The promise made by modern science, of knowing the truth and realizing a better world, disappeared with World War I, if not even before it. Rationalization produced a huge technical and bureaucratic apparel that was unable to provide meaning to individual and social life, already dominated by consumerism and conformism, by specialization and technical innovation, by curiosity and entertainment. Individual and social life headed towards the "night of the world," represented by an unvarying global society, homogenized and based on the continuous circle of production and consumption:

> The First World War shook Europe to its foundations. Men lost their sense of direction. The faith in progress decayed . . . Spengler's *Decline of the West* seemed to be much credible. But one had to be inhuman to leave it at Spengler's prognosis . . . Nietzsche's hope for a united Europe ruling the planet, for a Europe not only united but revitalized by this new, transcendent responsibility of planetary rule had proved to be a delusion. A world society controlled either by Washington or Moscow appeared to be approaching. For Heidegger it did not make a difference whether Washington or Moscow would be the center: "America and Soviet Russia are metaphysically the same." What is decisive for him is that this world society is to him more than a nightmare. He calls it the "night of the world." It means indeed, as Marx had predicted, the victory of an evermore urbanized, evermore completely technological, west over the whole planet—complete levelling and uniformity regardless whether it is brought about by iron compulsion or by soapy advertisement of the output of mass production. It means unity of the human race on the lowest level, complete emptiness of life, self-perpetuating routine without rhyme and reason; no leisure, no concentration, no elevation, no

withdrawal, but work and recreation; no individuals and no peoples, but "lonely crowds." (Strauss 1995a, 315–16)

Alongside his confrontation with the European crisis, Strauss did not abandon his engagement inside the Jewish community and continued to attend, although sporadically, Zionist congresses and the initiatives promoted by the *Lehrhaus* and the *Akademie* in favor of adult education. His residence in Berlin did not prevent Strauss from continuing his traveling through Germany. If anything, precisely due to his engagement at the *Akademie* and to his relation to the *Lehrhaus*, he conducted an intense educational activity among adult Jews of different provincial cities. Rosenzweig pushed him towards this "communitarian" pedagogical activity. Precisely by ideating the *Lehrhaus* and the *Akademie*, Rosenzweig asserted the necessity to conjugate, by means of a deep rethinking of educational models, academic research with education, and the diffusion of Jewish culture inside German-Jewish communities, often characterized by ignorance or indifference towards Jewish history. Therefore, Rosenzweig conceived the *Lehrhaus* as a place where professors and researchers could meet adult and young Jews looking for a deeper knowledge of their tradition, supporting such knowledge with a reflection on the sense that a re-appropriation of Jewish history could provide to contemporary individuals and social life. Rosenzweig had in mind the same perspective for the *Akademie*, which, however, progressively lost this kind of activity, causing him irritation. Right at the beginning of the appointment he received from the *Akademie*, between February and September 1925, Strauss was sent to Kassel with the purpose of offering courses, lectures, and seminars concerning Jewish themes. The *Akademie* renewed the appointment in 1927 and 1928 and Strauss employed his stays there to contribute also to the local Jewish community's journal, the *Jüdische Wochenzeitung für Kassel, Hessen und Waldeck*, where he published a long review to Hermann Cohen's collection of Jewish writings, contextualizing them inside his broader philosophical system (cf. Strauss 2012a, 118–27). Despite his limited knowledge of the Hebrew language, in 1925 Strauss taught a course of biblical Hebrew—with little success—conducted by reading the books of *Judges*, *Kings*, and *Amos*, which he also used to discuss theoretical issues of political Zionism. Closer to his abilities and interests was the seminar he held, still in 1925, on German Judaism after Mendelssohn. Inside this course, the participants had the possibility to give lectures on topics such as: "Judaism and Hellenism in the nineteenth century (Heine, Moses, Hess, Cohen)," "The image of Spinoza in German Judaism (Mendelssohn, Heine, Hess, Graetz, Cohen)," "Revelation and science," and "Judaism and the German State." This seminar continued in the second half of 1925, focusing on the topic "Religion and criticism of religion (from Spinoza's *Tractatus Theologico-Politicus*)." Evidently, the issue was at the time at the center of Strauss's studies for the *Akademie* and it remained the subject of his lectures in 1927 and 1928. In these later years, also the topics of the Law in Maimonides and of the relationship between faith and knowledge emerged (cf. Strauss 2012a, 128–31). They later were at the core of his book *Philosophie und Gesetz* (1935).

The *Akademie für die Wissenschaft des Judentums* in Berlin

The *Akademie für die Wissenschaft des Judentums* was founded in Berlin in May 1919, based on the programmatic idea that Franz Rosenzweig had shared two years earlier with Hermann Cohen.[1] It immediately structured as a research institute that, by granting scholarships to young researchers, dealt with the development of scientific studies on Judaism (from philosophy to the Talmud, from the Kabbalah to literature, from archaeology to biblical philology). Eugen Täubler was its first scientific director, maintaining the position from 1919 to 1923. Julius Guttmann succeeded him in 1923 and remained there until 1934, when the experience of the *Akademie* ended.[2] The *Akademie* meant to develop a tradition of historical and critical studies that had already deeply rooted itself in German Judaism at least from the first half of the nineteenth century, the *Wissenschaft des Judentums*. This tradition had made a decisive contribution to the rise of a Jewish historical and philological thought, dedicating great attention to the discovery and assessment of sources. Leopold Zunz had inaugurated it. Then, it had developed especially through the works of Zacharias Fraenkel, Abraham Geiger, Solomon Munk, and Moritz Steinschneider. This created the cultural conditions for the successive foundation of a Jewish academic research and teaching institution, the *Hochschule für die Wissenschaft des Judentums* (founded in Berlin in 1872 by Abraham Geiger, Hermann Steinthal, David Cassel, and Israel Levy, later directed by Leo Baeck, who was able to keep it alive until 1942). For the *Wissenschaft des Judentums*, the term "science" did not imply a critique of Jewish tradition or faith. It rather meant a method of historical and critical research applied to Jewish issues, expressing, on a theoretical level, the desire of renovation and liberation and the need of "self-conscience" and "self-comprehension" that the history of Jewish emancipation and Enlightenment expressed on the level of political and civic life in Germany.

Compared to the interpretation of the *Wissenschaft des Judentums* given by the *Hochschule*, the *Akademie* abandoned the traditional seminarian programs of education for rabbis and the education addressed to teachers, in favor of a greater attention to historical and philological research. Not only: the *Akademie* also renewed the intentions and guidelines of the *Wissenschaft des Judentums*, emphasizing its research's theoretical and non-evaluative dimension, without however denying the basic principles already expressed by the 1822 *Zeitschrift für die Wissenschaft des Judentums*. According to the *Zeitschrift*, the study of Judaism had to develop with modern historical and critical research techniques, applied to the different social and cultural contexts and to the different economic and political conditions in which Jewish communities lived. In this sense, Eugen Täubler and Julius Guttmann confirmed the intentions promoted by the *Akademie* highlighting the coexistence, inside the *Akademie*'s interdisciplinary research program, of two perspectives: the respect for Jewish tradition and the specialized and objective scientific accuracy of research. Indeed, research did not only have to serve the renewal of studies on Judaism, but it also had to serve a better knowledge of the various and diverse levels that made up the "Jewish world" and the "Jewish existence"—avoiding the pitfalls represented by apologetics or edifying parables. Therefore, the *Akademie* proposed to offer a reinterpretation of the "true" spirit of the principles of the *Wissenschaft des Judentums*, escaping the deadlock that historicism and the debate between science and faith had reached. Indeed, it was essential to create the conditions so that a new philosophical (and not only historical) understanding of the "living" sources of Jewish existence was made possible for Jewish communities, in a close relationship between "science" and "life." However, this relationship was not related to any specific "decision" in terms of religious belief or "national" will, nor was it considered the essence of Jewish life beyond any possible critical questioning.

Besides the yearly bulletin (*Korrespondenzblatt des Vereins zur Gründung und Erhaltung einer Akademie für die Wissenschaft des Judentums*, published between 1919 and 1930), the *Akademie* directly sponsored numerous publications. Among them, certainly deserves a mention the seven volumes (out of sixteen originally planned) of Moses Mendelssohn's complete writings, published from 1929 as a celebration of the two hundredth anniversary of his birth.[3] The *Akademie* also founded its own publishing house, the *Akademie-Verlag*, where it published its researchers' monographic studies, some of which also appeared in other publications.[4] Particularly important for an understanding of the *Akademie*'s cultural project and its research activity is the analysis of each issue of the yearly bulletin, the mentioned *Korrespondenzblatt* that appeared as the *Akademie*'s yearbook, which, as the editorial notes in the frontispiece of every single issue say, "has the task of making public the development of the scholarly work conducted by the Institute's researchers." The *Korrespondenzblatt*'s scientific structure upheld the interdisciplinary approach to the field of Jewish studies. Indeed, each issue contained contributions from various disciplines, from the history of Talmudic literature to the history of Jewish communities, from textual history and criticism (of the Talmud, Mishnah, Midrash, etc.) to Kabbalistic literature, from the comparative history of religions to the history of medieval philosophy, from demography to economic history.

The *Akademie* did not intend to deny the scientific and rational legacy of the traditional *Wissenschaft des Judentums*, but it aimed at the coexistence of free research with the recovery of the Jewish roots, intended as living roots, not simply fossils. Despite this, the *Akademie*'s enlightened program would have appeared cold and distant to many young German Jews coping with the failed promises of assimilation and in search for their Jewish identity. Indeed, the *Akademie*'s research program stood halfway between the enlightened tradition of liberal Judaism and the strong desire for religious, political, and spiritual innovation of the new movements of "return" to Judaism (first and foremost Zionism) surfaced at the beginning of the twentieth century. A third option, of course, lay in rabbinic orthodoxy, which considered all these emancipative or innovative tendencies as a sign of the Jewish spirit's decadence. The *Akademie*'s enlightened perspective did not prevent the participation of many young German Jews, animated by a deep spirit of renovation of Judaism and by a strong desire of return to Judaism. The nondogmatic atmosphere that characterized the institute favored the creation of a plural research environment, animated by research with different backgrounds: Zionist, liberal, neo-Kantian, and orthodox. Many of these researchers—among whom Gershom Scholem, Simon Rawidowicz, Fritz Baer, Nahum Glatzer, Haim Borodianski, Bruno Strauss, and Fritz Bamberger—found in the *Akademie* a fertile ground to produce essays and monographs. Leo Strauss was among them too.

The Assignment at the *Akademie*

Strauss became a researcher at the *Akademie* in February 1925, sponsored by Rosenzweig, who, being among the founders of the institution, as well as a central figure of German Judaism, expressed an authoritative opinion in his favor. Guttman, the director of the *Akademie*, also particularly favored Strauss's appointment there. He had met Strauss when the latter had attended his seminars on Maimonides in Berlin and had read his articles published on *Der Jude* and *Jüdische Rundschau*, especially the important 1924 essay on Cohen and Spinoza, where Strauss's abilities in the history of philosophy, in political philosophy, and hermeneutics were already clear. Guttmann was a neo-Kantian thinker, representative of a liberal Judaism similar to Cohen's. His aim as director of the *Akademie* was that of promoting "non-evaluative" scientific research. However, despite Strauss's strong criticism of Cohen's reading of Spinoza and of liberal Judaism, Guttmann believed the young scholar had the qualities to conduct research on the biblical hermeneutics of Spinoza's *Tractatus Theologico-Politicus*—one of the key points of Strauss's 1924 essay. Therefore, Guttmann entrusted Strauss precisely with this task, the first result of which was the essay *Zur Bibelwissenschaft Spinozas und seiner Vorläufer*, published on the *Korrespondenzblatt* (1926). In its brevity, the essay exposes the basic contents that later constituted Strauss's monograph on Spinoza. Indeed, it presents the primary targets of the criticism moved by Spinoza's biblical science (i.e., Maimonides, Calvin, and orthodoxy) and also announces the ongoing research on the predecessors of Spinoza's hermeneutics (Uriel da Costa, Isaac de La Peyrère, and Hobbes). More importantly, however, in his 1926 essay Strauss was able to identify the true object of his research, which shifted from Spinoza's biblical science to the conditions of possibility of that same biblical science. Strauss caught a glimpse of these conditions in the tradition of critique of religion, initiated by Epicure, continued by Averroes, Machiavelli, and Hobbes, and inherited by Spinoza, before it found its sociopolitical apex with eighteenth-century Enlightenment. Caused precisely by this shift in the entrusted research were Strauss's first contrasts with Guttmann, who did not approve the change and reminded Strauss—in vain—the original appointment he had received from the *Akademie*. Strauss finished his research in 1928, but Guttmann requested several corrections and integrations. On 22 May 1929, Strauss addressed a letter to Guttmann together with a new copy of his work, pointing out the places in which he had operated with corrections, but also asserting his intention not to intervene on other issues as requested by Guttmann[5]. The situation stalled until 1930, when Guttmann, after having further delayed the publication, decided to publish Strauss's first monograph: *Die Religionskritik Spinozas als Grundlage seiner Bibelwissenschaft. Untersuchungen zu Spinozas Theologisch-politischem Traktat*, dedicated to the memory of Franz Rosenzweig. It appeared as the second volume of the *Akademie*'s philosophical series. Strauss's friend, Gerhard Krüger—who had known the text in an almost complete form since 1928 (cf. Strauss and Krüger 2001, 377–38), published a review of it in an important German journal,[6] which granted the book some success, despite it appearing inside the limited German-Jewish world. The book even attracted Carl Schmitt's attention.[7] Given the resistance by Guttmann, due to his dissatisfaction for the work's theoretical perspective and the fact that the subject had changed from the original plan, Strauss had to write a brief preface, in which he acknowledged the shift in respect to the assignment:

> Regarding the assignment entrusted to the author by the *Akademie für die Wissenschaft des Judentums*, this work was to have as its object the Spinozian exegesis of the Bible. In the course of the investigation, the central core shifted, however, as was foreseeable from the beginning of the research, to the conditions that that exegesis makes possible and which essentially reside in the critique of religion. (Strauss 1930, VII)

In a letter addressed to Krüger on 7 January 1930, Strauss was more outspoken, accusing Guttmann of having adopted inquisitorial methods that resembled censure and of having deliberately kept his work on hold for over a year due to the "atheistic premises" that allegedly conditioned his interpretation of Spinoza's biblical science (cf. Strauss and Krüger 2001, 378–81). The conditioning would have been such that the book's results had become hardly comprehensible, having lost expressive clarity, and having made the structure more unclear.

Despite his conflict with Guttmann, Strauss received other appointments from the *Akademie*. Namely, in 1928 he became one of the editors of Mendelssohn's *Gesammelte Schriften*, directed by Ismar Elbogen, Julius Guttmann, and Eugen Mittwoch. Strauss edited and translated the three volumes of *Schriften zur Philosophie und Ästhetik*, two with Simon Rawidowicz, all under Guttmann's direction. A fundamental thinker for the history of modern Judaism, Mendelssohn was an author that

Strauss admired, but did not love. Strauss considered him the primary representative of "moderate Enlightenment," of the modern trend that (unsuccessfully) attempted to conciliate faith and reason, Enlightenment and orthodoxy, tradition and modernity. Mendelssohn was also the universally recognized father of the emancipation process of the Jews in the modern world and, consequently, the creator of the conditions for the *Wissenschaft des Judentums*, for assimilation and religious liberalism, the cultural and philosophical experience that Strauss criticized. Anyway, Strauss actively and diligently took part in the editorial work, producing an important section of the work. A part of it appeared between 1931 and 1932, while the rest remained unpublished, initially due to the *Akademie*'s financial problems and then to the Nazi persecutions. The remaining part only appeared in the 1960s and 1970s, although it had been ready since 1936–1937.[8] The texts edited and introduced by Strauss are among the most important ones published by Mendelssohn, especially *Morgenstunden* (1785) and *An die Freunde Lessings* (1786), dedicated to defending Lessing from the accusations he had received from Jacobi, according to whom Lessing was a devout admirer of Spinoza, and which—from 1783—had originated the *Pantheismusstreit*. In his studies on Mendelssohn, Strauss found a way to deepen his research on Lessing, the modern author he most admired, due to his ability to recover the Greek classics, and that, from the second half of the 1930s, provided him important inspiration for the elaboration of his theory of reticent writing. Moreover, inside the debate between Jacobi and Mendelssohn concerning Lessing's Spinozism, Strauss took sides with Mendelssohn, denying that Lessing was a follower of Spinoza *sic et simpliciter*.

Still for the *Akademie*, in 1928 Strauss began another research project dedicated to Gersonides's prophetology, with special attention to his work *The Wars of the Lord*.[9] Soon, a new contrast sparked with Guttmann regarding this second project. Already in 1929, Strauss's attention moved from Gersonides to Maimonides and his Islamic predecessors (Al-Farabi, Averroes, and Avicenna) as interpreters of Platonic political philosophy, with research that did not immediately produce publications, but that, condensed in some *papers* on Maimonides and medieval Islamic and Jewish philosophy written between 1931 and 1932, later became part of *Philosophie und Gesetz* (1935). His general interpretative framework for medieval philosophy quickly became clear. On 26 June 1930, Strauss proposed that Krüger organize a seminar in Marburg, briefly listing the "enlightened" characters of Islamic and Jewish medieval thought (different from Christian Scholasticism), which would be at the heart of his later publications: Law as a social and political system, rationalism founded on revelation, the recovery of political Platonism (cf. Strauss and Krüger 2001, 382–83). Strauss's growing attention for medieval Islamic texts favored his encounter with Paul Kraus, future husband of his sister Bettina, who in Berlin provided him with the necessary philological insight to deal with the study of the classics of medieval Jewish and Islamic philosophy (Al-Razi, Al-Farabi, Averroes, Avicenna, Maimonides, Saadia Gaon, Gersonides, and Abravanel). To this study, Strauss dedicated the days he spent at the *Staatsbibliothek* between 1929 and 1931.

Notwithstanding its broadness, plurality, and diversification, the research undertaken by the young Strauss in the 1920s and 1930s followed a compact and coherent logic. The crisis of modernity—in science, rationality, philosophy, and liberal politics—initially led him, on a philosophical level, to read Jacobi, among the authors that in the modern age most insisted on the limits of scientific reason and enlightened thought. On the theological and political level, his endorsement of political Zionism could answer at first his questions on sense and identity, in an anti-liberal perspective. However, in a second phase, political Zionism revealed its theoretical, religious, and political groundlessness. The convergence of these two directions, originated from a common root, brought Strauss to a polemical confrontation with Cohen, in whom the theoretical dimension of modern philosophy and the liberal perspective in politics and religion met. The result was predictable: for a reader of Nietzsche, like Strauss in the early 1920s, Cohen's position was untenable both on a philosophical-political level and on the level of Jewish tradition. There seemed to be no way out: even the most important authors—Heidegger and Rosenzweig—radicalized the modern crisis, showing aspects that not even Husserl, Weber, Freud, or Spengler had brought to light, without however offering *rationally* possible solutions. This was precisely the distinctive trait of Strauss's thought up to the 1920s: his substantially *rational* nature, notwithstanding his theological and political interests. Even during the Zionist debates he attended, his point of view was not *action* but *reflection*, which cost him a progressive exclusion from the *Kartell*, lived without sufferance, since Strauss himself realized that his path was neither theology nor politics, but philosophy. The intersection of all these interests—the crisis of philosophical and political modernity, the theological and political issue, Zionism, the "return" to Judaism—produced an almost predictable result: Spinoza. Strauss had to deal with the Dutch philosopher, especially to unravel the bundle of tangled and unsolved issues he saw in front of him. However, Strauss's *Destruktion* did not end with Spinoza, given that the analysis of the *Tractatus* confirmed what he had already perceived, that neither modern orthodoxy nor modern reason offered good reasons for one to embrace either of them in a lucid, convinced, and well-supported way. Up to 1928, when he completed his monograph on Spinoza, Strauss saw only debris around him: everywhere he looked he saw problems and critical issues, not solutions nor rays of light. He could certainly not find such solutions in Mendelssohn, who anyway constituted a natural arrival for a scholar who had worked on Spinoza and Jacobi. Where else could he look?

The years 1928–1932 represented a watershed for two reasons. On the one hand, Strauss's juvenile enthusiasm for radical political movements progressively faded and therefore his *radical* inclination assumed a *philosophical* dimension (while simultaneously embracing politically conservative inclinations). On the other hand, he began to sense that modern reason was not the sole model of rationality, since the *querelle des anciens et des modernes* precisely regarded two different models of rationality: the first, the pre-modern one, founded on moderate skepticism (which he later defined zetetic); the other, the modern one, based on a dogmatic skepticism. Two research possibilities appeared then, alongside Spinoza: on one side, the examination of modern philosophy's origins by means of a comparison with Hobbes's thought (a natural arrival point for Strauss, who had dealt with Spinoza and the theological-political problem) as the foundation of Enlightenment, positivism, and historicism. On the other side, the return to Maimonides and his Islamic teachers Avicenna, Averroes, and Al-Farabi as representatives of an "enlightened" rationalism that did not coincide with the modern one. Strauss took the final step in this complex and plural, yet organic and rational, path by combining these two possibilities. Indeed, in both cases the reference (of Hobbes's critique and of Maimonides's praises) was constituted by classical Greek philosophy, namely Plato, which therefore became the subject of Strauss's research. His phase of "change of orientation" concluded in 1932; between 1932 and 1935 Strauss initiated a new philosophical-political research perspective (the return to pre-modern classics), which accompanied him for the rest of his life.

Spinoza's Critique of Religion and His Biblical Science

The work that Strauss carried out on Spinoza for the *Akademie* was already present in the title of his 1930 monograph: Spinoza's critique of religion as the foundation of his biblical science. Strauss's analysis was not only limited to verifying the validity and legitimacy of Spinoza's biblical science, but rather it tried to find the *conditions of possibility* of that same biblical science, which ultimately lied in his radical critique of religion. In principle, no obstacle weighs on the foundation of modern biblical science precisely because Spinoza assumes that the Bible is a literary document like any other, which should be treated in a scientific way just like any other. The foundation of this critical assumption of revealed religion precedes any scientific constitution of Spinoza's hermeneutical method. The radical critique of religion is not a result of biblical science, but, vice versa, radical criticism of religion is the prerequisite of biblical science. For this reason, according to Strauss, enlightened critique of religion—founded by Spinoza—is only a peculiar, historically determined, stage of philosophical critique of religion in its complex, which originated with Epicure (cf. Strauss 1930, 3–20). Indeed, Spinoza's modern critique of religion operates an ancient epicurean motive that crosses the entire history of philosophy: from Democritus to Machiavelli, from Averroes to Giordano Bruno, from Uriel da Costa to Isaac de La Peyrère, from Gassendi to Hobbes, from Hume to Voltaire, from Feuerbach to Marx. It expresses the human beings' interest in freeing itself from the fear of ultra-terrestrial powers. Epicure's critique of religion traveled to the seventeenth century not so much in the form of a codified doctrine, but rather in the form of an original inclination of the heart and the mind that aims at finding a peace of the spirit. Compared to the ancient epicurean motive, between the seventeenth and eighteenth century, critique of religion shifted, both from an interest for the peace of the spirit to an interest for social peace and from a refusal of religion for its terrifying aspects to a refusal of religion for its delusive character. The fundamental aim of the enlightened revolt, therefore, consisted in the liberation from fear, in the reassurance about existence on earth, in the assurance of life.

The radical critique of religion claimed to be a scientific critique. Such scientific claim was never in doubt to the eyes of its supporters, not even when it occurred that religion was vigorously contrasted more for its harmfulness or wickedness than for the wrongfulness of its teachings.

Not even when these supporters were reminded that critique of religion is not limited to theoretical disapproval, but that it goes as far as practical rebellion. In Strauss's interpretation, the critics of religion of all ages expect that science may free them from religion. Aiming at a practical target, they do not distinguish their premises from their methods and from their results, which would not be possible without those premises. The scientific method serves a goal: freedom originated by the liberation from religion by means of a practical rebellion that precedes the method and that determines the results. Indeed, such freedom does not consist in beatitude of theory, of the "pure" research of truth, i.e., contemplative life, but rather in the happiness that derives from the search of a *reassuring* truth, be it the elimination of fear, the search for pleasure, or the pursuit of social peace. In this sense, Spinoza's biblical science is nothing but a means, oriented to a purpose *external* to science as well as religion, founded on prejudice (which is a *historical* category completely different from appearance and opinion, the consideration of which determines the birth of philosophy). In the *Tractatus*, biblical science serves an exclusively instrumental purpose towards the critique of revelation as a whole, which is in turn the necessary introduction to philosophy. The liberation of philosophy, in its being propaedeutic to philosophy, precedes philosophy's liberty. Spinoza's critique of religion splits into pre-philosophical critique and philosophical critique. Biblical science precedes, from a chronological point of view, the philosophical critique of religion, while, actually, philosophical critique of religion is the logical premise of biblical science (cf. Strauss 1930, 247–64). In this sense, Spinoza's enemy in his critique of the authority of the Scripture, with a propaedeutic and necessary act for the freedom of philosophy, is not Maimonides (cf. Strauss 1930, 129–81), but religious orthodoxy and, especially, Calvin, identified as the most radical opponent of the right to free philosophical research. Naturally, the propaedeutic point of view, with which Spinoza fights Calvin with his own weapons, i.e., biblical exegesis, *appears* to be decisive, while it is not such. What is decisive for the success of *Tractatus* is Spinoza's argument, which defines impossible anything that is not rationally verifiable and anything that eludes the eternal mechanical flow of nature. However, Strauss noted, there is no common ground between Spinoza and Calvin, on which a confrontation would be possible between the two different ways to experience the world, even though Calvin had no intention to give its faith a theoretical foundation (cf. Strauss 1930, 182–206).

Strauss raised many doubts about Spinoza's method, which cannot scientifically demonstrate the impossibility of miracles, but only their unknowability. Indeed, religious orthodoxy bases all its beliefs on the existence of an inscrutable and omnipotent God. Given such premise, which Spinoza cannot refute, revelations and miracles are possible. According to Strauss, this theoretical lack, however, does not concern Spinoza alone, but modern Enlightenment as a whole. Spinoza's critique of religion can demonstrate that the premises of orthodoxy—for instance, concerning miracles—cannot be *known*, but it cannot refute orthodoxy, which asserts the *belief* in those premises. Therefore, Enlightenment's battle against orthodoxy does not entirely hit its target and many doubts remain regarding its metaphysical and scientific foundation. Even the mature Strauss's words show the results that he had attained through his analysis of Spinoza's biblical science, founded on the critique of religion:

> If orthodoxy claims to know that the Bible is divinely revealed, that every word of the Bible is divinely inspired, that Moses was the writer of the Pentateuch, that the miracles recorded in the Bible have happened and similar things, Spinoza has refuted orthodoxy. But the case is entirely different if orthodoxy limits itself to asserting that it believes the aforementioned things, i.e., that they cannot claim to possess the binding power peculiar to the known. For all assertions of orthodoxy rest on the irrefutable premise that the omnipotent God whose will is unfathomable . . . may exist. Given this premise, miracles and revelations in general, and hence all Biblical miracles and revelations in particular, are possible. Spinoza has not succeeded in showing that this premise is contradicted by anything we know. (Strauss 1965, 28)[10]

Logic or experience cannot confute the premises of orthodoxy, at least not before the philosophical system is able to comprehend perfectly any mystery related to the world and to human life. However, in this sense, modern philosophy has come short of accomplishing a philosophical system based on radical reason. If God's "way" is not the "way" of human beings, then we cannot control God's "way" through experience, rationality, or experiment. Therefore, any attempt to scientifically prove the inexistence (or the existence) of God is essentially inappropriate. The criticism of religion is possible and legitimate only as a defensive criticism. However, if the results of modern rationalism do not maintain the promises of the modern project, also religious orthodoxy does not seem to demonstrate its validity. This is particularly true for Jewish orthodoxy, which cannot validate its uniqueness. According to Strauss, the result achieved by the test of the *Tractatus* does not provide the modern Jew with convincing arguments in favor of a return to Judaism. Indeed, not only does modern enlightened rationalism clearly shows its inadequacy, but orthodoxy also does the same, since one cannot know, but only *believe* in its premises. At this point—also considering the theoretical limitations posed by Zionism, Cohen, and Rosenzweig—Strauss's path appeared rather narrow:

> The victory of orthodoxy through the self-destruction of rational philosophy was not an unmitigated blessing, for it was a victory not of Jewish orthodoxy but of any orthodoxy, and Jewish orthodoxy based its claim of superiority to other religions from the beginning on its superior rationality . . . Other observations and experiences confirmed the suspicion that it would be unwise to say farewell to reason. I began therefore to wonder whether the self-destruction of reason was not the inevitable outcome of modern rationalism as distinguished from pre-modern rationalism, especially Jewish medieval rationalism and its classical (Aristotelian and Platonic) foundation. The present study was based on the premise, sanctioned by powerful prejudice, that a return to pre-modern philosophy is impossible. The change of orientation which found its first expression, not entirely by accident, in the article [on Carl Schmitt], compelled me to engage in a number of studies in the course of which I became ever more attentive to the manner in which heterodox thinkers of earlier ages wrote their books. (Strauss 1965, 30–31)

Beyond the Modern Crisis

A "change of orientation," as Strauss himself defined it, occurred in the years between 1928 and 1932. Without emphasizing such autobiographical assertion—since actual revolutions of thought are absent from Strauss's intellectual biography, characterized by a substantial thematic continuity and philosophical awareness, besides some obvious changes of mind and evaluations on single issues and authors—it is necessary to identify which theoretical point originated this "change." The monograph on Spinoza concluded the first phase of Strauss's studies, which led him to a critical analysis of the legitimacy of the foundations of philosophical and political modernity. The result of his work on the *Tractatus Theologico-Politicus*, starting from the conflict between philosophy and revelation, was not reassuring. The two opponents—modern reason and religious orthodoxy—both unveiled their unfoundedness and there did not seem to be any way of salvation from the crisis of modernity. In his analysis of the contrast between faith and reason, Strauss did not find an answer to the question "How should we live?," which not even political Zionism could answer coherently. However, Strauss did not mean to abandon philosophy, nor reason—nor did he mean to embrace Jewish orthodoxy—and he began to wonder if reason's self-destruction could be the inevitable result of modern rationalism, different from other forms of rationalism. Therefore, he meant to verify the existence of a possibility to elaborate a different form of rationalism that could avoid the pitfalls of relativism and nihilism by recovering the work of medieval Islamic and Jewish philosophers, Maimonides in particular, who represented a necessary outcome of his research on Spinoza. Thus, the answer to the question "How should we live?" moves from the theological-political level to a *philosophical* level, initially concerning medieval philosophers and later Greek philosophers. In this way Strauss began a skeptical, maybe even "atheistic," interpretation of religious orthodoxy, necessary for sociopolitical reasons, but not theoretically justified, which in the end shifted his theological-political interests on an evidently philosophical level. If, as Klein asserted, God and politics were the young Strauss's true interests (cf. Strauss 1970d, 1), following his "change of orientation," these topics remained central among his interests, but he added a new decisive lens through which he inspected them. The lens was philosophy.[11]

The historical-philosophical study Strauss began in 1928 on medieval thought—by reading the texts by Al-Razi, Al-Farabi, Averroes, Avicenna, Maimonides, and Gersonides available at the *Staatsbibliothek* in Berlin—had philosophical and political motivations, linked to the crisis of modernity and the contemporary theoretical urgencies. Besides the project on medieval philosophy, Strauss's studies on Spinoza also offered him another research path, related to the identification of the foundations of modern philosophical and political thought, which began in the seventeenth century, but which, to some extent, had some roots in the Reformation. It is not hard to understand the reasons that brought Strauss to Hobbes, considering Spinoza's dependence on the English philosopher, and considering that Hobbes enjoyed huge historiographical fortune in early twentieth-century Germany, spreading his appeal also to the young Strauss. He identified in Hobbes the key figure to understand the birth of modernity and to reopen the *querelle des anciens et des modernes*. Therefore, having ended his work on Spinoza, Strauss oriented his research in two different and complementary directions. On one side, medieval Jewish and Islamic philosophy as bearer of a different model of rationalism. On the other, Hobbes's political philosophy as the most representative of the modern conceptions of natural right and, more in general, of modernity, the nihilistic result of which was represented by Nietzsche. Nietzsche's atheism did not equate to traditional, or natural, skepticism, given that it inherited biblical morality and could only be conceived in a post-Christian perspective (as, after all, was the case for Heidegger's existentialism): Nietzsche's atheism differs from classical atheism because it considers that the "death of God" is like the setting of a sun, not a rebellion or a moral revolt against God. For Strauss, historical research on the roots of modernity did not have a merely antiquarian meaning, but, instead, it was necessary to understand how to avoid the "pitfall" that had spread inside the relationship between science and faith, between philosophy and politics. Therefore, Strauss's work appears as a historical "deconstruction" of the modern premises, in order to reopen the *querelle des anciens et des modernes*. Strauss only fully elaborated his famous assertions on the superiority of the ancient over the modern in the 1940s, when he was in the US. However, we can only understand them in their intimate origin considering the problematic context provided by early twentieth-century German philosophy, deployed in particular on the controversial relationship between philosophy, science, and politics in the modern world. Following the collapse of all philosophical systems, a strong awareness of the crisis that hit the sense and meaning of science and politics in the modern world characterized German culture, between nihilism and rationalization, reification, and massification, between *Kultur* and *Zivilisation*. Therefore, Strauss returned to Hobbes in the attempt to identify the foundation of the contradictions of the modern project, elaborated in their utmost evidence by Nietzsche and centered on the theological and political issue (cf. Strauss 1965, 1).

The "change of orientation" in his thought, which Strauss asserted he had condensed in a 1932 essay on Schmitt, actually regards a larger chronological scope, beginning in 1928, with the completion of his monograph on Spinoza, and comprising the analysis of several issues, all based on the new certainty that a return to pre-modern philosophy was possible. Firstly, as we have seen, he began two separate and complementary research projects on Hobbes and on medieval Islamic and Jewish philosophy, which both found their origin in the conclusions he had reached analyzing Spinoza's critique of religion and that both aimed at identifying the theoretical, philosophical, and political characters of modernity. Secondly, Strauss began a reflection on classical Greek philosophy, on Plato in particular, which subtracted him from the urgencies of the contemporary world (the situation of Judaism, etc.) and led him to a study on the *nature* of philosophy that absorbed him until the last years of his life. Such interest for classical philosophy—and especially for the issue of good life—was present in *Religiöse Lage der Gegenwart*, the text of a lecture he held on 21 December 1930 at the congress of the juvenile Zionist organization *Kadimah* in Brieselang, near Berlin (cf. *Religiöse Lage der Gegenwart*, in Strauss 1997a, 377–91). Despite its title and despite the occasion in which the text was read, in the essay Strauss insisted several times on the theme of the search for truth. Such theme had already been present in his "Zionist" writings, although in those occasions he had treated it making clear reference to current political debates, while now he dealt with it referring to Socrates and Plato (and we can only imagine the surprise of those taking part in the congress!). Obviously, the difference was not limited only to the discussed authors, but more in general the theoretical approach with which Strauss dealt with the theme of philosophical knowledge. Indeed, in the 1930 essay, we see the surfacing of Strauss's controversy against historicism, i.e., the modern ideology according to which there are no eternal truths, but only "historical" and "relative" truths. In this perspective, Strauss used the Platonic allegory of the *cave* to illustrate the obstacles to which the truth exposes philosophical research. He highlighted how these obstacles had changed in the modern age, not only from the natural obstacle to philosophize, but also from the peculiar epistemological position of modern philosophy and science, which lead to a "second" unnatural cave, determined by historicism's prejudices.

Strauss had already partly exposed this anti-historicist perspective in the essay *Der Konspektivismus* (1929), dedicated to the critical discussion—fierce and trenchant, at times in an embarrassing way due to the mocking tones—of the book *Ideologie und Utopie* (1929) by Karl Mannheim (cf. Strauss 1997a, 365–75; cf. also Strauss and Krüger 2001, 383–84). Strauss considered Mannheim a significant representative of the modern sophists, the primary philosophical expression residing in Heidegger's thought. The historicity of human condition does not make it possible to deal with philosophical issues "in general," but only in the present perspective, intended as a synoptic, or overall, sight, which outgrows all previous periods. Against Mannheim's "conspective" idea (from the Latin *conspectio*, intended here as "perspectivism"), Strauss asserted the total vacuity of the concept, given that, while it aimed at understanding the past from the perspective of the superiority of the present, it actually did not understand any distinction and built an empty faith in progress, void of any theoretical foundation. In the past, the opposition between different philosophical theories rested on the premise that there were right and wrong philosophical theories concerning the issue of *the* truth, valid for any time. The possibility of drawing the truth in the present was no longer available, because the orientation of every historicist theory, from the nineteenth century onwards, asserted the historical and social conditioning of any philosophical system. However, in this way, there was no longer room for any free thought and philosophy gave up confronting the issue of truth. A sociological diagnostics of the present had taken over the place reserved to metaphysics, while the intellectual had taken the place once held by the philosopher.

Strauss's anti-historicist polemic and the allegory of the *cave* are also present in his review to a book by Julius Ebbinghaus, published in 1931,[12] inside the letters he addressed to Krüger in November and December 1932 (cf. Strauss and Krüger 2001, 404ff., 420ff.) and in the book *Philosophie und Gesetz* (1935), becoming an essential trait of Strauss's thought. He also returned to anti-historicism on several occasions in the years he spent in the US. In his review to Ebbinghaus's book, Strauss asserts that the modern individual lives in a "second," "historical," and "artificial" cave, deeper than Plato's "natural" cave. In the present the obstacle to philosophizing is therefore "squared," because historicist relativism has determined the construction of a "second" cave (made of modern prejudices) from which it is necessary to ascend to the "first" cave (of opinion and appearance), to then attempt going out into the sunlight (metaphor of the search for truth). While Greek philosophy began with "things," modern philosophy begins with concepts: naturally, also beginning with "things" is problematic and entails the "natural" difficulties of philosophizing (the opinions that determined human existence in the "first" cave), but the obstacles that philosophy encounters in the present are by far greater, because "artificial" difficulties are added on to the "natural" ones. Therefore, it is necessary to *relearn* the fundamental issues by reading the texts of the past and *recovering* the philosophical lesson of Greek classics through the study of *history of philosophy*. Central to this purpose is historical research—different from historicism—that, in "deconstructing" modern prejudices, allows us to ascend from the "second" cave to the "first" cave. Thus, today we need a philosophical propaedeutic able to remove the "artificial" obstacles that stand on the way of philosophy and to reopen the *querelle des anciens et des modernes*. Strauss also asserted this in his essay *Die geistige Lage der Gegenwart* (1932), where—besides renewing his criticism of "historical conscience" and theories of progress—he seemed to retrace his personal intellectual biography in the 1920s, briefly pausing on three key moments. The first was the issue of the present from the perspective of the problematic situation of Judaism (namely political Zionism, cultural Zionism, and Rosenzweig's "return" to the Law). Secondly, the crisis of modernity, dealt with through the opposition between orthodoxy and Enlightenment. Finally, the recovery of a rationalism—like the one proper to Maimonides, but especially to Plato—able to present the question of good and justice. It is clear that these three moments correspond to three different phases of Strauss's thought in the 1920s (different phases, but tangled together and intended in a close relation, both chronological and theoretical). First, the "critical" involvement in Jewish movements, then the work on Spinoza as a key to interpret the foundations of modernity, and finally the "change of orientation" with the reopening of the *querelle* and the recovery of medieval and classical philosophy.

The Critique of Liberalism

Strauss had been reading Hobbes since the summer of 1922, when in Freiburg he attended Julius Ebbinghaus's lectures on the social doctrines of the Reformation and Enlightenment. Ebbinghaus's approach was unconventional, since it highlighted Hobbes's originality, releasing him from the stereotype of the materialist thinker, underlining the "resolution" (*Aufhebung*) of Kantian philosophy as the most significant part of his teaching. Therefore, the young Strauss found a theoretical interpretation of Hobbes, halfway between neo-Kantianism and Hegelianism, which directed him to identifying the English philosopher as a fundamental crossroad for modern thought, who, however, did not entirely answer his questions concerning the theological and political issue. Strauss found a more strictly *political* interpretation of Hobbes in 1927, when Carl Schmitt published the first edition of his essay *Der Begriff des "Politischen."* With this interpretation Strauss dealt by writing a long critical note on the third edition of *Der Begriff des "Politischen"* (1932), which appeared on the *Archiv für Sozialwissenschaft und Sozialpolitik* (cf. Strauss 1932b). The reasons for Strauss's approach to Schmitt did not only lie in the interpretation of Hobbes's thought. Given the political radicalism—with right-wing orientation—that animated the young Strauss in an anti-modern, anti-bourgeois, anti-liberal, and anti-capitalist direction, we clearly see why Schmitt's criticism of democracy and parliamentarianism became an inescapable reference for him. Strauss could only find the author of the *Politische Theologie* (1922) congenial to his thought, especially due to Schmitt's disdain of commercial and industrial society, of bourgeois culture, technology, and consumerism. Such sympathies clearly emerge also from the letters that the young Strauss addressed to Schmitt between March 1932 and July 1933—even after Hitler had become chancellor and Schmitt had officially entered the Nazi party! Strauss initially wrote to Schmitt to thank him for having supported his application to the Rockefeller Foundation. Then he wrote again to add some considerations to the review he had in the meantime published on the *Archiv*. Finally, he addressed him letters to request his help in being involved in a hypothetical critical edition of Hobbes's works directed by Carl Joachim Friedrich, which never actually began (cf. Strauss 1988).[13]

However, congeniality did not seem enough to avoid Strauss's criticism. Despite sharing Schmitt's underlying reasons, which lay in the criticism of liberal modernity, Strauss proceeded to verify the contradictions present in his position. Strauss's attention went to Schmitt's claim of the necessity and specificity of the *political*, used as a way to overcome the liberal paradox of an *anti-political politics* that aimed at its neutralization and de-politicization. However, Schmitt's critique of modern liberalism did not have its foundation, as it should have, in the critique of the modern concept of culture (*Kultur*). Across a tradition that moved from the *Geisteswissenschaften* to the *Kulturwissenschaften* (which Strauss interpreted as propaedeutic to *historicism*), modern philosophy—at the root of liberalism—has founded the idea of culture in *opposition* to nature, to later consider culture as an autonomous "value," as paramount creation of the spirit and the totality of human action. Schmitt's critique of modern liberalism did not confront this theoretical problem and remained on the surface, since it was limited to the critique of the outcomes of modern philosophy (i.e., liberalism), without facing its foundations. If the political is the natural, extreme, and fundamental *status* of the human being, it appeared to Strauss just as the first step—necessary, but not sufficient—towards a critique of the modern concept of culture (cf. Strauss 1932b, 734ff.). Against the liberal negation of the political, Schmitt intended to *reaffirm* the position of the political and *replace* the liberal system with another system of thought, able to *recognize* the political status and, on this path, to bring light back on the "order of human things." However, this reaffirmation, this substitution and this recognition were only the result of a *moral preference*, not of a theoretical criticism of the foundations of liberalism. The insufficiency of Schmitt's position was therefore evident to Strauss, since he was not able to free himself from the modern philosophical categories, thus confirming his permanence inside the context of thought determined by liberalism and by modern conception of culture: Schmitt remained tangled in the net of modern thought.[14]

If the foundation of culture is the state of nature, then Hobbes, according to Strauss's interpretation, was the first to determine the specific *modern* concept of culture, visible in the conception of the civil state as *opposed* to the natural state. Hobbes's characterization of the state of nature has a polemical value, in the perspective of its overcoming by means of a rational disciplining of human beings' will and desires. Indeed, the denial of the natural state means peace and security, obtained by means of the constitution of the State, which allows well-being and enrichment inside a context of moderate freedom. According to Strauss, then, Hobbes is the founder of the *modern ideal* of civilization (*Zivilisation*), meant as a rationally based cohabitation of humanity, which works with the aid of scientific progress until it becomes a community of production and consumption. Based on Schmitt's parameters, however, Hobbes is the ultimate "anti-political" thinker, given that the political (the opposition friend/enemy and the state of nature as a condition of war) according to the English philosopher has to be denied. Strauss read the difference between Hobbes and Schmitt in terms of a contrast between *negation of the political* and *assertion of the political*, between civilization and state of nature, peace and war, moderation and courage. The critique of modern liberalism cannot go through a simple opposition between moral preferences. Such critique reaches its scope only if confronted with the foundation of modernity initiated by Hobbes. He was the first to give a radical justification of the liberal principles, i.e., of bourgeois individualism, answering the question regarding the right life of the human being and the right order of society through the elaboration of the concept of *right*, meant as an individual inalienable demand (cf. Strauss 1932b, 737ff.).

A radical critique of liberalism is only possible based on a critique of Hobbes's philosophy, towards which the assertion of the political represents just the first step. Instead, Schmitt only aims at asserting the political intended as the real, fundamental, character of human life: the political is a *fact*, it is a *destiny*, which cannot be considered in an evaluative way, nor in a normative way, since it finds its justification in an analysis on the fundamentally dangerous character of human nature. The theme of *domination* (*Herrschaft*) fully expressed such an interpretation of danger. It is the true premise of Schmitt's recognition of the political. In Strauss's interpretation, Schmitt's opposition is not between pacifism and warmongering, nor between nationalism and internationalism, but between *authority* and *anarchy*. However, to justify the necessity of domination, Schmitt should challenge the idea (in Hobbes) of "innocent" human wickedness and recover the idea of wickedness as moral corruption (in a "theological" sense). Such an inversion, according to Strauss, did not occur. Moreover, the "animal" wickedness admired by Schmitt, considered by him as a "privilege," is actually a deficiency, which cannot be "recognized," but only "asserted." While in Hobbes the natural, and therefore innocent, wickedness is emphasized so that it can be fought, Schmitt speaks with sympathy of wickedness (cf. Strauss 1932b, 740ff.). But what is the meaning then of his affirmation of the political? According to Strauss, Schmitt affirms the political because the opposite liberal ideal is not rejected as utopian, but rather morally *detested*. Only politics can grant that the world does not become simple entertainment (*Unterhaltung*): Schmitt asserted the political because he saw in it the case of emergency (*Ernstfall*) that made human life solemn. The assertion of the political is the assertion of *morality* against any attempt of de-politicization that, reducing the opposition to a game, denies the commitment and seriousness of life. According to Strauss, Schmitt refused the ideal of civilization because he saw a threat to the seriousness of the moral engagement of the political. For Strauss, however, the problem did not concern the fight, or the lack of fighting, but *the matter* of the fight. On this point, related to peace and war, Strauss disagreed both with Schmitt and with liberalism. He opened a new way in the philosophical consideration of politics. Against liberalism's de-politicization and neutralization, Strauss raised the question of conflict on the purpose and sense of human life, lacking which there remains only the *means*—i.e., a technology that appears as an instrument only apparently neutral—certainly not the *aim*. Against Schmitt's "political" and his "case of emergency," Strauss recalled how the distinction between friend and foe can overcome its *status* of mere existential opposition, thus finding its rational justification, only if it assumes the issue of justice. Only the problem of the just—and not the political—can solve the problem of neutralization and de-politicization. If we want agreement at any cost, there is no other way than to completely get rid of the question of the just and deal only with the means: agreement at any cost is possible only when man renounces to ask the question of just and of good.

Schmitt's position is nothing but a reversed liberalism—the *moral* assertion of the political is the assertion of the state of nature—which signals his persistence inside the *normative* perspective typical of modern individualism, clearly determined by Hobbes's natural right. Indeed, Schmitt's criticism against the "humanitarian moral" is based on a *moral* judgment, fruit of a private preference (meant as a direct expression of modern subjectivity). However, according to Strauss, Schmitt hides this judgment, precisely because it is a *judgment of value*. Therefore, Schmitt's position does not leave the logic of liberalism and *Kulturphilosophie*, precisely because values do not have a binding character, given that it is possible to *choose* them. The assertion of the political expresses a *judgment*, in terms of *value*, in favor of the political, which is not a *fact*. Behind Schmitt's figure, another one stands tall: that of Max Weber. Thus, we understand the reason why Schmitt did not clarify the moral foundation of his interpretation of the political. Indeed, its *assertion* would equate the acknowledgement of a "profession of faith," the private and individualistic character of which would neutralize the reach of the political itself, intended as "destiny." Moreover, the uncritical assertion of the state of nature and the criticism against liberalism are, in Schmitt, just a propaedeutic action to a battle between opposed "spirits," i.e., anarchy and authority, atheism and faith. Precisely because Schmitt's last word is not the assertion of the political, but the "order of human things," the assertion of the political does not mean the assertion of war. Rather, it means the refusal of the safety granted by the status quo, which allows the recovery of the "intact and uncorrupted origin" of the "natural force of an intact conscience" against any representations of the eases and commodities of bourgeois life. In Strauss's interpretation, Schmitt's critique of liberalism only has the task of preparing the battle between the followers of the spirit of "secular anti-religious activism" and the supporters of faith in the authority and in providence, i.e., the battle between the followers of Bakunin and Donoso Cortés.

Against Schmitt's primacy of political theology, Strauss reaffirmed the primacy of the philosophical over the political and the theological. Political theology does not represent the solution, but rather the last crisis of modern rationalism. In other words, it represents the phase in which philosophy ceases to question itself in critical terms on the issue of theological-political belonging. Therefore, there is a profound interpretative difference between political theology and the theological-political problem. The first is a theoretical model, in which the justification of political power proceeds on a revealed theological foundation that bases the supreme sovereign authority and in which the political body expresses its religious and cultural identity, though secularized. The second is a theoretical model in which the justification of political power, though assuming the issue of religious dimension, proceeds on a secular basis. In this case, there is no faith or theological-confessional preference, since the conflicts between different political authorities are conflicts between different divine authorities, i.e., between different myths or foundational values of the political society. Such conflicts, for their nature, are intrinsically arbitrary, though justifiable on a historical or ethical level. Therefore, they are not so much theological controversies, but rather conflicts between ethical-political systems competing with one another, which implicate different and antagonist conceptions of justice. Moreover, political theology is quite different from political philosophy. Political theology answers the question of truth through direct and immediate reference to the truth of revelation, independently from any form of rational justification and giving theoretical foundation to the practice of obedience. Political philosophy, instead, is the search of truth on political issues through a form of human knowledge unconditioned by political belonging or religious faith, able to distinguish between what is *first for itself* and what is *first for us*. In this sense, the theological-political problem, but not political theology, is part of political philosophy. If Schmitt has been the founder of political theology in the twentieth century, then Strauss has been the founder of the political-theological problem. Indeed, according to Schmitt, but not to Strauss, politics decides on the issue of order, while for Strauss only philosophy can shed light on the sense of political order. Behind the political, according to Schmitt, stands "political theology." For Strauss, behind the political is the "theological-philosophical problem," i.e., political philosophy.

Chapter Three

Paris (1932–1933)

A Year in the "Ville Lumière"

Strauss's appointment as researcher at the *Akademie* in Belin ended on 31 December 1931, due to the growing financial problems of the institute, which could no longer afford a large number of researchers and contributors. Just few remained until 1934 (when the *Akademie* finally closed) and Strauss, because of his contrast with the director Guttmann, was not among them. An academic career in Germany was no longer possible. Despite Strauss's connections or relationships with numerous researchers and professors, his presence inside any university had always been of little significance and he could not count on any specifically academic credits. Even his seminars, his lectures, and his publications, which were already numerous and significant, were—from an academic perspective— too limited to the Jewish world to be considered valuable titles for an appointment in the university. Strauss was well aware of this, even though in some cases his aspirations for such a career surfaced, as in a letter he wrote to Krüger on 23 May 1931 (cf. Strauss and Krüger 2001, 385–86). The extreme difficulty of obtaining a *Habilitation* did not prevent him from looking for opportunities in different directions, with the aim of finding a stipend. Indeed, between 1931 and 1933 he tried to establish a contact with Friedrich Gogarten, Paul Tillich, Ernst Cassirer, Carl Schmitt, Julius Ebbinghaus, Erich Frank, and Paul Hinneberg. However, acting often in an agitated and careless way, he did not achieve anything. Among the few concrete possibilities, his attention focused on the fellowships offered by the Rockefeller Foundation, which financed long research stays abroad. In

December 1931, Strauss applied and—thanks to presentation letters written by Cassirer and Guttmann, as well as Schmitt (cf. Strauss 1988, 129)—in mid-May he received the news that he had obtained a yearly fellowship in social sciences, starting 1 October 1932, later renewed until 1 October 1934, for a research project on Hobbes's political philosophy. In October 1932, Strauss moved to Paris with the intention of attending the courses taught by Étienne Gilson and Alexandre Koyré on the relations between medieval and modern thought.[1] Strauss abandoned Germany for good. He would only return in one occasion, in the summer 1954, remaining there for just a few weeks during his journey towards Jerusalem (where Scholem had invited him as visiting professor): on that occasion, Strauss visited the Kirchhain cemetery to bring his respects to his father and the rest of his family. He then stayed in Heidelberg, invited by Gadamer, where he gave a lecture on the image of Socrates represented by Aristophanes, Plato, and Xenophon. Strauss moved to Paris with Miriam Bernsohn (recent widow of Walther Petry), whom he had met in Berlin in 1930 and married in Paris on 20 June 1933. With them lived Thomas Petry, born to Miriam in her second marriage (she had divorced her first husband). In Paris, the family experienced a chaotic series of relocations, living at first on rue Racine (at the Hotel Racine), then on rue de la Glacière (in the same house once occupied by Walter Benjamin), then on rue du Parc-de-Montsouris, and finally on rue Saint-Jacques.

In Paris, Strauss continued his studies on Hobbes and frequented the *Bibliothèque nationale*, also continuing the other research line he had taken up once he completed his book on Spinoza, on medieval Islamic and Jewish philosophy. Indeed, Strauss assembled his interpretation of Al-Farabi, Averroes, Avicenna, and Maimonides as representatives of "religious Enlightenment of the Middle Ages" between 1928 and 1934. Strauss's life in Paris, however, did not exclusively revolve around library catalogues and the obscurity of his modest homes. In Paris, it was easy to meet numerous German Jewish scholars ("Here is present the entire German-Jewish intellectual proletariat," Strauss wrote to Löwith on 19 May 1933). Moreover, Strauss frequented the international intellectual community that lived in the *Ville Lumière*, inside which he became acquainted with numerous thinkers, in particular Jacob Gordin, Bernard Groethuysen, Georges Gurvitch, Fritz Heinemann, Paul Kraus, Sylvain Lévi, Jacques Maritain, Shlomo Pines, and Abel Rey. In the letters he wrote during these years, Strauss expressed special interest and appreciation for the lectures and the works of Étienne Gilson, Alexandre Koyré, Louis Massignon, and André Siegfried.[2] Moreover, through Koyré, Strauss became good friends with Alexandre Kojève, with whom he maintained a continuous philosophical dialogue and exchange of letters for the rest of his life. The German context and his relations there, however, were not distant: during Easter 1933, for instance, Strauss hosted his friends Gadamer, Löwith, and Krüger in Paris. Strauss and Gadamer had met in Marburg in 1921. Klein favored their encounter, introducing Strauss to Gadamer, at the time entrusted with the administration of the library. The initial exchanges between the two were not friendly. Quite the opposite: in his memories, Gadamer speaks of Strauss as a shy young man, emotional and distrustful, whom it was easy to offend without intention. Strauss, on the other hand, seemed to demonstrate an even greater aversion for Gadamer, a young student already proud of his early academic success (cf. Gadamer 1978, 1984). Such animosity, however, did not prevent them from discussing philosophical and methodological issues concerning the interpretation of Plato and Aristotle and from maintaining a relationship regarding different issues related to private and academic life. A change in their relationship—from a simple acquaintance to friendship—occurred in Paris, when Strauss introduced Gadamer to Kojève during an evening spent together at a Jewish restaurant. In light of this renewed friendliness, which did not end with Gadamer's return to Germany, we can understand the reasons of the (failed) attempt made by Gadamer—as well as by Löwith and Krüger—to find a German editor of Strauss's book on Hobbes, which instead appeared, translated into English, in Oxford in 1936.

However, besides these frequentations, Strauss's intellectual and friendly reference point in Paris was Kojève, with whom he initiated a long debate on the nature of philosophical and political modernity, the outcomes of which appear in their critical dialogue between the end of the 1940s and the mid-1950s on Xenophon's *Hiero*, as well as in their long correspondence. Strauss and Kojève—who in 1933 began his famous Hegelian seminar at the *École Pratique des Hautes Études*, completed in 1939, attended by intellectuals such as Raymond Aron, Georges Bataille, Roger Caillois, Henry Corbin, Jacques Lacan, Michel Leiris, Maurice Merleau-Ponty, and Raymond Queneau—also discussed the project of writing a book together, dedicated to the confrontation between Hobbes and Hegel. Despite the book not being accomplished, Strauss's writings (cf. Strauss 1936c, 57–58, 105ff., 122–23) contain mentions in this sense, since he evidently considered such confrontation a key moment of modernity. To Kojève, Strauss also confided his unimpressed, almost nauseated and annoyed, impression for the "disorderly" Parisian lifestyle (cf. Strauss and Kojève 1991, 222ff.). An impression that grew stronger when Strauss could compare it to the London lifestyle, which he experienced, with greater pleasure, from the first days of January 1934.

The First Writings on Hobbes

Despite Paris not being the city where it was possible to work on Hobbes's manuscripts, Strauss studied the English philosopher's works in depth, in order to carry out what he had agreed to do with the Rockefeller Foundation and because he identified in Hobbes's political philosophy a decisive turn in the history of philosophical and political thought. Strauss had been reading Hobbes since 1925, when he began working on Spinoza's biblical science, of which he traced ancient (Epicure and Averroes) and modern (Uriel da Costa and Isaac de La Peyrère) antecedents, among which Hobbes, who played a primary role in the definition of biblical hermeneutics as a tool for the critique of religion. Through Spinoza, since 1928, Hobbes was at the center of Strauss's philosophical and political reflection on modernity. Indeed, also thanks to Krüger's insistence, from 1930 Strauss tended to frame his writings on Hobbes in a larger historical and philosophical context, reaching even a comparison with Kant (cf. Strauss and Krüger 2001, 382, 387, 394, 404–7) and using them as a reference point for his critique of Schmitt's essay *Der Begriff des "Politischen."* Still in the early 1930s, Strauss's work plan concerning Hobbes remained undefined.[3] On the one hand, inspired by his previous work on Spinoza, Strauss was focusing again on the research concerning the critique of religion in Hobbes. On the other hand, the comparison between Hobbes and Plato progressively emerged as the place where it was be possible to measure the distance between modern and classical political philosophy. Finally, the connection between Hobbes and modern liberalism became clearer. These different research questions regarding Hobbes characterized Strauss's studies during his stay in Paris. However, only the last two made it into the monograph he dedicated to Hobbes in 1936.

The first writing Strauss entirely dedicated to Hobbes dates from his stay in Paris and consists in a long review of Zbigniew Lubienski's book on Hobbes.[4] The core of Strauss's interpretative paradigm of Hobbes, intended as the founder of modern liberalism due to the concept of natural right and the artificial creation of political society by means of a pact, is already present and discussed (cf. Strauss 1933). According to Strauss, anyone who is unable to accept a nostalgic, reactionary, or theological perspective of politics, despite being conscious of the radical crisis of liberal democracy, has to confront Hobbes. Since the English philosopher is the founder of philosophical and political modernity, it is necessary to verify the characters of the pre-modern model of thought *opposed to* which Hobbes built the modern model. Historical research is necessary to this purpose. Not a simple learned reconstruction, nor a reinterpretation based on historicist methodology, but rather a research that is able to recover "objectively" a form of knowledge of the past, in order to allow a renewed analysis of fundamental philosophical questions. Despite this interpretation, which featured in Strauss's studies on Hobbes also in later years, the provisional character of his position between 1932 and 1933 is demonstrated by the presence, inside this review, of two considerations concerning Hobbes's politics (not present in the contemporary *Anmerkungen* to Schmitt's book on the "political") that Strauss later not only abandoned, but even completely overturned. Firstly, Strauss studied the modern form of the State through the reconstruction of the principles of Hobbes's theory on the conflict between "political" and "economic," respectively founded on vanity and the fear of violent death. However, this separation made by Strauss of the different foundations Hobbes attributed to politics and economy, stemming from the analysis of the theory of passions, is entirely provisionary and temporary. Indeed, inside the book *The Political Philosophy of Hobbes* (1936), Strauss considered both key principles of Hobbes's theory of passions (vanity and the fear of violent death) as characteristic of modern politics, thus considering political economy just as a "consequence" of the new moral principle expressed by Hobbes's philosophy. Secondly, inside this review Strauss alluded to a similitude between Hobbes's dichotomy vanity–fear of violent death and the Christian dichotomy *superbia-humilitas*. To the point that it is possible to speak about a laicization of faith in Hobbes, and in modern thought in general, which seems to recall the paradigm of secularization presented by Schmitt in his *Politische Theologie* (1922). Also in this second case, it is clear that Strauss later dropped this interpretative line in favor of a reading of the modern as *novum* in respect to ancient philosophy and Christianity. Notwithstanding these provisionary assertions, however, inside this long review Strauss mentioned two guidelines that became central in all his later interpretations of Hobbes. On the one hand, the necessity to confront Hobbes with Plato's political philosophy. On the other hand, the presence, in Hobbes's theory, of an anti-traditional and anti-Aristotelian philosophical core.

In the early 1930s, Strauss's confrontation with Hobbes unfolded on numerous topics, among which the most treated ones were the critique of religion, moral theory, natural right, and the theory of the State. The amount and depth, even philological, of Strauss's studies on Hobbes testify to the centrality of the English philosopher in the development of Strauss's thought. His efforts were not limited to what he published, but also included what Strauss wrote between 1931 and 1933–34, which, though unpublished, constitutes useful studies to understand the genesis of *The Political Philosophy of Hobbes* (1936) (cf. Strauss 2001a, 193–215, 263–369). In these studies, Strauss anticipated some central themes of his anti-historicist (identified in the concept of "historical conscience") and anti-positivistic (identified in Kelsen's legal positivism) polemic, which merged in his 1940s studies on modern hermeneutics and political philosophy, in particular in his essays on Locke and Rousseau, before finding a systematic formulation in the book *Natural Right and History* (1953). Strauss wrote *Die Religionskritik des Hobbes* in 1933–34, originally planning it as an essay to obtain a degree at the *École Pratique des Hautes Études*, but he actually never used it in this sense (cf. Strauss and Krüger 2001, 431, 435). As he did in his monograph *Die Religionskritik Spinozas*, also in his writing on Hobbes Strauss presented the critique of religion as a condition of possibility for modern biblical science and for the illuminist historical and critical method. As for Spinoza, also in Hobbes's case, regarding the relationship between biblical science and critique of religion, Strauss distinguished pre-philosophical critique (on a hermeneutical level equal to the critique of the hermeneutical Scholastic tradition) and philosophical critique (equal to the critique of the Scripture, i.e., directly of the sacred texts). Despite Hobbes's polemic being apparently towards the critique of the Scholastic tradition, he addressed his actual critique to the Scripture, i.e., revelation and prophecy, destitute of any foundation. In this perspective, the central point expressed by Strauss consisted in understanding Hobbes's critique of religion not in light of the materialistic or scientific principles of his natural philosophy (of Galilean set up), but in light of the *moral* principles of his *political philosophy*.

The two 1931 writings—*Disposition. Die politische Wissenschaft des Hobbes* and *Vorwort zu einem geplanten Buch über Hobbes*—are brief and unfinished, but still significant. In the *Vorwort*, Hobbes's name appears only few times, because Strauss's main purpose is to raise philosophical objections against legal positivism, represented by Hans Kelsen and Carl

Bergbohm. Particularly interesting is Strauss's outspoken polemic against Kelsen, whom he identifies as the primary representative of *modern* critique of the theory of natural right. The polemic against the *Rechtspositivismus* characterizes also the first part of the *Disposition*, which offers a reasoned schematization of a tentative outline for a book on Hobbes. After Kelsen, Strauss's polemical target is in this case the interpretation of Hobbes proposed by Dilthey, centered on the analysis of the permanence of motives of ancient stoicism in the thought of the English philosopher (in this sense, Strauss was careful to clearly separate Hobbes from Grotius). Therefore, Strauss's Hobbes was, already from 1931, a radically anti-traditional philosopher, founder of Enlightenment and of the modern ideal of progress, precursor of utilitarianism, the "ancestor" of Voltaire and of the protagonists of the *querelle des anciens et des modernes*, creator of the modern contrast between nature and culture (*Kultur*, of which *Zivilisation* constitutes a further and decadent stage) through which the possibility of the conquest of nature is determined, with the direct consequence of the affirmation of human omnipotence.

The Return to Pre-Modern Philosophy

Besides prosecuting his research on Hobbes, during his year in Paris Strauss turned his attention towards medieval Islamic and Jewish philosophy, which became the model of thought through which, for the first time, he realized that it was possible to recover pre-modern philosophy, in order to use it as a tool to overcome the modern crisis. Before the return to classical Greek philosophy, namely to Plato, which occurred especially during the 1940s, Strauss confronted Maimonides's thought and that of his Islamic predecessors concerning the theme of prophecy, intended not as a theological issue, but as a philosophical-political one. These studies—initially focused on Maimonides's and Gersonides's prophetology—had begun in Berlin in 1928 and in 1931 they had appeared in the lecture *Cohen und Maimuni* (cf. Strauss 1997a, 393–436) and in the essay *Maimunis Lehre von der Prophetie und ihre Quellen*, published in 1934. The essay also constituted the basic structure for the last chapter of the book *Philosophie und Gesetz*, published in 1935, but written, although partially and discontinuously, even during the years in Paris.

We can define the philosophical path undertaken by the young Strauss, especially through his interpretation of the "Spinoza case," as a progressive approach to Maimonides on one side and to Hobbes on the other, considered as representatives of two different models of rationalism. From this perspective, the year spent in Paris constitutes a decisive turning point, during which Strauss developed the fundamental interpretative lines that later brought him to publish, between 1935 and 1936, his works on Maimonides and Hobbes. With the completion of his book on Spinoza, in 1928, Strauss concluded a phase of his studies, focused on the problematic situation of Judaism inside the crisis of modernity. In this first phase, two research trends were present, which later guided Strauss's work in the 1930s: one concerning the analysis of the philosophical foundations of the *theological-political problem*; the other concerning the opposition between modern natural science and the modern ideal of civilization. Strauss respectively published the results of these different, but complementary, research trends in *Philosophie und Gesetz* (1935) and in *The Political Philosophy of Hobbes* (1936). The analysis of Spinoza's Enlightenment led Strauss to verify its theoretical unfoundedness precisely where it claimed to be a *system of knowledge*. In the meantime, however, the theoretical inadequacy of religious orthodoxy in responding to Spinoza clearly emerged. Therefore, from 1928, Strauss had the necessity to define a different model of Enlightenment, capable of identifying a balance between philosophical radicalism and political conservatism, between the search for truth and the necessity to accept common opinions, between philosophy and the city, between Athens and Jerusalem. In *Philosophie und Gesetz*, Strauss identified the traces of such enlightened model in the medieval Islamic and Jewish thinkers (Al-Farabi, Averroes, Avicenna, and Maimonides) in a way that presents a fundamental characteristic: revealed religion did no longer have, as it did in the 1920s, a theoretical value, but rather a *political* one.

Philosophie und Gesetz is an eccentric book for many reasons. Eccentric, because it declines in a historical-philosophical form—in particular by aiming at the analysis of the theological-political problem through the prophetology of Maimonides and his Arabic sources—philosophical and political questions of extreme relevance in the development of twentieth-century European thought (on the legitimacy of political power, for example). Eccentric, because it reconstructs a model of the history of Western thought by drawing new borders and, above all, new junctions between European, Arabic, and Jewish cultures that allow an original reinterpretation of the development of philosophical modernity. Eccentric, because it intertwines theological, philosophical, and political issues against the backdrop of a critical analysis of contemporaneity. Finally, eccentric because it is almost unconventional—due to its genesis and internal architecture—

even within the Straussian intellectual biography itself. Probably because of this eccentricity, *Philosophie und Gesetz* was for a long time, among the Straussian volumes, one of the least studied and considered by critics, both at the level of historical and theoretical research. Yet authoritative readers have left clear traces of its significance: just think, for example, of Löwith's considerations on the decisive question of the relationship between philosophy and the history of philosophy in the age of nihilism—a question reactivated by the Heideggerian idea of *Destruktion*—as well as of the considerations contained in the correspondence between Benjamin and Scholem especially regarding the status of the philosophy of religion and the theological-political problem.

The structure of the book itself, apparently uneven, does not help the reader, who tends to find it a book published for a particular circumstance. Such an impression is partly justified: Strauss wrote the book's chapters at different times between 1931 and 1935 and even the publication proceeded in a non-organic way. Moreover, having to give a general description of *Philosophie und Gesetz*, it would seem appropriate at first glance to point at the irregularity of its structure. The first chapter deals with the critique of modernity, followed by a historiographical chapter on Jewish culture that presents a critique of Julius Guttmann's book *Die Philosophie des Judentums* (1933). The third chapter concerns the issue of the relationship between philosophy and revelation inside the history of medieval Islamic and Jewish philosophy. The book ends with a long discussion in the fourth chapter of the theological-political issue in Maimonides. However, this initial impression of irregularity does not correspond to the truth. Quite the opposite. Looking at the book's structure from the perspective of Strauss's intellectual biography, we can note how inside it the author treated, for the first time, some central themes of his thought. The relationship between Athens and Jerusalem, the criticism of the modern world, the definition of socio-political root of esotericism, the theological-political problem, the relationship between philosophy and history of philosophy.

Apparently, the book corresponds to a trend of studies related to the history of medieval Aristotelian tradition (from Averroes to Maimonides, from Avicenna to Gersonides) that enjoyed good fortune among Jewish scholars in Weimar Germany, especially due to the studies by Cohen and Guttmann. Only apparently, though. Indeed, Strauss's work contains a dense and outspoken critique of any modern interpretation of the medieval Aristotelian tradition elaborated after Mendelssohn. Not by chance are Cohen and Guttman among the main targets of Strauss's critique. Strauss criticized them both on the level of historical research (medieval Jewish philosophy, and Maimonides in particular, is not the forerunner of modern philosophy and *Kulturphilosophie*) and on the level of theoretical consideration (the idea of revealed religion expressed by religious liberalism loses its transcendence to become the product of human interiority). Even though the author presents it as a research into the history of philosophy, *Philosophie und Gesetz* is actually a book in which Strauss builds, *through* an original reading of medieval philosophy, a strong philosophical and political interpretation of the modernity. This interpretation—through the construction of two great categories, named "Enlightenment" and "orthodoxy"—seriously takes into account the impossibility of an immediate return to orthodox Judaism (the theoretical foundations of which are mined by Enlightenment), as well as the impossibility of accepting the relativism resulting from the transformation of modern rationalism into historicism, i.e., modern sophistry. However, compared to his book on Spinoza, Strauss moves his perspective to a new theoretical and philosophical-political frontier, represented by his "change of orientation": the possibility to overcome the modern crisis by identifying a different model of rationality. Therefore, Strauss's critique has a double target. On one side, Enlightenment, in its multiple forms (from Spinoza to Kant, from Descartes to Cohen). On the other, the plurality of Jewish movements (from religious liberalism to the *Wissenschaft des Judentums*, from political Zionism to Rosenzweig's *neue Denken*) that in different forms have tried to appease Enlightenment and orthodoxy, ever since Mendelssohn. These movements have depreciated the effective reach of the truths of faith, transforming them from objective to subjective truths, interiorizing them and betraying the original spirit of Judaism intended as revelation. Despite the importance of the references made to Maimonides in his book on Spinoza's critique of religion, the young Strauss's path towards the author of the *Guide of the Perplexed* was rather complex, at least until when, one day in 1929, at the *Staatsbibliothek* in Berlin, he read a passage from Avicenna:

> Maimonides was, to begin with, wholly unintelligible to me. I got the first glimmer of light when I concentrated on his prophetology and, therefore, the prophetology of the Islamic philosophers who preceded him. One day, when reading in a Latin translation Avicenna's treatise *On the Division of the*

Sciences, I came across this sentence (I quote from memory): the standard work on prophecy and revelation is Plato's *Laws*. Then I began to begin to understand Maimonides's prophetology and eventually, as I believe, the whole *Guide of the Perplexed*. (Strauss 1970d, 3)

Strauss began to think that the guiding idea shared by Greek, Islamic, and Jewish philosophers was precisely the idea of the divine Law intended as a unique and total law that was, at the same time, religious, political, and moral law.[5] According to this, the doctrines of medieval Islamic and Jewish philosophers resulted based more on Platonic than Aristotelian philosophy. Naturally, this is not so much the case of logic and metaphysics—in which Aristotle was the undisputed master of Islamic and Jewish philosophers—but rather of the *foundation* and *purpose* of philosophy and politics, which are Platonic. The central theme of Maimonides's philosophical and political rationalism, as well as of that of his Islamic predecessors, was not the opposition between faith and knowledge, but between philosophy and Law. Indeed, the theme on which Plato and medieval thinkers agreed was the idea of a rational Law, of a Law that aims at its own perfection as well as that of humankind. Such Law, however, can only be of divine origin. For this reason, it is necessary to begin the interpretation of Platonic philosophy not from the *Republic*, but from the *Laws*. Plato's considerations on the divine laws provide medieval thinkers the starting point whence they can philosophically understand revelation, thus expressing the philosophical, skeptical, foundation of faith in revelation.

The philosophical declination of the theological-political problem is central in Strauss's studies on Maimonides in the 1930s. Strauss's Maimonides is, like Cohen's Maimonides, a Platonic thinker. However, differently from Cohen (who depreciated any Aristotelian reference), Strauss attributed the Platonic character of Maimonides's thought to its political basis and not to its theoretical dimension, for which, instead, Aristotelian theory was the primary reference. Strauss's Maimonides is an Aristotelian from a theoretical point of view, while he is a Platonist from a theological-political point of view, which deals with *prophetology* (following the example of the *falasifa*, the medieval Islamic philosophers) developing two different but complementary arguments regarding the relationships between philosophy and revealed religion. On the one hand, Maimonides underlines the necessity of the *legal* foundation of philosophy, a justification of philosophy in front of revelation, intended as the

Law that regulates actions and opinions, so the entire social order. On the other hand, Maimonides considered the necessity of the *philosophical* foundation of the Law, because the practical usefulness of the revelation cannot disregard the supremacy of theoretical life over political life. These themes were absent from Greek philosophy due to the absence of revelation and had also been absent from Jewish (or Islamic) philosophy up to that point due to the absence of philosophy. It is only with the *falasifa* and with Maimonides that the problem posed by revelation became *the* problem of medieval philosophy, precisely because revelation constituted the starting point for philosophy as a "fact" on which social order is possible. Medieval philosophers did not understand revealed religion as a *scope of validity* nor as a *direction of the conscience*, nor as a *scope of culture*—as did the idealistic, historicist, and existentialist philosophies of the early twentieth century—but rather as a *Law*. In this sense, medieval Enlightenment became the philosophical model that guided Strauss in the interpretation of the theological-political problem through the fracture between ancient and modern[6]. Maimonides's rationalism (and that of medieval Islamic philosophers) was the model that allowed the uncovering of modern rationalism as "sophistry," responsible for the process of historicization, politicization, and ideologization of philosophy.

The Legal Foundation of Philosophy

Strauss's Maimonides is always a "political" thinker. He solves the different metaphysical and theological topics contained in the *Guide of the Perplexed* from a specific political perspective, the Platonic one, which embodies the relationship between philosophy, religion, and politics. Despite Strauss only defining the hermeneutical question towards the end of the 1930s, he connected the theological-political problem to esotericism already in *Philosophie und Gesetz*. Actually, in this phase of Strauss's reflection, it seems more correct to speak about elitism rather than esotericism.[7] Indeed, the theme of reticence is declined here not so much on the level of philosophical writing, but on the level of government and legislation, i.e., the control of the populace, incapable of understanding theoretical truths and therefore in need of learning knowledge and rules by means of a metaphorical and imaginative language. There are numerous passages inside which the theme of the "double truth" (public vs. private) emerges in the prophetological analysis of medieval Islamic and Jewish philosophers (Al-Farabi, Averroes, Avicenna, Maimonides, Gersonides, and Yehuda ha-Levi). However, in none of these passages does Strauss focus on the issue of reticent writing as a form of philosophical education. On the other hand, he highlighted the necessity to maintain the truth secret for reasons of political prudence and public convenience. However, Strauss did not characterize such elitism with mystical inclinations, nor did he base it on reactionary principles. Although he admitted that inequality is an unavoidable character of political society, still it is not "naturalized" neither in the relationship between governors and governed, nor in the relationship between the "few" and the "many." Not by chance, Strauss defined the position of medieval Islamic and Jewish philosophers as "religious Enlightenment of the Middle Ages," hinting at a decisive distinction from the modern Enlightenment of Descartes, Hobbes, Spinoza, and Voltaire. Maimonides and his Islamic predecessors are skeptical thinkers, rationalist philosophers who deal with the relationship between philosophy, politics, and religion in a perspective that is at the same time (privately) radical and (publicly) moderate, clearly different from the moderns' anti-religious radicalism. Not by chance, Maimonides—following Averroes and Avicenna—developed a legal foundation of philosophy, meaning a justification of philosophical activity (and of its limits) in front of the court of revelation. For medieval philosophers, it was possible to debate the content of revelation, the immortality of the soul, the creation of matter and other things. However, there could be no debate on the truth of revelation and on the duty to obey it. The recognition of revelation's authority is the premise of philosophical activity, which finds its condition of possibility inside it from a historical-social perspective (cf. Strauss 1935, 68ff.).

The human being's perfection is only possible in contemplative life. Therefore, revelation orders philosophical activity, making the philosopher responsible in front of the Law. Thus, revelation, becoming the main topic of philosophical investigation, alongside everything else that exists in the natural and human world, authorizes and frees philosophical activity. Revelation is a fact that precedes philosophical activity. It is necessary for a legal foundation of philosophical activity able to answer the following question: if the Law given by God is sufficient to lead life to its true purpose, then what is the meaning of philosophical activity? In the answer to this question, Strauss's Maimonides finds the justification for pursuing a "pagan" activity such as philosophical activity even inside a monotheistic world, because the purpose of the Law coincides with the purpose of philosophy: the happiness of the human being, rendered possible by knowledge of truth, gained through contemplative life. Therefore, philosophy is free, even if not absolutely. Philosophy is free in the study of the natural world "beneath the skies," not in the study of the "skies," where the *pre-written* truths of the Law, inaccessible to human reason, have a central role (as, for instance, concerning creation). Philosophy's freedom rests on its connection, i.e., on *the primacy of the Law*. For Maimonides and the other medieval thinkers, it was not a question of expanding the light, of educating the people on rational knowledge. Furthermore, for them the esoteric character of philosophy was absolutely necessary, contrary to what happens with the modern Enlightenment. The esoteric character of the "religious enlightenment of the Middle Ages" finds its foundation in the primacy of theoretical life, just as the exoteric character of the modern Enlightenment finds its foundation in the primacy of practical reason.

The Philosophical Foundation of the Law

There is also another problem, complementary to the one discussed above, concerning Maimonides, as well as the *falasifa*. Indeed, if a legal foundation of philosophy is necessary, the *philosophical foundation of the Law* is equally necessary, meaning the rational justification of revelation, which becomes a philosophical theme in the doctrine of prophecy (cf. Strauss 1935, 87ff.). By highlighting the *political*, i.e., *practical*, role of the revelation, Strauss identifies in prophetology the place where the Law becomes an *object* of philosophy. The revelation represents the perfect order, both theoretical and practical, the founder of which, the prophetical legislator, is not only a prophet, but also a philosopher and a political leader. It is essential for the prophet to possess a perfect intellect, a perfect moral habit, and a perfect imagination, to the purpose of deliberating on theoretical truths, community habits, religious beliefs, and political institutions. Prophecy's relevance is not so much metaphysical as it is practical, i.e., political, and it is connected to the creation of a good legislation and a rightful government, which are both essential conditions to attain the revelation's original purpose: moral and spiritual perfection of the human being. Given that the revelation communicates the theoretical truths, the prophet must possess a perfect intellect. However, since revelation also contains beliefs necessary to common life—beliefs that, however, are not *true*—and since the language of philosophy is not proper to communicate revealed truths to the multitude, the prophet also has to dispose of a perfect imaginative ability. This ability allows him to use a metaphorical language, often necessary for the public explanation of the revealed truths. The purpose of prophecy is essentially *political* because the prophet has the duty to establish a society inside which the human being may attain its supreme perfection: *theoretical life*.

For Strauss's Maimonides, the prophet is the founder of the ideal state. This assertion shows the connection Maimonides made, following the *falasifa*, between prophetology and *Platonic* political philosophy. Indeed, only the prophet can fulfill the conditions that Plato demanded for the concurrence of philosophy and political power. The prophet is the historical and concrete image of the philosopher-king who establishes a community specifically oriented to the human being's perfection: theoretical life. Revelation finds its justification in being the necessary condition for an ordered community life according to the model of Platonic politics. This, in turn, is the condition for theoretical life to exist, faced with its social, political, and religious responsibilities. Despite living his search for knowledge in complete freedom, the philosopher has to be aware of the necessity of a legal justification of philosophy, of living under the prophet's political direction. The prophet, differently from the philosopher, is a master and a guide at the same time. Indeed, "logical" and "chronological" primacy do not coincide. Theory, not politics, is the greatest good, but politics, not theory, is the "first" good, because the human being, as a political animal, can only live inside a society. Maimonides asserted without doubt the primacy of theoretical life, but what has logical primacy (philosophy) does not have chronological primacy (proper to political life, which is the Law prescribed by the Revelation) and vice versa. In other words, the assertion of the chronological primacy of theological-political life does not erase the assertion of the logical primacy of theoretical life, precisely because theoretical life, in its being *virtue* and *happiness*, is the greatest good, but not the first good. In short: Aristotelian theory is not conceivable if not inside a Platonic state. The fundamental difference between Plato and Aristotle only appears in the way in which they deal with philosophy intended as the human being's highest perfection. Aristotle made it completely free; or, rather, he left it in its natural freedom. Plato, on the other hand, did not allow philosophers to spend life in philosophical activity, intended as persistence in the contemplation of truth, because he "forced" them to worry about others, so that the political community may be "just." The Platonism of Maimonides and the *falasifa* is given by their withstanding of the Law. However, once allowed by the Law, they are free to do philosophical activity in complete Aristotelian freedom (cf. Strauss 1935, 117ff.). They justify their philosophical activity in front of the court of the Law, drawing from the Law the *authorization* for philosophical activity, intended as a legal *obligation* to philosophical activity, only capable of justifying the *rational usefulness* of the Law.

Jerusalem or Not?

From the 1950s, especially following the publication of *Natural Right and History* (1953), Strauss's name was often associated with the "party" of the ancients in the *querelle des anciens et des modernes*. In his criticism of modernity, Strauss turned to Maimonides and the Islamic philosophers, before Plato and Aristotle, considering them models of a philosophical rationalism capable of finding a solution to the crisis of philosophy and politics in modernity. This explains—together with the personal acrimony, stratified by now, dating back to the events that delayed the publication of the book on Spinoza Strauss had prepared for the *Akademie*—Strauss's violent attack against Guttmann's book *Die Philosophie des Judentums* that takes up the whole second chapter of *Philosophie und Gesetz*. Strauss planned and wrote this part of the book in an almost definitive version during his stay in Paris. His attack against Guttmann does not concern a peculiar historical or theoretical issue, but rather encompasses Guttmann's reading and interpretation of medieval Jewish philosophy as a whole. The author of *Die Philosophie des Judentums* is guilty of completely historicizing medieval Jewish philosophy due to the use he makes of modern premises (such as the idea of "religious conscience") typical of the whole tradition of religious liberalism. Reading Maimonides as Guttmann does—i.e., through the lens of the *Wissenschaft des Judentums*, of the neo-Kantian "religion of reason" and of the modern "philosophy of religion"—means, according to Strauss, completely misunderstanding the sense and meaning of medieval philosophy.

Strauss was not prudent in his polemic against Guttmann. Since September 1933, through Klein in Germany and Scholem in Jerusalem, he had been circulating his profoundly critical essay, both to delegitimize Guttmann's interpretation and to support his candidacy as chair of medieval Jewish philosophy at the Hebrew University of Jerusalem. Guttmann was the favored candidate for the position (other candidates included

Simon Rawidowicz, who had edited with Strauss, between 1931 and 1932, the two volumes of *Schriften zur Philosophie und Ästethik*, inside Mendelssohn's *Gesammelte Schriften*). Scholem tried to favor Strauss, through a series of direct interventions, testified also by a letter he addressed to Strauss on 29 November 1933 (cf. Strauss and Scholem 2001, 704–6). On 7 December 1933, Strauss tried to reassure Scholem regarding the appropriateness of his publications and of his knowledge of medieval Islamic and Jewish philosophy, but he did not conceal his incertitude regarding his ability to speak Hebrew (cf. Strauss and Scholem 2001, 706–9). On the same day, without warning Scholem, Strauss addressed a letter to Krüger (cf. Strauss and Krüger 2001, 436–37) requesting him to contact Rudolf Bultmann, who in turn should intercede for him with Buber. The latter valued Strauss from a scientific perspective, but also had a certain animosity towards him, after all understandable, given the bitter criticism with which the young Strauss had addressed him inside Zionist contexts. Strauss's request—promoted also by Klein—failed, as did the efforts made by Scholem, who worked under false premises, having underestimated two factors: firstly, Guttmann's renowned academic and institutional importance, having directed for many years the *Akademie* in Berlin; secondly, the problem represented by Strauss's strong criticism of political Zionism, which certainly could not be completely unknown in Jerusalem. The outcome of the assignment of the chair was catastrophic. Despite his friendship with Fritz Baer and the sympathy that David Hartwig Baneth showed for him, and despite Scholem's continuous effort in his favor, in January 1934 the university finally appointed Guttmann (cf. Strauss and Scholem 2001, 710ff.).

Actually, the result did not upset Strauss too deeply, although the issue of financial sustainability was certainly important. Since 1932, his continuous daily concerns clearly emerge from his correspondence with friends. To the point that he even wrote he feared for his own "earthly future" (cf. Strauss and Krüger 2001, 386, 388, 391–92; Strauss and Klein 2001, 468ff., 485ff.). These concerns created a load of tensions that—as always—fell onto Miriam, as Klein pointed out scolding Strauss for his anxiety and for his excessive emotional charge (cf. Strauss and Klein 2001, 456). However, the negative result of the appointment in Jerusalem also represented a liberation from the possibility of a job that Strauss would have certainly accepted for "material" reasons, but for which he would have experienced as a strong limitation to his true philosophical interests for Hobbes (cf. Strauss and Klein 2001, 485), not to mention the fact that

Strauss had no intention of making concessions in favor of religious orthodoxy, not even after the failure of his candidacy in Jerusalem (cf. Strauss and Scholem 2001, 711). Therefore, Strauss's attempt to find an academic appointment in Jerusalem corresponded to an objective necessity, but not to an intimate aspiration. Indeed, in his correspondence with Scholem, it seems like theoretical issues attracted Strauss much more than academic politics. Scholem, instead, showed great interest in defending Strauss's candidacy, while neglecting the philosophical and theoretical issues—such as the relationship between myth and the Kabbalah, the political character of prophecy, the nature of medieval rationalism etc.—to which Strauss often brought his attention.

A demonstration of Strauss's intellectual independence from an academic chair in Jerusalem is also present in the introduction to *Philosophie und Gesetz*, written in 1935, when Strauss was in Cambridge. Guttmann had already obtained the chair in medieval Jewish philosophy,[8] but the perspectives for an appointment in Jerusalem were still open, possibly for other chairs in philosophy of religion. Scholem—who deeply praised Strauss's work—was progressively acquiring influence and prestige among the faculty of the Hebrew University and he invited his friend not to neglect any chance to strengthen his position as a scholar of Jewish philosophy, given that, within a year or two, there could be other chances in Jerusalem. Still, the introduction Strauss wrote for his book on Maimonides—published for the eighth centenary of Maimonides's birth, as a testimony to the many celebrations organized in Germany, despite Hitler, by Jewish communities—definitively certified Strauss's impossibility to move to Jerusalem, as Scholem's words to Benjamin in a letter dated 29 March 1935 testify. Inside this letter, Scholem asserted that with the publication of *Philosophie und Gesetz*, Strauss determined his own academic "suicide" in Jerusalem, because this work begins with an outspoken profession of atheism, motivated in a detailed way, declaring that atheism was the most important Jewish watchword.[9]

The events connected to the contrast between Strauss and Guttmann did not end here. The contrast had a significant backlash on 2 June 1952, when Scholem wrote to Strauss announcing that Guttmann's widow had left the library owned by her husband, who had died in 1950, to the Hebrew University. Among Guttmann's papers, there were some portions of a long essay in response to Strauss's critique (cf. Strauss and Scholem 2001, 726ff.). On 22 June, Strauss replied to his friend telling him he had known from Guttmann in person about the response to the critique to his interpretation of Maimonides he included in *Philosophie und Gesetz*, which had intentionally been left unfinished. Therefore, the issue of the typewritten response seemed not to interest Strauss. Moreover, Scholem too lost interest in it, given that he lost the text during the weeks that followed. Only on 7 November 1972, Scholem wrote to Strauss that he had found the typewritten document, written between 1940 and 1945. Despite being unfinished, the text was long and well organized, thus publishable, although with annotations provided by Scholem himself and by Nathan Rotenstreich. On 17 November 1972, Strauss asked Scholem to send him a copy of the document, which he received promptly before the end of December. Without this copy, Strauss would not have been able to read the essay, given that it was published only after his death.[10]

The chapter of *Philosophie und Gesetz* concerning Guttmann is not only relevant for biographical reasons. From the beginning of the text, Strauss dealt with two issues that characterized his entire philosophical path. Firstly, he asserted that history of philosophy has a *philosophical* meaning, since it allows the recovery of lost forms of knowledge that can grant us tools to overcome the modern crisis. Secondly, Strauss proposed a radical critique of the idea of *progress*, which Guttmann instead defended in respect to the passage from medieval Jewish philosophy to modern Jewish philosophy (after Mendelssohn). According to Guttmann, modern philosophy is more suitable than medieval philosophy to express the "interior world" of faith, because medieval philosophy privileges Greek philosophical conceptions over the biblical conception of God, while modern philosophy has recovered the traditional conceptions of Jewish faith. For Strauss, instead, since Judaism is essentially revealed religion, i.e., *Law*, medieval philosophy is closer to Judaism than modern philosophy.

The writing against Guttmann is also relevant because it represents a new critique of the modern idea of "culture," already expressed in his essay on Schmitt, where the modern concept of culture is criticized on the basis of the political. This time, instead, Strauss notes that Guttmann, following Kant and Schleiermacher, asserts that the purpose of philosophy of religion is the analysis of religious conscience or, more precisely, the limitation of the "context of validity" of religion in respect of all the other contexts of culture. According to Strauss, religion cannot be sufficiently understood inside the concept of culture, which expresses a way for the human spirit to produce, while religion is not a product of the human being, but it is *given* to it. This demonstrates that it is a "burden" for philosophy of culture. The other burden for philosophy of culture is, according to Strauss, the political. Religion and politics are the facts that transcend culture, or in other words, they are the *original* facts. Radical critique of the concept of "culture" is only possible in the form of a "theological-political treatise," which—if it does not want to lead to an identical foundation of modern culture—has to maintain a tendency exactly opposite to the seventeenth-century theological-political treatises, namely those written by Hobbes and Spinoza (Strauss 1935, 31–32). The problem posed by religion cannot be understood from the conceptual background elaborated by *Kulturphilosophie* of neo-Kantian orientation. However, it cannot even be understood by Rosenzweig's *neue Denken*, nor by philosophy of existence (which, in *Philosophie und Gesetz*, Strauss criticizes confronting the thought of Friedrich Gogarten), since religion is *revelation* and not human activity. The attempt made by Strauss to understand again the *original* meaning of revealed religion intended as Law justifies the long historical *excursus* on medieval Islamic and Jewish philosophy through which Maimonides's thought appears as the model of rationalism that escapes the pitfalls of historicist relativism and political nihilism.

Chapter Four

London and Cambridge (1934–1937)

Years of Ups and Downs

On 7 January 1934, Strauss moved to London, together with his wife and her son. His initial accommodations were in a small hotel between Montague Street and Russell Square, with a view of the British Museum, which he immediately started visiting to study the literature on Hobbes, as well as his manuscripts. The renewal of his fellowship at the Rockefeller Foundation prompted his transfer from Paris to London. Strauss had to finish his research project on Hobbes's political philosophy, and it was clear that he could not accomplish such research in Paris, not just because Hobbes's manuscripts were unavailable, but also because there were no scholars in France working on the author of the *Leviathan*. Even Gilson advised Strauss to move to England and suggested contacting John Laird, who studied Hobbes's thought (cf. Strauss and Krüger 2001, 431). Strauss was happy to move to London. Just a few days after arriving in England, he wrote to his friend Kojève describing the very pleasant conditions he found there: public order, people's discretion, a civil and austere atmosphere, measured political life[1]—even delicious food, with the exception of wine! (cf. Strauss and Kojève 1991, 222ff.). England was the state that received the greatest praises from Strauss, both for the sobriety of its literature (according to Strauss, William Thackeray and Jane Austen were preferable to Dostoevsky) and for the austerity of its habits. Strauss did not make similar comments about Germany nor about France (nor would he later have any for the US). It is possible that the political conservatism that characterized English political culture (visible, for instance, in the image of the *gentleman*, which Strauss later mentioned in his writings on Greek classics from the 1950s and 1960s) played an important role in Strauss's preference for England. Strauss used particularly praising terms when writing to Klein on 14 February 1934, having visited Oxford, where he met Cassirer (cf. Strauss and Klein 2001, 493). From an urban perspective, Oxford reminded Strauss of Tübingen. Esthetically, not only did the city offer great splendors, but Strauss also appreciated what appeared to him as a great respect for the past, accompanied by a likewise great opening to the world and the future. Strauss ascribed this trait to all English history, determined by an "empiricist" attitude. No other people revered past experiences, as the English did, in the precise moment they were about to engage in new experiences.

In London, however, Strauss had no friends—his relationship with Cassirer was rather cold—and therefore, in the first stages, he exclusively nurtured his academic relations via correspondence, maintaining contacts with the German academic world. Notable is some of the few exceptions to these exclusively epistolary contacts, namely the public lectures he held in a number of small Jewish associations in London (during one of which he made the acquaintance of Raymond Klibansky) and the encounters with Hans Jonas, from January 1934. The two scholars discussed Spengler and Heidegger, as well as their respective current research interests, which, in Jonas's case, concerned Gnosticism (cf. Strauss and Klein 2001, 490, 494). Even in England, the German world remained present for Strauss. In the letters he exchanged with Klein, Kojève, Krüger, and Löwith, the names mentioned—besides the common friends in Paris, among whom were Alexandre Koyré, Jacob Gordin, Fritz Heinemann, Abel Rey, and Georges Gurvitch—were often of more or less known German scholars: Fritz Bamberger, Ernst Bloch, Friedemann Philipp Boschwitz, Emil Brunner, Martin Buber, Rudolf Bultmann, Ernst Cassirer, Hans Philipp Ehrenberg, Julius Guttmann, Hans Jonas, Paul Ludwig Landsberg, Simon Rawidowicz, Franz Rosenzweig, and Julius Stenzel, as well as Gadamer and Heidegger, whose speech for the nomination as rector of the University of Freiburg was often specifically mentioned. Strauss's letters, instead, almost never referred to the concrete political events that were occurring in Germany. When they did, it is because Klein and Löwith, who were living in Berlin and Marburg respectively, mentioned them. It is almost as if Strauss wished to erase these problems from his life. Strauss's solitude grew in intensity, despite the pleasantness of English society. Strauss had never taught at a university and had never received appointments that required social relations, with the exception of the Zionist congresses and the lectures and didactic activities for adults he had taken part in during his youth. In the last few years, however, he dedicated his life exclusively to study and individual research, which he conducted in a foreign land, without any real personal relations, neither for friendship—with the exception of Kojève—nor for work. Therefore, his life was solitary not just in the generic sense of the term, but also because, not having any appropriate audience to address, he was forced to write—in the silence of his humble homes—for faceless, future, and unknown readers.

Like in Paris, also in London, where he remained for the whole of 1934, before moving to Cambridge in January 1935, Strauss often changed accommodation. Having left the small hotel in early February, he moved to an apartment on Elsworthy Road, then—at the end of May—to Primrose Hill Road. The economic issues, and therefore the problem of an academic placement, remained urgent: "Some influential English professors do, I believe, take an interest in me—but whether and how that interest will manifest itself in terms of bread, cigarettes, and the like, is another matter entirely . . . If I had a modest income, I could be the happiest man in the world" (Strauss and Kojève 1991, 227). The professor Strauss referred to almost certainly was Richard H. Tawney, who taught economic history at the London School of Economics. Strauss met Tawney shortly after his arrival in London, thanks to a reference letter written for him by Henri Sée, and immediately received his deep appreciation for his research project on Hobbes.[2] In the following months, Tawney managed to find Strauss an appointment, although precarious, in Cambridge (cf. Green 1995). The limited duration of the Rockefeller fellowship—renewed to Strauss up to October 1934, then transformed into a substantial economic integration to the meager wage he earned at Sidney Sussex College in Cambridge from 1935—did not grant him the possibility to make any long-term project. There were no prospects in France and returning to Germany had become impossible, both for the lack of job opportunities and for the installation of the Nazi regime. The possibility of an appointment in Jerusalem had already faded and adventures in other countries (among which Italy, suggested by Löwith) were improbable. There remained just a small hope in England, which, however, soon vanished. After this, Strauss saw just one possibility: the US, either inside the academic world (in this sense he received Tawney's help) or among Jewish institutes (regarding which he asked his friend Scholem for advice). In this latter direction, Strauss wrote on several occasions, since 1932, to Cyrus Adler, presenting his research work in a way that, in a letter dated 30 November 1933, already appears almost as a first intellectual autobiography.[3] In this letter Strauss writes about his own studies on the theological-political problem in Spinoza, which led him, on the one hand, to the medieval Jewish predecessors of Spinoza (in particular Gersonides and Maimonides) and, on the other hand, to the political philosophy of Hobbes. During the research on these sources, it was outlined the direction of his future studies on the theory of prophecy in Islamic and Jewish philosophy of the Middle Ages, through which he verified the connection between the Islamic and Jewish teaching on the prophecy and Plato's *Laws*.

In the high sea of intellectual emigration, between 1932 and 1936, the letters Strauss exchanged with his friends—Klein, Löwith, Kojève, Scholem, Krüger—give voice in a continuative way to the deep concern for economic sustenance and professional placement, often shared, for similar reasons, by his correspondents, who even considered Strauss as an important access point for the Rockefeller Foundation. Klein and Löwith—but even Eric Voegelin, who did not personally know Strauss—wrote to him on several occasions to ask for suggestions, contacts, and information to obtain a fellowship, often receiving precious advice, crowned by success. From these long exchanges concerning the scarce job opportunities that a young German Jewish philosopher could find, Strauss's disillusioned opinion surfaces, the opinion of an "emigrant" in life and thought concerning the intrinsic ineffability of human events and the misery of political issues. The news that, since December 1933, had been arriving from Kirchhain piled on these concerns. The family commercial activity seemed to be heading towards ruin and the health of Strauss's father appeared unstable. Unable to return home and persuaded that the letters he received from his family members were filled with lies, Strauss asked Klein to verify the situation in person, telling him he was aware that "I will never be able to see my dad again" (cf. Strauss and Klein 2001, 484, 487–88). Sadly, this last observation turned out to be true since Strauss would not return to Germany before 1954. However, the concerns regarding his family's conditions had been exaggerated. On 26 January 1934, Klein wrote to reassure him: his father was older and was trying to sell the family business, but there were no dramatic urgencies. If anything, Klein invited Strauss to write home, reassuring his family of *his own* conditions and of the fact that he was no longer concerned about them. Notwithstanding this partial reassurance, uncertainty was the distinctive trait of Strauss's feelings during his years in England, even when—acknowledged, from

1935, as one of the greatest experts of Hobbes in Europe—some English academics, such as Tawney, Ernest Barker, and Harold Laski, worked hard to find solutions for his situation. Their efforts, however, were in vain, at least as far as England was concerned. Despite the solidity of his studies on Hobbes, Strauss could not find a stable position and—thanks to Barker—he only managed to achieve a small yearly wage at Sidney Sussex College in Cambridge, renewed for a second year and matched by the Rockefeller Foundation. The consequences on Strauss's mood are understandable: "The economic situation is serious. I have a grant until October 1 [1935], which does not exceed the minimum for bare existence. It remains an open question whether it will be renewed for another year. After that it is certainly over. Where we turn then, only the gods know. I have no luck" (Strauss and Kojève 1991, 231).

Despite such uncertainty, and the apprehension deriving from it, worsened by Miriam's and Thomas's unstable health, Strauss's studies on Hobbes continued with great results, also thanks to a careful study of Hobbes's manuscripts preserved in libraries in London, Cambridge, and Oxford, as well as in the Duke of Devonshire's private library in Chatsworth. To this latter library, he gained access thanks to an intercession made by Tawney, who believed Strauss one of the best scholars working on Hobbes.[4] "His Grace, the Duke of Devonshire has allowed me to consult Hobbes's *Nachlass* (not yet published) which is deposited in his castle in Derbyshire (southwest of Liverpool). I will go there in early March, for a few days, without Miriam, because we have to save," Strauss wrote to Klein on 14 February 1934 (Strauss and Klein 2001, 493–94). Regarding his approach to Hobbes's early writings, Strauss wrote to Klein on 9 April (cf. Strauss and Klein 2001, 495–96). On the same day he also wrote to Kojève:

> I have become a real Hobbes philologist: Mss., etc. The Hobbes-edition project is not entirely hopeless—the Master of an Oxford College is prepared to sponsor it—and hence also myself. In the most recent Hobbes book, by John Laird, Professor in Aberdeen, to which Gilson called my attention—the book is better than Lubienski's, but not good, not as good *as that by Tönnies*—I am described in connection to our joint *Recherches* article, as "a very competent writer" . . . Most important: I may *perhaps* (!) have found Hobbes's hitherto entirely unknown first writing—a collection of 10 essays, the first five of which deal with vanity and related phenomena. In the worst case, the ms.

was written under Hobbes's influence by one of his disciples. The decision will be reached in about a week. (Strauss and Kojève 1991, 225)

Strauss's interpretative path on the foundation and genesis of Hobbes's political philosophy turned to Hobbes's "first writings," meaning those preceding 1640, when Hobbes wrote the *Elements of Law Natural and Politic*. Therefore, Strauss studied Hobbes's translation of Thucydides (1628) and two collections on Aristotle's *Rhetoric* (1635), as well as letters and autobiographical writings (while he made no use of the 1627 poem *De mirabilibus Pecci* nor of the brief scientific treatise *Short Tract on First Principles* written in 1630–32, since these were inconsistent with the philosophical-political theme). Aiming at identifying the traits of Hobbes's early thought, in the phase that preceded his acquaintance with Galileo's science, Strauss mostly focused on the Chatsworth manuscript, mentioned in his letter to Kojève. The manuscript appeared written in Hobbes's style, although it did not belong to Hobbes's writings. Following the finding of this manuscript, in 1934 Strauss submitted a proposal to Cambridge University Press for the publication of a new edition of Hobbes's letters and early writings.[5] However, the editorial board declined the proposal since it found it uncertain precisely on the level of philological reliability. Moreover, the optimism that Strauss expressed in writing to Kojève about the attribution of the manuscripts at issue—entrusted to the College of Arms—was destined to frustration. There was disagreement among the experts, which delayed their pronouncement. Despite this, on 3 June 1934, Strauss wrote to Kojève a letter filled with euphoria for the philological and philosophical results he had gained, asserting that the attribution of the manuscript to Hobbes was by then certain. His optimism, however, was frustrated again, despite still on 10 October Strauss continued writing to Klein about the possibility to publish a book with Hobbes's unedited texts (cf. Strauss and Klein 2001, 529). Indeed, in the preface to *The Political Philosophy of Hobbes*, although Strauss reaffirmed the accuracy of his philological work, he was forced to use cautious terms, asserting that it was not possible to attribute the manuscript to Hobbes, despite its content being inspired directly by him, given that Hobbes had been the tutor of the author of the essays:

> The manuscript in question is entitled "Essayes" and was composed by W. Cavendish . . . The "Essayes" are the ear-

lier and much shorter manuscript version of *Horae subsecivae*, anonymously published in 1620. As the "Essayes" and the *Horae subsecivae* are based on some essays of Bacon's which were not published before 1612, they must both have been composed between 1612 and 1620. *Horae subsecivae* was traditionally attributed to "Lord Chandos" or to "Lord Chandish, after Earle of Devonshire" . . . The (nominal or actual) author of the "Essayes" and very probably also of the *Horae subsecivae* can be nobody else but W. Cavendish, afterwards 2nd Earl of Devonshire. Now, this W. Cavendish was Hobbes's pupil and friend. Hobbes lived with him as his author and secretary from 1608 until 1628, therefore also during the whole period within which the "Essayes" and the *Horae subsecivae* can have been written. (Strauss 1936c, XII–XIII)

We would only later know, but only after almost sixty years, that Strauss, and not the College of Arms, was actually right.[6] However, despite the obstacles posed by the philological issues concerning attribution, Strauss's research continued, as well as his writing of a book on Hobbes, a first version of which was already finished in November 1934. Strauss definitively completed the book in May 1935. Along with it came the great satisfaction of having identified the basis and genesis of all modern philosophy, as he wrote to Klein on 10 October 1934 (cf. Strauss and Klein 2001, 523–54). The editorial affair, however, was far from over. Strauss's text, entitled *Hobbes' politische Wissenschaft*, was in German and initially thought for a publication in Germany, since the English translation would mean additional costs for the potential publisher. Therefore, on 12 May 1935 Strauss wrote a long letter to Krüger and Gadamer to present the structure of the book, chapter by chapter, and the results of his work on Hobbes, requesting their help to find a German publisher (cf. Strauss and Krüger 2001, 443–47). Strauss's attempt did not have a positive outcome, nor did the attempts made by Klein in Germany and the Netherlands. Löwith also helped Strauss to find a German publisher. Or at least, he comforted him with some advice, as we read from their correspondence in 1935, when Löwith did his best to suggest different publishers in Germany—also through the mediation of the elderly Ferdinand Tönnies—Italy and France. Not even this friendly care could lift Strauss's mood, who had grown rather skeptical on the possibility of finding a publisher in Germany (cf. Strauss and Löwith 1988, 185–86). Notwithstanding these difficulties, the book finally appeared in England, especially thanks to the mediation made by Tawney and Barker—the latter also wrote a preface—in the translation made by Elsa M. Sinclair, under the title *The Political Philosophy of Hobbes. Its Basis and Its Genesis* (1936). The proposals contained inside it ignited a long-lasting debate—we could say still open today—but the scientific community immediately recognized, unanimously, the solidity of Strauss's work, to the point that the book received numerous reviews between 1937 and 1938.[7] In particular, Michael Oakeshott, one of the most prominent English thinkers, reviewed the book in 1937, defining the work—notwithstanding a number of critiques of Strauss's interpretation of Hobbes—a book of great importance, written by an author that, although young, was already "a leader" in the field of Hobbesian studies and had produced "the most original book on Hobbes which has appeared for many years."[8]

Modernity as a Problem

In the years he spent in Paris, London, and Cambridge, Strauss dedicated most of his research to Hobbes, without however neglecting the other research project he had begun in 1928, once completed his book on Spinoza: medieval Islamic, and Jewish philosophy. This research, however, proceeded in a less organic and systematic way than the one developed on Hobbes. Indeed, on medieval philosophers Strauss wrote some essays, without however having the programmatic intention of publishing an effective monograph. Despite this, a monograph—*Philosophie und Gesetz* (1935)—appeared. It was the result of a fortunate trail of positive factors, as Strauss himself acknowledge in a letter addressed to his friend Scholem on 14 December 1934 (cf. Strauss and Scholem 2001, 714). In this letter, Strauss communicated that, thanks to the mediation of Buber and Simon, Schocken Verlag had taken an interest in publishing his essays on Maimonides and he asked Scholem to favor this possibility by writing to Salman Schocken, the owner of the publishing house. The apparently "fortuitous" appearance of *Philosophie und Gesetz* contributed to keeping this work almost unknown for a long time. A work dedicated to an apparently Jewish topic written by a Jewish author, published in Nazi Germany by a Jewish publishing house on the threshold of the tragedy that would hit German Jews, it only circulated among Strauss's friends (Klein, Kojève, Löwith, Scholem, Krüger, Koyré, Buber, Simon, Gadamer,

Benjamin) and a very small circle of scholars interested in medieval thought (Fritz Baer, Paul Kraus, Julius Guttmann, Simon Rawidowicz, as well as Shlomo Pines and Georges Vajda, who reviewed it for the journals *Recherches philosophiques* and *Revue des études juives*[9]).

Strauss had not considered in advance the eight-hundredth anniversary of Maimonides's birth, but the publisher did not miss the occasion offered by the celebration. The chance was too big not to catch it. Before the end of January 1935, Strauss made the last corrections to the essays he had already finished (corresponding to chapters II, III, and IV) and, in the first half of February 1935, he wrote the introduction (chapter I), allowing the publisher to print the book by the end of March. Despite its "fortuitous" character, the book is actually very important for the philosophical-political and theoretical themes it treats, and it is very significant in the context of Strauss's intellectual development. It represents the first, true, and accomplished expression of the "change of orientation" that characterized his thought, following the writing of the book on Spinoza, between late 1920s and early 1930s. Indeed, in *Philosophie und Gesetz*, Strauss identified, for the first time in a systematic way, a model of rationality—represented by medieval Islamic and Jewish philosophers—able to elude the crisis of the modernity founded by Descartes and Hobbes. Such a perspective is placed—in chapters II, III, and IV—inside a research that is only apparently historical-philosophical (the Islamic sources of Maimonides's thought and the Platonic sources of medieval Islamic and Jewish philosophy) and historiographical (hermeneutical methodology to read medieval texts), but which rather has a theoretical and philosophical-political scope. Such perspective of criticism of modernity appears in an outspoken way in the book's *Introduction*—defined as "audacious" by Strauss in person—that represents a true anti-modern manifesto, both from a philosophical-political and a theoretical-scientific perspective. The target of Strauss's critique was modern rationalism, i.e., Enlightenment, and, against modern Enlightenment, Strauss recovered Maimonides's medieval Enlightenment. The purpose of *Philosophie und Gesetz* is to elaborate an argument in favor of medieval rationalism, or rather to raise a suspicion against the modern prejudice against pre-modern rationalism. For Strauss the critique of the present, the critique of modern rationalism, understood as a critique of modern sophistry, is the necessary beginning of the search for truth.

In fact, this was the true focus of the question posed by *Philosophie und Gesetz*: which rationalism was still possible *after* Nietzsche? In other words, which rationalism was still possible after the final crisis of orthodoxy and Enlightenment? According to Strauss, the answer was not the rationalism of Descartes or Hobbes, nor that of Mendelssohn or Cohen, not even Rosenzweig's "new thought" or Heidegger's existentialism or Carl Schmitt's decisionism. The merit—the great merit—of Strauss's Nietzsche is that of having *theoretically* caused the collapse of Enlightenment, both the radical one, represented by the line Descartes-Hobbes-Voltaire, and Mendelssohn's moderate one. After Nietzsche—on a theoretical level—a "return" to orthodoxy is no longer possible, but the defense of Enlightenment is equally impossible, both in its neo-Kantian version and in its positivistic or historicist version. Naturally, according to Strauss, Nietzsche does not represent an answer to the theological-political problem, due to the risk of exalting authoritarianism, but he certainly represents the decisive opportunity to bring clarity to the crisis—not fortuitous, but rather necessary—of modern philosophy. From this perspective, Strauss's Nietzsche unmasks both any positivistic illusion of the possibility of progress and any neo-Kantian illusion of the relationship between ethics and theory of knowledge. With an anti-modern fury that represents one of the highest moments of his *philosophical radicalism* and with a "hieratic" and "somber" prose, which is reminiscent of Nietzsche's own writing, Strauss goes as far as to doubt not only the moral legitimacy of the Enlightenment, but also the reliability of the foundations of modern science. Modern science results only in a historically conditioned comprehension of the world, which opens a pitfall on the crisis of modern rationalism. The nature, "free from purposes and values," of modern natural science cannot provide anything to human beings concerning "purposes and values." Modern natural science's "being" does not contain in itself any reference to "shall be." Therefore, if modern natural science cannot justify the modern philosophical-political ideal, the spontaneous question it raises is asking whether, instead, this philosophical-political ideal is not actually the basis of modern science. In this case, Enlightenment is not so much justified by a new knowledge as by a new faith (cf. Strauss 1935, 18ff.).

In his book on Spinoza, Strauss uncovers the unfoundedness of modernity, without however pointing out any alternative solution. In his book on Maimonides, instead, he opens the way towards a recovery of a different form of Enlightenment, of rationalism, the *pre-modern* one represented by Maimonides and the *falasifa* (while in later works he identifies it primarily in Plato), intended as a possible "ultramodern" answer to the crisis of modernity. Given that the "defensive" critique of

Enlightenment catches the theoretical deficiency of orthodoxy, Enlightenment is necessary; however, it is not sufficient on its own. Strauss's first step in this direction consists in verifying pre-modern rationalism, which, before becoming the rationalism of Greek classics, in particular from the 1940s, in *Philosophie und Gesetz* is the rationalism of medieval Islamic and Jewish philosophers. This does not mean nostalgically "repeating" antiquity, honoring tradition or nurturing an antiquarian attitude towards the past, but building a model of rationalism, a new Enlightenment, through which it becomes possible—for the *moderns*—to leave the draughts of relativism and nihilism from which modern philosophy has led. Only a process of "deconstruction" can render the premises of modernity inoperative since Nietzsche has uncovered their failure. In this way, Strauss transforms a *philosophical* problem into a *historical-philosophical* problem, and vice versa, explicitly building a philosophical model of the history of philosophy. In this perspective, inside the introduction to *Philosophie und Gesetz*, he draws a long-period image of the birth, development, and crisis of modernity, crossing theoretical and political, ethical and religious, scientific and anthropological themes. The introduction to the book looks like a programmatic manifesto and constitutes an exception compared to the way Strauss generally wrote his texts. Indeed, specific references to passages, texts, works, and authors are almost absent here, while Strauss often structured his writing on punctual references—sometimes, especially in his later years, in a deliberately "obsessive" way—to the works he analyzed. However, the introduction to *Philosophie und Gesetz* also constitutes the interpretative pillar of modernity, inside which Strauss's specific studies on Plato and Xenophon, Al-Farabi and Maimonides, Machiavelli and Hobbes, Spinoza and Locke, Rousseau and Burke, Cohen and Weber, Heidegger and Schmitt find their sense. Indeed, entire passages from this introduction, translated into English with just few differences from the original text, returned in his *Preface* (1962) to the American translation of his book on Spinoza, published in 1965. This demonstrates that those contents continued to stand for the critical analysis of modernity, even after thirty years.

However, according to Strauss, modernity develops in different phases. The first stage of modernity—founded by Descartes, Hobbes, and Spinoza and brought to success by the Enlightenment—is now over: during the second stage of modernity, in the nineteenth century, doubts about the results of civilization have become doubts about the possibility itself of civilization. For Strauss, the crisis of modernity—identified in the

"Promethean" short circuit between philosophical skepticism and scientific dogmatism—consists precisely in the end of the faith according to which the human being can progress towards ever greater freedom by subduing nature. The modernity therefore ends in nihilism. When the faith in improvement and the faith in progress vanished, religious representations are then rejected not because they are terrible or because they are illusory, but almost paradoxically because they are desirable and consoling. Religion is not a tool created by the human being to make life more difficult; rather, it is a means of escaping the loss of hope in life. Thus, a new form of virtue is created, which—in Nietzschean terms—prohibits any escape from the misery of life and which accepts the misery of man without God. But the new Nietzschean concept of "intellectual honesty" is very different from the classic concept of "theory," which indicates the love for the search for truth. Philosophy, in its classical sense, is not the search for a *determined* truth, be it reassuring or terrifying. It is the search for truth in and of itself, whatever it may be, against opinion and appearance.

We should read Strauss's interpretation of Hobbes on this background. Strauss confronted a theme that runs through early-twentieth-century German culture: modernity as a problem. Strauss's work was not isolated. Hobbes's figure and work played a fundamental role in the history of German philosophical, political, and legal culture between the nineteenth and the twentieth century, especially in reference to the debate on the interpretation of the modern world, both on a theoretical and a historiographical level. Indeed, numerous eminent authors dealt with the teachings of the English philosopher, especially in relation to two central issues for German culture: the critique of political modernity and the crisis of the State; the comprehension of the specificity of Western rationalism. These authors attempted to pursue interpretative lines that aimed at freeing Hobbes's work from the worn-out categories of "absolutism," "materialism," "empiricism," and "sensualism." Inside this context, from a philosophical perspective, Hobbes became one of the founders of modern rationalism, centered on the geometrical-mechanistic character of the new natural science. On the political level, he became one of the most prominent authors of the theory of State and public right. The list of German authors that dealt with Hobbes between nineteenth and twentieth century is long, to the point that we can assert that German culture had a greater credit than the English one in recovering Hobbes. To give a general idea of the large and complex context that surrounded Strauss's work, it is sufficient to mention the names of: *in primis* Ferdinand Tönnies—who also edited

Hobbes's *Behemoth* and his *Elements of Law Natural and Politic*, as well as other minor writings and numerous letters—and then Friedrich Albert Lange, Wilhelm Dilthey, Otto von Gierke, Lorenz von Stein, Rudolf von Jhering, Friedrich Jodl, Werner Sombart, Georg Jellinek, Heinrich Cunow, Friedrich Meinecke, Ernst Troeltsch, Ernst Cassirer, Carl Schmitt, Julius Ebbinghaus, Cay von Brockdorff, Max Horkheimer, Franz Borkenau, Eric Voegelin, and Helmut Schelsky. Therefore, Strauss's research on Hobbes represented a chapter inside this larger mosaic constituted by Hobbes's fortune in Germany. In turn, this constituted a chapter of the larger German debate on modernity, which crossed the main concepts—rationalization, reification, progress, leveling, massification, nihilism—used to interpret the processes of modernization of European societies, resulting in the construction of dichotomies that polarize the opposition between tradition and modernity: community/society, *Kultur/Zivilisation*, soul/machine, spirit/technique. In Germany, in fact, philosophical and historiographic research on the genesis, development, and crisis of modern civilization constitutes a real obsession which, exploded with Nietzsche, does not fail to present itself in the authors—from Max Weber to Thomas Mann, from Freud to Spengler, from Stefan George to György Lukács—who most influenced the German culture in the early twentieth century. In this sense, Strauss's confrontation with Hobbes was not the result of an occasional historical or philosophical choice, but rather of the necessity to confront the highest expression of the philosophical-political paradigm of modernity.

Hobbes and the Foundation of Modern Political Philosophy

To understand the innovative character of Strauss's book on Hobbes—which still today, almost a century after its publication, constitutes a fundamental text inside the critical literature on the English philosopher—it is important to pay attention to the subtitle, which focuses on the *basis* and on the *genesis* of Hobbes's political philosophy. Strauss identifies the *moral*—not scientific—basis that lies at the foundations of Hobbes's political theory and of the entire modern political philosophy. The result of his study does not constitute an isolated result in his thought. Indeed, the theme of the moral basis of modern philosophy is also central of his 1930 monograph on Spinoza, dedicated to showing how Spinoza's biblical science actually stems from a prejudice linked to the critique of religion. It is also central in his 1935 book on Maimonides, in the introduction to which he asserts that modern science has a moral rather than theoretical basis. Strauss's target in these years constitutes the identification of the theoretical and political limits of modernity, given that the only scientifically supported result of the Enlightenment consists in its "defensive" criticism of orthodoxy (the truths of which can be believed, but not *known*). These common traits characterize Strauss's three monographs on Spinoza, Maimonides, and Hobbes. They develop on three different and complementary levels, on which Strauss verified the unfoundedness of modernity: the hermeneutical level (especially in the book on Spinoza), the theoretical-scientific level (especially in the book on Maimonides, but also partially in the one on Hobbes), and the philosophical-political level (especially in the book on Hobbes, but also frequently in *Philosophie und Gesetz*). Strauss, however, did not conceive his critique just as a *pars destruens*. Already halfway on this path (in the years 1928–32, once finished the book on Spinoza and while he was working on medieval philosophy and on Hobbes), Strauss became aware of the possibility of overcoming modernity—in the form of a "return"—recovering the lesson of pre-modern philosophy and reopening the *querelle des anciens et des modernes*.

Strauss was aware of having reached an overall vision of his research on Hobbes—demonstrating the moral basis of Hobbes's (political) philosophy—at least since 3 June 1934, when he wrote a letter to his friend Kojève summarizing in just a few lines the sense of his whole work on the formation and development of Hobbes's thought:

> In his "youth" i.e., until he was 41, that is to say before he became acquainted with Euclid and *thereafter with Galileo* etc., Hobbes had been influenced by four forces: Scholasticism, Puritanism, Humanism and the aristocratic atmosphere in which he lived. Relatively early—let us say at the age of 22—he broke with Scholasticism. But the break with Scholasticism does not mean he broke with Aristotle. Aristotle, albeit not the scholastic Aristotle, still remains the philosopher for him. But the center of gravity has already shifted: from physics and metaphysics to ethics and rhetoric (the teaching about the passions). The place of theory is taken by "heroic virtue" (modified Aristotelian magnanimity), that is to say, virtue . . . That is the first point. The second is that (under Bacon's influence), while he *in principle* acknowledges ancient, Aristotelian ethics and the

inquiry into virtue, his focus shifts to the function of virtue and the inquiry into the *use* and *life with others* . . . Hence *history*, which *exhibits instances* of moral life, assumes greater importance than does philosophical doctrine with its exclusively abstract precepts . . . In this way Hobbes's later break with Aristotle becomes radically intelligible . . . The aristocratic principle is honor, fame, pride. This criticism, the principle of which is *puritanical* origin, by which honor, fame, and vanity are singled out and devalued, requires a revolution in basic moral concepts that results in the antithesis vanity-fear. The further, most important and most difficult task is then to show how the *project* of a *mechanistic*-deterministic account of nature arises from this *new* moral principle. The essential middle term here is the significance attached on a priori grounds to the *sense of touch*, which now becomes the most important sense. That is simply the as-it-were "epistemological" expression of the fact that the fear of (violent) death becomes the moral principle. (Strauss and Kojève 1991, 228–29)

The modern ideal of civilization is intended as a rationally based cohabitation of humanity, which works and produces with the help of scientific progress, in its bourgeois-capitalistic as well as in its socialist versions. However, if the modern political philosophy inaugurated by Hobbes is the result of a moral preference and not of scientific knowledge, then such ideal of civilization does not have a basis that has the statute of truth. To reach this conclusion, Strauss analyzes the genesis and development of Hobbes's thought, avoiding being misled by the *mechanical philosophy* that apparently constitutes the *Leviathan*'s theoretical structure and that seems to give a scientific cover to the new morality and to modern politics. Hobbes's political philosophy does not rest on the application of the new Galilean scientific method to politics, but rather in his specific moral conception, which is clear in his theory of passions. It is essentially independent from the new natural science because its principles concern moral knowledge, made possible by the anthropological analysis of passions, not by the geometrical analysis of figures and movements. Hobbes's political philosophy, based on principles recovered through anthropological experience, does not need a natural science. Through the analysis of the theory of passions it is possible to identify the anthropological and moral motives that recur in Hobbes, in his early writings (where there is no reference to Galilean science) as well as in the later ones. Therefore, it is possible to verify that these motives were already present in the English philosopher *before* he embraced the perspective of mechanical philosophy. In any case, they are *independent* from it. Hobbes is the first philosopher that consciously inaugurates the modern tradition of *right* as distinct from the ancient concept of *law*. Moreover, Hobbes's natural right, intended as a source for morality and politics, is not only different from the natural law of the classics, but it is also different from the principles of the naturalistic tradition typical of mechanical philosophy. The decisive trait of Hobbes's political philosophy does not lie in the application of the method of modern science to politics, but in its specific moral conception. No matter how much Hobbes highlighted his attempt to solve the issues of political philosophy by means of natural science's methods and arguments, there remains a fundamental difference between the two theoretical perspectives. According to Strauss, Hobbes's political philosophy was essentially independent from natural science (cf. Strauss 1936c, 151ff.).

Far from proposing once again the old image of the author of the *Leviathan* as the adorer of absolutism, Strauss identifies in Hobbes's theory of passions the roots of liberalism and modern culture, because the *individualistic* character of natural right constitutes a turning point in respect to Platonic and Aristotelian theories of natural law. Therefore, Hobbes was the true founder of liberalism, and it was precisely for this reason that anyone who aspired to radically criticize or justify liberalism—as Strauss already asserts in his critical review to Schmitt's *Der Begriff des "Politischen"*—necessarily has to confront Hobbes. Right from the start of his *The Political Philosophy of Hobbes* Strauss declares his own program:

> We must raise the more precise question, whether there is not a difference of principle between the modern and the traditional view of natural law. Such a difference does in fact exist. Traditional natural law is primarily and mainly an objective "rule and measure," a binding order prior to, and independent of, the human will, while modern natural law is, or tends to be, primarily and mainly a series of "rights," of subjective claims, originating in the human will. (Strauss 1936c, VII–VIII)

Against Plato and Aristotle, Hobbes's conception of natural right expresses a subjective claim, independent from any obligation or law, which becomes, in turn, the origin of any form of obligation. Hobbes maintains the idea of natural law, but he separates it from the idea of human perfection, so much that the foundation of natural law is no longer—as in Aristotle—in the human being's purpose, but it is in the human being's origin, in natural right. Such anti-teleological perspective confirms, according to Strauss, Hobbes's role as the founder of modern liberalism. If the State does not have the function of promoting virtue or good, but rather that of safeguarding the natural right of each human being, then the State's power finds its limit in the individual natural right, unpassable and inviolable. If liberalism is the political doctrine that considers rights as the fundamental political fact and that identifies the function of the State with the protection and safeguard of those rights, then Hobbes is the founder of liberalism.

Strauss builds his interpretation of Hobbes's political philosophy trying to analyze—also philologically—the genesis of his thought (cf. Strauss 1936c, 30ff., 44ff.). There exists a profound difference between Hobbes's humanistic education and his philosophical education. While his initial humanistic education, between 1596 and 1602, focused on Greek and Latin historians and poets (Homer, Demosthenes, Euripides, Thucydides, Livy, Cicero, Seneca, Tacitus), his philosophical education unfolded under the sign of Aristotle. At Magdalen Hall in Oxford, between 1603 and 1607, Hobbes studied Aristotelian logics and physics, without, however, drawing any element of interest from them. He did not delay in manifesting the first signs of intolerance for the Aristotelian philosophy taught in Oxford, where the metaphysical dimension of his thought was emphasized, presenting it by means of the Scholastic system of *disputationes*, which Hobbes reputed responsible of creating "empty subtleties" and "senseless devises" devoid of scientific and civil use. Hobbes acted on these signs of intolerance towards Aristotelian philosophy by going back—in the 1610s and 1620s—to humanistic studies, during which, however, he abundantly also used Aristotle's *Rhetoric*. Indeed, Strauss ascertained that, at least until the date of the composition of the preface to his translation of Thucydides (1628–29), Aristotle was for Hobbes *the* philosopher of morality and politics, the teachings of whom were condensed in his *Rhetoric*. Besides moral and political Aristotelian philosophy, another tradition is present in the thought of the young Hobbes, defined by Strauss as "aristocratic." Indeed, alongside the progressive abandonment of metaphysics in favor of practical philosophy, an aristocratic conception of virtue, intended as heroic virtue and courage, *honor*, emerged inside Hobbes's writings.

This "juvenile" moral conviction did not pass on to his mature writings, where the distance between the aristocratic virtue of honor and Hobbes's conception of fear of violent death as the source of justice becomes clear. The elaboration of Hobbes's political philosophy expresses a progressive departure from the original recognition of honor as a virtue (i.e., from the original recognition of aristocratic virtue): Hobbes moved further and further away from the recognition of aristocratic virtue to finally reach the foundation of a bourgeois morality. At the end of the process of abandonment of aristocratic virtue, Strauss asserts that inside Hobbes's political theory the origin of justice does not lie in magnanimity, always connected to a form of "honorable" superiority, but rather in the fear of violent death, connected to some form of natural equality. The development of Hobbes's political philosophy is therefore equivalent to his progressive moving away from the juvenile acceptance of aristocratic virtue and the progressive definition of the bourgeois morality (cf. Strauss 1936c, 108ff.).

This passage from aristocratic morality to bourgeois morality did not depend on Hobbes's endorsement of the new Galilean science, but on his theory of human nature, based on two postulations: natural appetite and natural reason. In Strauss's interpretation, natural appetite is defined as different from animal instinct, since it is limitless and indefinite, and for this reason originates an insatiable and irrational desire for power. Vanity indicates human desire to find pleasure in considering its own recognized superiority. The result of this passion is desire of recognition of superiority over the others, intended as a peculiar condition of honor. The postulation of natural reason, instead, asserts the principle of self-preservation, considered as fear of violent death. Since death is the supreme and primary evil, the human being has an intrinsic natural purpose, that of fleeing death by the hand of other human beings. Indeed, in Strauss's interpretation, according to Hobbes there is a *summum malum* (violent death), but there is no *summum bonum*: life is the "first" good, i.e., what makes all other goods possible, but it is not the supreme good, since this latter one does not exist. Vanity is a passion that, in pushing the human being towards growing triumphs in respect to other human beings, with the purpose of self-satisfaction, creates a world of unimaginable pleasures and pains. The human being that chases the pleasures of recognized triumph loses the awareness of the "first" good, the preservation of life, and can only gain it again when he perceives the resistance of the concrete world on his own body through an unexpected offense. The ideal condition for self-knowledge is the unexpected danger of violent death. The claim and recognition of superiority always leads to disdain and desire to offend, to a physical fight that can become a fight for life or death. The danger of violent death appears every time that a confrontation with another human being occurs. On the medium and long range, it is not so much fierce fight that grants preservation of life, but rather the acquisition of allies. One can obtain allies in two ways, either by force or by means of a pact. In this sense, the sole true postulate of natural reason, through which the human being achieves a peaceful life, is fear of violent death, which reveals itself to be a *rational passion* (cf. Strauss 1936c, 8ff.).

Hobbes based his political philosophy on a passion—the fear of violent death—that is unconditionally applied. His political philosophy is in harmony with passions because it is in harmony with the strongest among them. In Strauss's reading, the fear of violent death takes up a *moral* meaning. It is different from all other non-moral reasons that can originate, in a "technical" sense, law and the State. This distinction allows a systematical differentiation between justice and injustice, allowing a distinction between the human being's *natural appetite* and its *natural right*. The basis of Hobbes's political philosophy consists in the morally characterized antithesis between *unjust* vanity and *right* fear of violent death, not in the naturalistic antithesis between animal appetite and desire of self-preservation, both morally indifferent. Strauss concludes that a coherent naturalism would be the ruin of Hobbes's political philosophy, to the opposite of what occurred in Spinoza. A coherent naturalist philosopher, Spinoza abandons the distinction between power and right and professes the natural right of all passions. Hobbes, instead, in virtue of the moral—not naturalistic—basis of his political philosophy, asserts the natural right only of the fear of violent death. The antithesis between nature and will, power and right, is an essential element of Hobbes's political philosophy. In opposition to Spinoza, the English philosopher does not renounce the possibility to distinguish between natural right and natural appetite, maintaining that political philosophy and natural philosophy are separate.

The Modern Ideal of Civilization and the Bourgeois Morality

Strauss turns to Hobbes in the attempt to recover the origins of modernity, in order to identify the roots of its crisis. Far from interpreting Hobbes as the standard-bearer for absolute monarchy, Strauss interprets him as the founder of liberalism, of bourgeois morality, and of capitalist way of living, highlighting the *puritan* inspirations that recall Max Weber's proposal on the relationship between Calvinist ethics and capitalist rationality. Indeed, the ideals of Hobbes's political philosophy does not represent the ideals of the aristocracy, but rather the utilitarian desires of the new middle class. The passage from vanity to fear represents the passage from aristocratic virtue to bourgeois virtue. The utilitarian tone of Hobbes's morality—the quest for peace as a condition of possibility of a comfortable life—determines that the fundamental purpose of the State is *security*, which allows welfare and freedom of personal enrichment. The conditions to exercise such interest of the new middle class is rendered possible only by obedience to political power, which is the condition for peace and therefore for *work and accumulation* in a perspective of capitalist rationalization. The individualistic principle on which the State-Leviathan is based shows that public power is a "tool" at the service of citizens and of their desire to lead a comfortable and peaceful life. Work and accumulation, commerce and industry, freedom and capital are the characteristics of the modern ideal of civilization, which finds in Hobbes's philosophy the earliest coherent philosophical justification:

> Hobbes' political philosophy is directed against the aristocratic rules of life in the name of bourgeois rules of life. His morality is the morality of the bourgeois world. Even his sharp criticism of the bourgeoisie has, at bottom, no other aim than to remind the bourgeoisie of the elementary condition for its existence. This condition is not industry and thrift, not the specific exertions of the bourgeoisie, but the security of body and soul, which the bourgeoisie cannot of itself guarantee. For this reason the sovereign power must be permitted unrestricted power. (Strauss 1936c, 121)

The progressive substitution of aristocratic virtue (honor, courage, and magnanimity) with bourgeois virtue (self-preservation, pleasure, and usefulness) appears inside the development of Hobbes's political philosophy. The basis of moral utilitarianism lies in a passion—fear for violent death—that leads the human being to prudence and brings him to experiment the hedonist utility of security. Without fear for violent death, it would not be possible to build a political order that creates the social conditions to pursue individual pleasure. Therefore, Hobbes is a defender of bourgeoisie even when he attacks it—for instance in the *Behemoth*. He does not attack bourgeoisie in and of itself, but rather for its wrong political action, directed against its own interests. If the new middle class precisely understands its own interest, it unconditionally obeys secular power, since peace is the necessary condition to pursue individual welfare through a competitive selfishness with an economic foundation. Liberalism and capitalism find their basis in the bourgeois morality that Hobbes shaped:

> Not only does Hobbes not attack the middle class, which is sensibly aware of its own interests, he even provides it with a philosophical justification, as the ideals set up in his political philosophy are precisely the ideals of the bourgeoisie. It is true that he condemns the desire "to grow excessively rich," but "justly and moderately to enrich themselves" is "prudence in private men." It is true that he condemns the exploiting of the poor, but he takes it for granted that "a man's labour also is a commodity exchangeable for benefit." (Strauss 1936c, 118)

Once abandoned the terrors of the state of nature, the desire for self-preservation, expressed in the form of fear for violent death, survives in the form of competition and it is directed to the creation of lasting comfort and a pleasant life. Therefore, the recipients of Hobbes's political philosophy are not aristocrats longing for honor and glory, but citizens devoted to practical well-being and to a reassuring hedonism. Hobbes's State is born to grant peace and security and thus to create the conditions for a certain and granted definition of *property*, which cannot be defended in the state of nature, since everything is at anyone's legitimate disposal. Through the connection between peace and work, fear and pleasure, security and property, Strauss's Hobbes is the founder of bourgeois morality.

Such hedonist and secular image of the human being does not casually develop inside Hobbes's thought, since it corresponds to his criticism of religion, namely of *providence*. Indeed, inside Hobbes's thought, Strauss identifies the image of a human being who recognizes his own salvation only in the progressive improvement of the world. Awakened to a serious awareness of its real position inside an indifferent world, abandoned by a nature that is neither ordered nor ordering, but which instead constitutes the principle of disorder and danger (evidently in the condition of the state of nature), the human being understands that his duty is to build his own world, against nature and against providence. The human being has no reason to be grateful to the "first cause" and, rather, has to acknowledge its own original miserable condition, due to the concrete world's violent resistance, without creating illusions regarding its natural condition and without putting together vain dreams. Since the human being is exposed to a nature that is completely uninterested in its prosperity or misery, it has no alternative but to help itself. The human being is unsuited for vain contemplation. Rather it is suited for the conquering of nature, the only endeavor that can grant refuge from the condition of solitude in the outside world.

From Political Philosophy to Political Science

The dissatisfaction with Aristotelian tradition of the "first" Hobbes also appears, according to Strauss, in his "juvenile" turning to the philosophy of history. History burst into Hobbes's thought through the issue of the *effectiveness* of the rational precept. In his humanistic phase, Hobbes did not discuss the content of traditional philosophical precepts but dealt with their practical *application*. The purpose of history consists in teaching prudence to men in a methodical way, highlighting not what men should do, but what they actually do. Therefore, according to Strauss, Hobbes already has doubts on the effective ability of traditional philosophy well before he learns about the perspectives opened by the new science. Indeed, Hobbes considers history a remedy to Aristotelian philosophy's fundamental deficiency, the abstractness of its political and moral perspective, given that, in their everyday lives, humans do not adhere to norms dictated by a transcendent order. The theme of the efficacy of rules does not concern only Hobbes's humanistic phase, but also his mature years. Indeed, Hobbes's political philosophy aims at solving the problem posed by history's appearance in Aristotelian philosophy. However, with the formation of the *new* political philosophy, history returns to its philosophical insignificance. The premise that causes Hobbes's turning towards history—the problem of applying traditional precepts and their efficacy—constitutes the basis for Hobbes's political philosophy once it reaches its accomplishment. Not only does it deny the applicability of Aristotelian norms, but also their *validity*. The new political philosophy teaches an *applicable* morality, since, studying passions—that govern the life of all human beings—a definition of universal norms becomes possible (cf. Strauss 1936c, 93ff.).

Hobbes's *moral* conception—based on his political philosophy—precedes, according to Strauss, the manifestation of the English philosopher's scientific interests. However, the clear awareness of the deep fracture with philosophical tradition that is implied in Hobbes's new and revolutionary moral conception only surfaces with his discovery of Euclid. The English philosopher only becomes fully aware of the incompatibility of his conception with the Aristotelian conception finding out the incompatibility of the new science with traditional science (cf. Strauss 1936c, 165ff.). According to Strauss, however, there is a similarity, but not an identity, between the conception of nature that stands as the premise to Hobbes's philosophical-political writings and the conception of nature in his scientific writings. Only an "incoherent" naturalism is compatible with Hobbes's political philosophy. However, despite Hobbes's assertions that his political philosophy is an exact science, Strauss identifies an insurmountable obstacle: the adoption of mathematics and geometry as universal models creates problems not only on an anthropological level (with the destruction of man's natural purposes), but also on the political level:

> Political philosophy must be just as exact and accurate as the science of lines and figures. But exactitude in political philosophy has a scope and significance quite different from that of mathematics; exact passionless mathematics is indifferent to passions; exact passionless political philosophy is in conflict with the passions. (Strauss 1936c, 137)

Hobbes's dominating interest for the applicability of norms determines his use of Galileo's "resolutive-compositive" method (cf. Strauss 1936c, 130ff.). If the form of the State is deducible from its matter, which is the human being radically deprived of any education, then nothing other than human nature interferes in political science. However, in Strauss's interpretation, the adequacy of the "resolutive-compositive" method in the field of physics does not constitute an argument in favor of its validity in the field of political philosophy, which, differently from physics, has to produce artificial bodies. Moreover, the use of such a method implies the reduction of political philosophy to a *technique*: "The procedure of political philosophy is much less like the procedure of physics than that of the technician, who takes to pieces a machine that has broken down, removes the foreign body which prevents the functioning of the machine, puts the machine together again" (Strauss 1936c, 152). The adoption of the Galilean method requires the systematic elimination of the issue of the State's *purpose*, meaning the systematic elimination of the issue of *good*, which is clear in the subordination of natural law to natural right. According to Strauss, all this implicates a redefinition of the functions and limits of the idea of sovereignty. Against classical political philosophy, Hobbes defines the space of political power not in the terms of reason, but in terms of *will*. The role of political reason is not uncovered by the rationality of who detains sovereign power, but rather by his or their will (cf. Strauss 1936c, 157ff.). What detains sovereign power is not the "head," i.e., the ability to deliberate and plan, but the "soul," i.e., the ability to lead inside the State. In this way, through the reformulation of the categories of natural right and sovereignty, Strauss's Hobbes opens the road to *formal ethics*, following the relativistic turn from philosophy to history, which is visible in the primacy attributed to the definition of directly effective and applicable norms. Between positivism and historicism, modern political philosophy becomes, on the one hand, *political technique* (which is clear in Hans Kelsen's legal positivism) and, on the other hand, *ideology*, which is an apology of the existing social order (clear in Carl Schmitt's decisionism). This modern deviation—in its being a new sophistry—is, according to Strauss, the exact opposite of what occurs with classic political philosophy.

A New Reading of Platonic Philosophy: Al-Farabi

During the years he spent in England, Strauss focused his studies on Hobbes, in a substantial but not exclusive way. Indeed, his interest for medieval Islamic and Jewish philosophy remained alive, since they constituted a privileged reference for the criticism of modernity and—independently from the negative outcome of Strauss's candidacy at the Hebrew University of Jerusalem—they could favor the perspective of an appointment inside one of the research centers connected to the Jewish world, especially in the US. The studies on medieval philosophy always remained one of the primary pillars of his thought, from the 1920s to the 1960s. However, inside this long-lasting research, his interest towards single authors changed. In the second half of the 1920s, central in Strauss's studies was Maimonides—due to the issues connected to biblical hermeneutics, especially in opposition to Spinoza—as well as Gersonides and Avicenna, for the interpretation of prophetology. In the early 1930s, the primary figures were Maimonides and Averroes, with Avicenna in a secondary position and Gersonides and Al-Farabi in the background. From the second half of the 1930s, instead, Maimonides and Al-Farabi were at the center of the studies conducted by Strauss—who also dedicated sporadic attention to Isaac Abravanel and Yehuda ha-Levi—while progressively forgetting Averroes, Avicenna, and Gersonides. Strauss found in Maimonides the key figure to comprehend medieval philosophy and to build a rationalism that could be able to avoid the dangers of relativism and nihilism into which modern philosophy had fallen. However, as the years passed, also thanks to Paul Kraus's suggestions, Al-Farabi acquired growing importance in Strauss's thoughts, to the point that Strauss mentioned him among his teachers during the last lecture he held on 1 December 1967 at Chicago University (cf. Anastaplo 1976, 35). Finally, Al-Farabi became the model and inspirer of Strauss's last book, dedicated to the interpretation of Plato's *Laws*, which he wrote in a way that closely resembles Al-Farabi's writing in his *Compendium Legum Platonis*.

In Strauss's interpretation, Al-Farabi is the first author to "translate" Platonic political philosophy in the world of revealed religion, without losing its theoretical specificities. Therefore, he represents a central moment in the history of philosophy, more important than Avicenna and Averroes, both as the founder of philosophy in the Islamic world and as the interpreter of Plato and Aristotle (as well as Maimonides's "teacher"). Strauss's readings of Al-Farabi show a substantial interpretative continuity. Yet, we can subdivide them into two different periods, the first comprised between the years 1928–1936, the second between the years 1937–1957. It is possible to point out at least two themes among the ones that are common between the two phases. Firstly, Al-Farabi is neither a neo-Platonic philosopher nor an Aristotelian contaminated by neo-Platonic conceptions. He is a skeptical philosopher—aware of the *opposition* between reason and revelation, philosophy and religion—who accomplishes an original composition of political Platonism and theoretical Aristotelian philosophy. In this sense, he constitutes a fundamental turning point in the history of political philosophy, because, as the founder of philosophy in the Islamic world, where the fortune of Platonic political thought flourishes, he also has profound effects on humanist and Renaissance cultures, as well as on Maimonides. Secondly, an original declination of the relationships between philosophy, religion, and politics, is present in Al-Farabi's thought. This expresses the (Platonic) dialectics between esotericism and exoterism that characterizes all pre-modern philosophical-political thought.

Other themes, instead, more specifically pertain to either of the two phases of Strauss's thought, which are primarily separated by the accomplished formulation, between 1930s and 1940s, of his theory on reticent writing. The discussion on the relationship between philosophy and revelation (intended as the Law that rules the entire social order, not as a system of dogma) belongs to the first phase (1928–1936). Strauss identifies it especially in the *Book of the Opinions of the Inhabitants of the Virtuous City*. In this phase Al-Farabi—intended especially as the teacher of Avicenna, Averroes, and Maimonides—is a moderate skeptical philosopher, who considers esotericism necessary especially for political reasons (the populace is not able to understand theoretical truths, therefore has to learn the fundamental truths exclusively through imaginative and metaphorical screens built by the prophet, intended as the leader of the community). Instead, the elaboration of a meticulous methodology to read the philosophical texts of the past based on the "hermeneutics of reticence" (cf. Momigliano 1967) pertains to the second phase (1937–1957). In this period Al-Farabi—of whom Strauss especially read the *Compendium Legum Platonis* and *De Platonis Philosophia*, which became the hermeneutical models through which he read Plato—is a radical skeptical philosopher. He presents, between the lines, the conflict that opposes philosophy and the city (since philosophy is the quest for happiness and knowledge in a form that is hardly compatible with the needs of socio-political order) expressed by Platonic political philosophy in an exemplary way.

During his years in England, Strauss dedicated less attention to Al-Farabi than he did to Maimonides. Despite this, in *Philosophie und Gesetz*, Al-Farabi's primacy in the recovery of Platonic political philosophy, of the *Laws* in particular, remains in the foreground. His recovery of the *Laws* allows the identification of the essentially *political* nature of prophecy in view of the quest for the perfect city (cf. Strauss 1935, 98ff.). The importance of Al-Farabi in Strauss's thought rapidly grew and it strengthened his image as founder of medieval Islamic political science.[10] Already the year after publishing *Philosophie und Gesetz*, Strauss published a long essay on the political science of Maimonides and Al-Farabi—under the title *Quelques remarques sur la science politique de Maïmonide et de Farabi* (1936)—to reaffirm the specificity of medieval Islamic and Jewish philosophers concerning political science, intended as the philosophical discipline that treats the revealed law. In this essay, however, there are some thematic and interpretative novelties in respect to *Philosophie und Gesetz*. In this occasion, Strauss uses Maimonides's *Treatise on Logic*, as well as the *Guide of the Perplexed*. Strauss insists more than once on the deep influence played on the author of the *Guide* by Al-Farabi, both as a direct source and as a mediator of Plato's teachings. Moreover, Strauss engages in a meticulous analysis on the problems connected to the division of sciences in the *Guide* (speculative philosophy vs. practical philosophy, with further internal subdivisions, as the one between ethics, economy, and politics regarding practical philosophy) with the purpose of demonstrating the centrality of political science for the understanding of the divine law. In this way he presents a perspective that was later abandoned, for instance, by Isaac Abravanel.[11] More specifically, Strauss concludes that, in a central issue such as *particular providence*, Maimonides follows more closely Plato than the Torah.

Inside this essay, there are also novelties regarding Al-Farabi. Firstly, Strauss means to underline—much more than he does in previous writings—the importance of Al-Farabi as the founder of philosophy in the context of revealed religion and as Plato's "heir." His Platonizing politics constitute the starting point to comprehend the thought of all the *falasifa* and of Maimonides, even when they recall Aristotle's physics. In this way, Strauss underlines the absolute necessity to deal with Al-Farabi—and with his original composition of political Platonism, through the interpretation of the *Republic* and the *Laws*, and Aristotelian physics and metaphysics, through the interpretation of the *Metaphysics*, *Physics*, *Categories*, and *Prior Analytics*—to comprehend the skeptical thought of medieval Islamic and Jewish philosophers.[12] Concerning Al-Farabi's political philosophy, Strauss underlines the fundamental difference between ethics and politics, with the latter having primacy over the former. Indeed, ethics does not deal with the distinction between virtues and vices, or between good and bad actions, but the distinction is possible only in relation to the human being's ultimate purpose, the true happiness, which coincides with theoretical knowledge. Since virtue is only good when it is a means to reach true happiness, the distinction between true and false happiness *precedes* the distinction between vices and virtues. However, true happiness cannot exist outside a political community (not necessarily a perfect city: it is possible to achieve true happiness, contemplative life, even inside an imperfect city). For this reason, Al-Farabi, in the book on *Political Regime*, puts (Platonic) politics, not ethics, at the basis of (Aristotelian) theory. Moral virtue is an auxiliary means, a necessary condition, but *not sufficient*, to achieve speculative virtue: happiness is knowledge and comprehension of theoretical truth, superior in dignity to good actions. Thus, the search for happiness does not pertain to ethics—a science that Al-Farabi does not mention in his *De scientiis*—but rather to politics, which, therefore, must not only deal with civil organization, but also with divine things, given that there is no true beatitude without the knowledge of the beings separated from matter. Since it is not possible to separate politics from philosophy, on one side, and politics from religious science, on the other side, in Al-Farabi, politics has "chronological" primacy over jurisprudence (*fiqh*), or the practical and legalistic science of the Law, as well as on apologetics (*kalam*), or the theoretical and demonstrative science of the Law. Politics is superior to ethics and religion, while in respect to philosophy has a "chronological" primacy, which, however, does not erase the "logical" primacy of philosophy intended as the search for truth, the only thing able to realize happiness in contemplative life.

Chapter Five
New York (1937–1948)

A New Beginning

Once he concluded his work on Maimonides and Hobbes, notwithstanding the success his book dedicated to the latter received, Strauss went through a difficult personal time. Indeed, a feeling of uncertainty regarding his research piled on the usual concerns for his economic problems and the precarious situation of his academic appointments. Unable to tell what and where his future would be, it was hard to plan on the medium and long term the engagement in new broad research. Even a theoretical aspect that was clearly positive (the interdisciplinary character of his research, between political philosophy and history of philosophy, Jewish studies, and history of ideas) risked constituting an impediment to his candidacies at universities and research centers, which could misinterpret his continuous crossing of the borders between philosophy, politics, and religion. "Lay" universities considered him a religious thinker, while Jewish institutes saw an atheist philosopher. History departments considered him a philosopher, while philosophy departments considered him a historian or a scholar of religions.

The feeling of estrangement was particularly strong during these years, but it was actually always present in Strauss's intellectual biography. Indeed, throughout his philosophical career, Strauss can be defined as a "stranger," always split between different worlds and never at home in any of them. We can prove this statement even just by means of a superficial scan of his intellectual path. In the 1920s, Strauss sympathized with Zionism, but actually perceived its limits and could not seriously consider immigrating to Palestine. He had a strong interest in dealing with religious issues, despite the fact that no religious faith inspired his research. He felt the fascination of conservative German culture, which, however, he could not embrace due to its antisemitic character. Furthermore, he worked at the *Akademie* in Berlin, but without sharing the post-enlightened ideals that animated it. In the 1930s, Strauss lived in Paris and London as a precarious intellectual and an immigrant, without knowing his future, but often looking back at German culture, the philosophical and political questions of which continued to guide his research on modernity. In the 1940s, in New York, despite obtaining his first official appointment as a professor, Strauss suffered from living inside the culturally progressive context of the New School, while still fully taking part in the institute's didactic and editorial activity. He formulated the hermeneutics of reticence while teaching students who, in general, were not very competent. He held lessons and lectures criticizing the German culture that had made Nazism possible, while in the meantime he considered US society to be the ultimate result of mass culture. In the 1950s and 1960s, in Chicago, Strauss became an appreciated professor and achieved great renown for his publication and for his ability to attract students, but he never received a chair in philosophy. He began to have some notoriety, but he experienced a growth in the hostility against his anti-positivistic critique. He wrote books on the classics of Greek philosophy, printed by important publishers, which, however, only a circle of friends and students appreciated. In conclusion, Strauss's intellectual biography can be defined as a sort of permanent exile, always split across several borders.

There was no chance for a stabilization in England, not even a temporary one. The only possibility Strauss had was to find an appointment in the US, the country towards which Barker directed him with conviction.[1] However, the situation was not simple, despite Tawney's active interest. Strauss had never conducted any teaching activity, his public speaking suffered from an excessive shyness, he displayed a distrustful and introverted character and, finally, his English was not excellent (conditioned by a strong German accent). An initial attempt to present himself at the University of Chicago—thanks to Tawney, who introduced him to John Ulrich Nef—was unsuccessful. In October 1936, as a guest lecturer in a university course of English history, Strauss gave a lecture that Conyers Read, the professor teaching the course, described in an ambivalent tone. The contents were excellent, but Strauss's way of speaking was inadequate for the standard of American students. His English was hard to follow, and his personality lacked charm. According to Read, at this time Strauss was more adequate teaching specialist seminars and PhD courses. He could only succeed in teaching university courses once he had gained some teaching experience (cf. Sheppard 2006, 75). Strauss had better luck in establishing a contact with Salo Baron (professor of Jewish history at Columbia University) when he sent him his work on Maimonides. Indeed, from autumn 1937, after a brief period at Bard College in New York, Strauss became research fellow and editorial assistant at the History Department of Columbia University in New York, where, on 7 February 1938, he held his first seminar on Aristotle's *Politics*. Then, in Autumn 1938 (thanks to Tawney's and Laski's interest), Strauss moved to the Graduate Faculty of Political and Social Science of the New School for Social Research in New York, where he remained until 1948, initially as a lecturer in political science (until 1941), then as an associate professor of political science. The situation at the New School was not easy at first. The director, Alvin Johnson, was not well disposed towards him and hoped Strauss could find a new appointment elsewhere after spending a couple of years in New York. To avoid the risk of remaining without a job, since 1939 Strauss made efforts to strengthen his academic curriculum, delivering lectures in other institutions and universities, establishing contacts with some influential American professors, such as Mortimer Adler, Scott Buchanan, and Richard McKeon (cf. Strauss and Klein 2001, 566–67, 587).

In the 1940s, Strauss accepted a number of appointments as visiting professor and speaker in conferences at St. John's College (1939, 1946), Union College (1939), Hamilton College (1939–40), Amherst College (1940), Syracuse University (1940), Wesleyan University (1941), Bryn Mawr College (1946), and Hartford Theological Seminary (1948). At this last institution, on 8 January 1948, he gave a lecture under the title *Reason and Revelation* (cf. Strauss 2006b), which repeated some of the themes already treated during the lecture *Jerusalem and Athens* held at the General Seminar of the Graduate Faculty (at the New School) on 13 November 1946, where he exposed in a systematic way the core of the opposition between Athens and Jerusalem, i.e., between philosophy and religion, which characterized his thought until his death. Strauss highlighted the limits of knowledge that are visible in the opposition between reason (in the version elaborated by Plato's and Aristotle's classical philosophy) and revelation, the opposing epistemological statutes of which clarify that revelation cannot claim the statute of knowledge and that philosophy cannot claim the possibility to achieve a systematic explanation of being. These are two incompatible alternatives, which are forced to cohabitate. They have different opinions concerning good, the correct way to live life, and happiness. The presence of these two alternatives, both incomplete and both unable to refute the opposite option, has granted in the past the liveliness of Western culture, endangered in modernity by the coming of an "a-philosophical" science and an "a-scientific" philosophy, which assert atheism while denying the search for truth.

The opposition between philosophy and religion is present throughout Strauss's thought, from the 1920s to the 1970s. He often treated it in the form of the "theological-political problem." It was central in the book, planned in 1946 but never realized, *Philosophy and Law: Historical Essays*. Here Strauss meant to gather a number of already published essays—one on reticent writing from 1941, one on Maimonides from 1941, one on Yehuda ha-Levi from 1943 and one on Al-Farabi from 1945—the text of some lectures he had given at the New School concerning medieval philosophy and on the relationship between Athens and Jerusalem, as well as a number of unpublished essays on Socrates, Maimonides, Spinoza, Lessing, and the *Pantheismusstreit*. According to his plan, the collection included an introduction dedicated to the modern crisis and the condition of Judaism in modernity (cf. Strauss 1997b, 467–70). Already from the title it is clear that the project returned to the intentions of *Philosophie und Gesetz*, reviewing and updating them in the light of the dialectics between esotericism and exoterism, without however changing the general frame, based on medieval Islamic and Jewish philosophy intended as *the* model of philosophical rationalism. Despite the importance of the reference to medieval philosophy, the project also included a brief but dense reference to Socrates, which would be the basis of Strauss's studies in the 1960s and 1970s, which focused on philosophy as a *style of life*: "While Aristotle was generally considered *the* philosopher, the representative of the philosophic attitude, or of philosophy as a human possibility, was not so much Aristotle but Socrates" (Strauss 1997b, 468).

On the family level, the years spent in New York were not easy, despite the good academic appointment. When, in autumn 1937, Strauss moved to New York, his wife Miriam and the young Thomas remained in Cambridge, since Strauss's initial appointment was only temporary and his wage rather meager. His concern—almost an anguish—for his loved ones was visible and persistent. In the letters Strauss addressed to his friend Klein—who was in England—from January to May 1938, he repeatedly asked for detailed information both on his wife's and son's state of health and on their financial condition, sometimes receiving not completely truthful answers, which Klein wrote to avoid increasing his concerns (cf. Strauss and Klein 2001, 544ff.). Faced with this situation, Strauss returned to Cambridge in June 1938 to organize the whole family's transfer to the US. They arrived in New York on 12 September. The reunification of the family did not positively affect Miriam's health, but at least favored the couple's good mood, although the economic problems increased and Strauss was forced, between 1938 and 1940, to borrow money from Klein. Personal problems, however, were not limited to economic issues. The news coming from Germany were increasingly concerning. In November 1938 the synagogue in Kirchhain was destroyed and Strauss's father tried to obtain a visa for England or the US. His attempt was in vain, partly because his son was not able to find the necessary economic guarantee for the affidavit requested by German authorities. In January 1942, in Cairo, aged only 41, Strauss's sister Bettina died, due to complications from giving birth to little Jenny. Just few days later, in Kirchhain, Strauss's father died, after a stroke. Later that year, in June, the Nazis began the deportation of the Kirchhain Jewish community: all of Strauss's relatives—including Johanna Lomnitz, his father's second wife—died in concentration camps. In 1944, in Cairo, Strauss's brother-in-law, Paul Kraus, died, leaving little Jenny an orphan, whom Strauss's family soon adopted in New York. Thankfully, there was at least one piece of good news: in 1944, Strauss became an American citizen.

Despite all these problems, Strauss never abandoned the study of the opposition between the ancients and the moderns nor of medieval philosophy, which he had successfully conducted in Paris and England. The years he spent in New York were very productive, from a scientific point of view, given that there he formulated the main themes that characterized his thought in a complete and organic way: the recovery of Platonic political philosophy, the difference between ancients and moderns, the relationship between Athens and Jerusalem, the critique of modern natural right. A number of these themes were the natural development of studies he had already previously conducted, but their mature elaboration only occurred during the years Strauss spent at the New School. In particular, the issue of reticence in philosophical writing—intended as a representative feature of the difference between political and philosophical life—had taken shape already in the late 1930s. Strauss had organized it in a complete form since 1938, when he developed his studies on Herodotus's *Histories*, on Thucydides's *History of the Peloponnesian War*, and Xenophon's *Cyropaedia*, as well as on Plato's *Laws* (cf. Strauss and Klein 2001, 557ff., 566ff.), asserting that classical texts should be read through the dialectics of esotericism and exoterism. Still in 1938, he began writing a number of texts on the reticent writing of Xenophon, Maimonides, and Lessing.[2] This was before he published, in 1941, his famous essay on hermeneutics and persecution (cf. Strauss 1941a), whose themes were also anticipated by a lecture given on 6 December 1939 at the Union College under the title *Persecution and the Art of Writing*. Inside his essay on Xenophon (which originated from a lecture given at St. John's College in Annapolis in May 1939), Strauss wrote of "writing between the lines" and analyzed the contents of the *Constitution of the Lacedaemonians* in light of the structure of the text. He dedicated special attention to the omissions and contradictions the author used to express, in a veiled way and in order to avoid persecution, a number of substantial critiques of Lycurgus's legislation, of the Spartan educational system and of the Spartan hierarchy of virtues (cf. Strauss 1939, 504ff., 512ff., 518ff.). In conclusion, Strauss declared that the work, far from being a praise of Sparta, actually was a satire of Spartan morality and habits. Inside this essay, Strauss presents the necessity—for philosophers—to dissimulate their skepticism towards the city's gods and asserts the superiority of wisdom over politics. However, this was not the only essay that shows Strauss's interest for Xenophon, since between 1938 and 1940 his correspondence with Klein is filled with numerous passages in which Strauss identifies a number of key issues that make of Xenophon a classic for philosophy. Indeed, according to Strauss, Xenophon's Socrates was identical to Plato's Socrates: both versions of the *Apology* constitute the defense of philosophy facing the city (cf. Strauss and Klein 2001, 559, 566–67, 569, 572, 574, 580, 586).

The issue of reticent writing explicitly and organically appeared in the 1939 essay *Exoteric Teaching* (published posthumously: cf. Strauss 1986), dedicated to Lessing. According to Strauss, Lessing is one of the last representatives of the classical distinction between esotericism and exoterism, which completely disappears after him and which concerns the distinction between the imperfection of political life and the perfection of contemplative life, self-sufficient to lead to happiness. After Lessing, the issue of exoterism seems not to appear again in philosophy, to the point that not even Schleiermacher's interpretation of Plato makes any mention of the issue of exoterism, despite speaking about different levels of understanding. Strauss's scientific production, however, was not limited to this. Once he elaborated on the new hermeneutics, between 1941 and

1946 Strauss published a number of essays (especially on Plato, Al-Farabi, Maimonides, and Yehuda ha-Levi), in which he directly tested his theory of reticence on pre-modern texts. He then also applied his theory to some classics of modern thought (Rousseau and Spinoza) and finally wrote his first American book (*On Tyranny*, 1948, with a preface by Alvin Johnson), dedicated to Xenophon's *Hiero*. Moreover, in these years Strauss laid the groundwork for a broad research on natural right—from classical Greece to the twentieth century—which would become the core of his main works in the 1950s. In this perspective, the lecture *Natural Right* that Strauss gave at the permanent seminar of the Graduate Faculty on 9 January 1946 and then again at St. John's College in Annapolis is particularly significant (cf. Strauss 2018a, 221ff.). Such landscape of studies is further enriched by other research Strauss dedicated to the opposition between the ancients and the moderns, which he led in New York since 1937, writing texts that remained unpublished, but became base material for his work in the 1950s, especially *The Origin of Modern Political Thought* (1937) and *On the Study of Classical Political Philosophy* (1938) (cf. Strauss 2018a).

Strauss's work in the 1940s is also significant because another pillar of his reflection consolidated during this period: anti-historicism. From an editorial point of view, Strauss's anti-historicist polemic reached its peak in the 1950s. However, the basis for his position—already present in his thought from the early 1930s—became organically structured in this period and Strauss expressed it in numerous essays and lectures during the 1940s, among which was the lecture *How to Study Medieval Philosophy* given on 16 May 1944 at the Fourth Institute of Biblical and Post-Biblical Studies. Here, besides contesting any form of "idealizing" interpretation of medieval Islamic and Jewish philosophy, Strauss claims the importance of building an "objective" historical research, able to abandon any prejudice in favor of contemporary thought (cf. Strauss 1996c). He reasserts the critique he had already moved against the theoretical and interpretative positions of Cohen, Rosenzweig, and Guttmann concerning the superiority of modern philosophy over medieval philosophy. Directly connected with the polemic against historicism is Strauss's critique of social positivism. Also in this case, Strauss's polemic reached its peak in the years he spent in Chicago, but already in New York it had gained a clear methodological precision in written texts and lectures that constituted the preparation for the texts that later composed *Natural Right and History* (1953). In this sense, we should understand the lectures he gave at the General Seminar of the Graduate Faculty: *Historicism* (26 November 1941), *What Can We Learn from*

Political Theory? (July 1942), and *The Frame of Reference in the Social Sciences* (1945). Here Strauss highlights how the modern separation of science and philosophy was fatal not only in itself (with the reduction of philosophy to ideology and of science to technology), but also in regards to politics, which, separated from philosophy and science, becomes only the reign of consent, of conformism, or of force (cf. Strauss 2018a).

After the end of World War II, especially after 1946, Strauss reconnected with two old friends, Löwith and Kojève. The latter, in the meantime, had become a high official of the Ministry of Economics in France, as Robert Marjolin's collaborator. With Kojève, Strauss began a dense exchange of publications. Strauss sent Kojève his essays on Yehuda ha-Levi (1943), Al-Farabi (1945), and on classical political philosophy (1945). Meanwhile, Kojève sent Strauss his book *Introduction à la lecture de Hegel* (1947), edited by Raymond Queneau on the notes taken during the seminars and lectures on Hegel that Kojève had given at the *École Pratique des Hautes Études* in Paris between 1933 and 1939. In their correspondence between 1946 and 1948, the two friends briefly wrote of their common acquaintances—Koyré and Klein, Löwith and Eric Weil—and exchanged biographical information and brief philosophical reflections on their recent works. A dialogue began between Strauss and Kojève that, in the early 1950s, became a true philosophical-political debate concerning *On Tyranny*, the book on Xenophon published by Strauss in New York in 1948.

The correspondence with Löwith between 1946 and 1948 is dense in significant philosophical discussions concerning the state of classical philosophy and the *querelle des anciens et des modernes*. Strauss often made assertions that repeated positions he had expressed in his essay *On Classical Political Philosophy* (1945) and his critical review to John Wild's study of Plato inside the essay *On a New Interpretation of Plato's Political Philosophy* (1946). Several biographical issues emerge from this correspondence. Firstly, Strauss attempted to help his friend find an appointment in the US that could improve his current position at Hartford Theological Seminary, trying to favor Löwith's arrival at the New School (cf. Strauss and Löwith 2001, 658, 671ff.). Moreover, on some occasions, inside this correspondence Strauss showed signs of intolerance for the American context, as he outspokenly wrote in a letter dated 10 January 1946:

> As you can see from my handwriting, I am not at all well. One grows older and older, and nothing gets finished. Life here in this country is terribly hard for people like me. One must struggle

for the most modest working conditions, and one is defeated in every battle. I would like to print my study of Socratic politics, which you mention. But it is impossible to print it here. If I had time I would translate it back into the original language and try to have it published in Switzerland. Here, what does not fit the pattern is lost. (Strauss and Löwith 1983, 105)

However, independently from such polemical considerations, this phase of Strauss's intellectual biography was particularly positive and fruitful in themes and perspectives. Besides a strong attention towards Plato and Al-Farabi and besides the mature formulation of his reticent hermeneutics, Strauss worked in an original way on classical political philosophy, on the criticism of historicism and social positivism, on the tradition of natural right, on the connection between relativism and nihilism and on the relationship between Athens and Jerusalem. Despite publishing a relatively small number of essays (and just one book) in the twelve years he spent in New York, his research and the material he elaborated in this period were of central importance for his whole intellectual career.

The "University in Exile"

From 1938 at the Graduate Faculty Strauss found an academic appointment that for the first time included both research and teaching. Moreover, he became an editor of the journal *Social Research*, published by the New School for Social Research and directed by Hans Speier (whom Strauss had met in 1929 in Berlin). For this journal, between 1939 and 1948, Strauss worked as an editor as well as a contributor, publishing important essays on Plato and Rousseau, on classical political philosophy and hermeneutics, also contributing thirteen reviews of books that concerned his research interests: Greek classics, early modern philosophers, the opposition of ancient and modern, history of political philosophy, and contemporary German philosophy.

As associate editor of *Social Research*, in January 1942 Strauss made the acquaintance of Eric Voegelin, thanks to an article that Voegelin submitted for publication. The journal rejected the article in February 1943, due to its form (cf. Strauss and Voegelin 1993, 5ff.). The article was too long and appeared as a chapter of a larger work that Voegelin was writing. Between 1942 and 1943 the correspondence between Strauss and Voegelin was rather dense. Having known about Voegelin's project to write a book on modern politics, Strauss suggested he should change his proposal for *Social Research*, advising him—in vain—to present an essay on sectarian mentality in politics. The letters exchanged between Strauss and Voegelin also contain discussions of several philosophical-political themes. Against his "mythological-religious" approach to classical philosophy (and to Plato in particular), Strauss asserted that Plato did not intend to build a myth, but rather a science of the soul and of the state, based on the issue of truth. Moreover, in his letters dated 24 November 1942, 20 December 1942, 13 February 1943, 9 May 1943, and 11 October 1943, Strauss claimed the necessity of reopening the *querelle des anciens et des modernes*, since—in light of the modern crisis—the essence of classical philosophy (in particular of Platonic and Aristotelian *politike episteme*) was not Greek, but rather universal. Moreover, a philosophical movement able to radically contest the Cartesian subjectivist foundation had never really consolidated in modernity, with the sole exception of Husserl, who, in his essays *Philosophie als strenge Wissenschaft* (1911) and *Die Krisis der europäischen Wissenschaften und die transzendentale Phänomenologie* (1936), had really tried to find a "new beginning," *integre et ab integro*. In the last two letters, Strauss praised Husserl, regarding whom, Voegelin remained skeptical. Besides some negative comments on Husserl's critique of *naturalism*, according to Strauss, phenomenology represented the most radical critical analysis of *modern* science, in the direction of the restoration of philosophy intended as a "rigorous science," not as a "system." This presupposed the recovery of the Platonic-Aristotelian discussion on the problem of "foundation." It was not an antiquarian issue, according to Strauss. The construction of a new social science in an anti-positivistic perspective, had to go through the recovery of classical political concepts (virtue, good, justice) that the modern age had refused, from Machiavelli to contemporary historicism (with the only partial exception of neo-Thomism). Stemming from these interpretative differences concerning Plato and Husserl, Strauss and Voegelin developed an intense exchange, both intellectual and personal (cf. Strauss and Voegelin 1993, 36ff.). This dialogue—which lasted until the 1970s—had its apex when Strauss's book *On Tyranny* appeared in 1948 (he had been working on it since 1944), which Voegelin reviewed, with a follow-up to his review written by Strauss.[3] The book was already finished in 1945 and Strauss asked Barker for advice on a possible English publisher.[4] However, aware of the great difficulties in this sense, on 16 October 1946 Strauss also requested Voegelin's suggestions.

All this occurred while Strauss was teaching at the New School for Social Research, which seemed an ideal context for an exiled intellectual like him. The New School was founded in 1919 by professors such as Charles Beard, John Dewey, Alvin Johnson, and Thorstein Veblen, with the aim of promoting freedom of teaching and independence of research in an institutional context dedicated to the development of progressive thought and to the education of adults. From 1933, the New School created the University in Exile (renamed in 1935 Graduate Faculty of Political and Social Science, the institute where Strauss was appointed) with the purpose of offering a place where the intellectuals and professors fleeing from totalitarianism-dominated Europe, especially Germany, could find refuge. In many ways, Strauss was at home at the Graduate Faculty. Indeed, for the first time he could hold university courses and seminars in a continuative way, using his abilities as a teacher as well as those as a researcher. Moreover, Strauss had always been attentive to the importance of offering educational paths for adults who intended to approach philosophy and politics. Strauss cultivated this interest already in the 1920s at the *Freies Jüdisches Lehrhaus* and he continued to pursue it until the 1960s, when he delivered lectures and lessons at the Hillel House and at the University College in Chicago. Finally, yet importantly, Strauss was happy of having found an academic appointment in a context that granted freedom of thought. However, at the Graduate Faculty, Strauss also found elements of discomfort. Firstly, the intellectual context, though eclectic, was dominated by Marxism and by "positivist" social sciences, the furthest possible positions in respect to his political conservatism and his Socratic and Platonic philosophizing. The researchers and professor with whom he cohabited inside the Graduate Faculty often appeared to him as "contemporary sophists," aligned on progressive fashionable themes and incapable of distinguishing between free thought and political militancy. One of the few exceptions, among his colleagues, was Kurt Riezler, whose critique of economic and technocratic cosmopolitism Strauss appreciated. Strauss later recalled the theme in his commemoration of his late friend, delivered at the General Seminar at the end of 1955 (cf. Strauss 1956a). Secondly, the excessive proximity of philosophy and politics—visible also in the *intelligence* assignments for strategic agencies of the American government received by numerous German intellectuals—appeared suspicious and dangerous to Strauss for the nature itself of philosophy, which Strauss was at the time reading in light of his hermeneutics of reticence. The ideological corruption of philosophy at the service of politics did not regard totalitarian regimes alone, but it also concerned liberal societies, in which the necessity to "write between the lines" remained still extant, to avoid the dangers of conformism and persecution (as McCarthyism was about to demonstrate), determining the dominion of a vulgar and low mass culture. Finally, Strauss was far from his colleagues—philosophers, political scientists, sociologists—at the Graduate Faculty in his interpretation of the phenomena of nihilism and totalitarianism, which had provoked the collapse and tragedy of Europe. In order to understand these phenomena, Strauss had turned to classical authors such as Plato and Xenophon, while his colleagues looked in the direction of psychoanalysis, economy, or sociology.

Despite these differences, Strauss regularly contributed to the activities of the Graduate Faculty's General Seminar, which, in the years 1941 and 1942, was devoted to the interpretations of the causes and characters of Fascism and Nazism. This public seminar gave room to the exposition of the working activity that some teachers of the Graduate Faculty had been conducting. A specific working group had been created inside the Graduate Faculty to study Germany and collectively discuss the research on what could be identified as the "German issue." The list of professors who took part in the General Seminar shows its multidisciplinary composition: Arthur Feiler (economics), Eduard Heimann (sociology), Erich Hula (political science), Horace Kallen (philosophy), Felix Kaufmann (law), Jacob Marschak (economics), Carl Mayer (religious studies), Kurt Riezler (philosophy), and Albert Salomon (sociology) regularly met, together with Strauss, to present the results of their philosophical-political and sociological research for students and colleagues. In this context Strauss presented, at least once a year, a paper (on German nihilism and German political culture) that generally put together contemporary reflections with broader research on German history and political culture. During the meetings of this seminar, some students began to identify Strauss as their "teacher": Joseph Cropsey, Harry V. Jaffa, David Lowenthal, Henry Magid, and Howard B. White who defined the seminar meetings "a convocation on Mount Olympus" (Smith 2009, 25).

The meetings of the General Seminar were not exclusively devoted to German issues. Between 1939 and 1941 and from 1943 to 1949, Strauss delivered numerous lectures on Hesiod, Plato, Xenophon, Al-Farabi, Yehuda ha-Levi, Spinoza, Rousseau, and Lessing, some of which resulted in publications. Besides these public lectures, Strauss also held some seminars dedicated to Greek classics (for instance, Plato's *Phaedo* and Aristotle's *De anima*), modern classics (especially Descartes's *Passions of the Soul*) and natural right. An interesting aspect of these seminars consists in the fact that—as suggested by the interdisciplinary, didactical, and research model promoted by Alvin Johnson—Strauss often developed them together with colleagues, among whom Solomon Asch, Philips Bradley, Alexandre Koyré, Alexander Pekelis, Kurt Riezler, Albert Salomon, and Alfred Schütz. Still, Strauss's didactical activity was even larger, having to teach at least two courses for each academic year. If until 1937 Strauss's didactic experience was rather weak, from 1938 it absorbed a lot of his energy, without, however, diminishing his research activity, given the number of studies conducted during the 1940s. From the New School's records, we know that, on average, Strauss taught two courses each year. The broadness of his interests was reflected in the variety of titles, of which the following are just some examples: Plato's *Laws* (1938); Aristotle and Later Ancient Political Thought (1939); Political Philosophy from Hooker to Spinoza (1939); Persecution of Freedom of Thought in Classical Antiquity (1939); European Thought from Locke to Burke (1940); Absolutism and Constitutionalism, Ancient and Modern (1941); Natural Law and the Rights of Man (1942); Religion and the Rise of Modern Capitalism (1943); Utopias and Political Science (1943); The Philosophy of Aristotle and the Teaching of the Bible (1943); The Declaration of Independence (1944); Idealism and Empiricism on the Basis of Plato's Dialogue *Theaetetus* (1944); The United States Constitution (1945); Interpretation of Plato's *Republic* (1945); Morals and Politics in Plato's *Protagoras* (1946); The Social Philosophy of Thomas Aquinas (1947); Principles of Liberal Democracy (1947); Philosophy and Revelation (1947); Plato's Political Philosophy and Its Metaphysical Foundations (1948); Analysis of Selected Writings and Speeches by Edmund Burke (1949).[5]

However, during these years, despite the intense didactical and research activity, Strauss also looked outside of the New School. Encouraged by Tawney, who again wrote to Nef, in 1942 Strauss put together his application for a position as professor in Chicago, still without luck (cf. Green 1995). Robert Maynard Hutchins, chancellor of the University of Chicago, was in excellent terms with Tawney, who, also through Nef, suggested hiring Strauss as professor of political philosophy, since his interests were not only focused on Hobbes, but had extended to the whole history of natural right, using a historical and philosophical approach to politics and social sciences.[6] Despite Tawney's interventions on Hutchins and Nef—Tawney's letters contain praising and detailed judgments on

Strauss's intellectual abilities and his historical-philosophical knowledge—both the departments that could receive Strauss refused his appointment, or at least manifested a strong indifference. At the Department of Political Science (where Strauss actually later arrived, in 1949) the two directors in charge in that period, Charles Merriam and Leonard D. White, opposed a firm refusal to the recruitment of Strauss. The Department of Philosophy, instead, dominated by the figure of Richard McKeon, manifested a total disinterest. Such disinterest was also repeated in 1949 and in the following years, when Strauss became a full professor at the University of Chicago, but in the Department of Political Science and with a chair in political *science*, not political *philosophy*. The disinterest and hostility shown by the Chicago philosophers towards him always remained a source of great bitterness for Strauss.

Thoughts on Germany

In the early 1940s, what was going on in Europe, especially in Germany, conditioned the American cultural context. The phenomenon of Nazism represented a fact so new and disturbing that public discourse often turned to the reasons that had made such a horror possible. American universities did not draw back from this debate, least of all the New School, which, especially through the General Seminar of the Graduate Faculty, dealt with the issues connected to the experience of World War II. On 26 February 1941, Strauss took part in the activity of this permanent seminar by giving a lecture on German nihilism (cf. Strauss 1999), which he immediately related to Nazism. However, while he regarded this latter phenomenon as miserable, dishonorable, and transitory (Strauss was certain that Germany was going to lose the war), German nihilism demonstrated to have much more solid and deeper roots, the fascination for which was also moving to other Western countries, with the risk of culturally colonizing them despite the German defeat in war. Strauss immediately identified the feature that distinguished German nihilism from other forms of nihilism: it is not absolute, because it wishes to destroy *modern civilization* "only" in its moral inclination, not in its technical means. The target of Strauss's critique is therefore clear: the "reactionary modernism" (or "conservative revolution") of Oswald Spengler, Ernst Jünger, Arthur Moeller van den Bruck, and Carl Schmitt, even Heidegger. Some themes that already appear in his critical review to *Der Begriff des "Politischen"* returned in the analysis of this nihilist position: the defense of closed society against open society, the importance of seriousness of existence and of the "case of emergency" (*Ernstfall*), the safeguard of moral life, the dislike of internationalism and commercial society, the refusal of cosmopolitism, capitalism, and communism. Alongside this philosophical-political analysis, Strauss also ventured into a brief historical-sociological analysis that explained the success gained by German nihilism in 1920s' Germany, especially among the youth. Everything was founded on the weakness of the Weimar liberal-democracy, on the absence of roots in German culture and on the inability to give emotionally captivating answers to the Germans coping with post-war difficulties. Faced with such crisis, the Germans felt the presence of two alternatives: either the return to a pre-modern "imperial" political condition, romantically sublimated; or the advent of a planetary society—either capitalist or communist—only devoted to the production and consumption of goods, which represent the entertainment and the pleasure that characterizes soulless societies: "What they [the young Germans] hated, was the very prospect of a world in which everyone would be happy and satisfied, in which everyone would have his little pleasure by day and his little pleasure by night, a world in which no great heart could beat and no great soul could breathe" (Strauss 1999, 360). Therefore, Strauss refused to identify nihilism and militarism. There was, of course, an affinity between these two sensibilities, but they did not share the same root, because German nihilism expressed a trait that belonged to the most intimate history of German culture, i.e., the criticism of modernity:

> Germany reached the hey-day of her letters and her thought during the period from 1760 and 1830; i.e., *after* the elaboration of the ideal of *modern* civilisation had been finished almost completely . . . The ideal of *modern* civilisation is of English and French origin; it is not of German origin . . . One can define the tendency of the intellectual development which as it were exploded in the French Revolution in the following terms: to lower the moral standards . . . Against that debasement of morality, the thought of Germany stood up . . . Opposing the identification of the morally good with the object of enlightened self-interest however enlightened, the German philosophers insisted on the *difference* between the morally good and self-interest, between the *honestum* and the

utile; they insisted on self-*sacrifice* and self-*denial* . . . Germany saw no way out except to purify German thought completely from the influence of the ideas of modern civilisation, and to return to the premodern ideal. National Socialism is the most famous, because the most vulgar, example of such a return to a pre-modern ideal. (Strauss 1999, 370–72)

Against this nihilistic degeneration of Germany, Strauss praised the measure and moderation of the English, who have never loved radical fractures and who, although modern, have nonetheless maintained a sharp attention on the principles of classical culture and on politics inspired by ancient virtues.

The lecture on German nihilism, however, was not the earliest testimony to Strauss's interest in presenting the problems of German culture linked to the rise of Nazism to an American public. Already on 27 April 1940, at the Creighton Philosophical Club of Syracuse University, during a lecture on *The Living Issues of German Postwar Philosophy* he exposed the main traits of German philosophy's anti-modern perspective (cf. Strauss 2006a). There was an aspect in which German anti-modernism reached its peak: the criticism of modern science. It was clear to Strauss that there was a difference between the long-range German cultural context, which determined the constitution of an anti-modern attitude, and cultural positions such as those held by Schmitt and Jünger that, on the brief period, had favored the rise of Nazism. Thus comes the surfacing of the importance of Spengler's work, intended as the ultimate representative of German critique of modernity from the perspective—unsustainable, according to Strauss—of relativistic historicism, inside a larger path of philosophy of history, which led to the domination of *historical conscience* over reason. Such outcome of German culture—from Hegel to Nietzsche, from Spengler to Heidegger—is ambivalent and contradictory. On one side, it accomplishes the crisis of modernity initiated in the seventeenth century, reducing any human knowledge to a historically conditioned knowledge, which is therefore never true. On the other side, it appears as a radical critique of modern civilization, since it highlights the limits of science, incapable of providing a dimension of sense to human existence and to answer the question "why science?," without which any political choice is possible. Strauss identifies the way out in the recovery of classical political philosophy. He has already elaborated his anti-historicist critique and, clearly distinguishing between historical research and historicism, he highlights the importance of hermeneutical methodology in the reading of texts of the past, the only method that allows the reconnection with other ways to find truth, the Platonic and Aristotelian ones, very different from those that had led to the bankrupting of modernity.

In these lectures on German culture, an internal contradiction in Straussian thought clearly emerges. On the one hand, numerous philosophical criticisms of the political foundations of German culture that allowed the advent of Nazi barbarism are explicitly formulated here. On the other hand, it is evident that, in his critique of liberal and democratic modernity, Strauss does not embrace a progressive orientation, but rather places himself on conservative positions so as to show a certain sympathy towards the radicalism of right-wing thinkers against the domination of technique and economics that characterizes Europe in the early twentieth century, in both its capitalist and communist version. It is a denunciation against mechanization and rationalization, against the uprooting and reification that is already present in Spengler and Heidegger, in Schmitt and Jünger, (but also in Tönnies, Simmel, and Weber). Strauss makes this complaint his own, accentuating the dichotomies between community and society, *Kultur* and *Zivilisation*, soul and forms, spirit and machine.

It is true that Strauss is concerned with distinguishing carefully between the anti-modern perspective in a purely political key (the one that is at the origins of Nazism) and the anti-modern perspective in a purely theoretical or philosophical key (the one that he elaborates and embraces in a convincing way). This distinction, however, does not always manage to remain clear and, above all, the rejection of modern philosophy is not irrelevant to the rejection of modern politics (of liberal democracy, for example), even though Strauss tries to keep these two perspectives separate. According to Strauss, one cannot escape from the crisis of bourgeois society by using the socialist and communist perspective which, on the contrary, takes the premises of modernity to its extreme consequences, underlining the depersonalizing, technocratic, and bureaucratic dimension of a society without a soul and without morals. From the crisis of bourgeois society—and therefore from the advent of a planetary society dominated by the economy, trade, and production—we must recover a model of premodern theoretical and practical rationality. By all means, according to Strauss, this recovery does not correspond to the concepts of community, of *Kultur*, of soul or of spirit of which Spengler and the other thinkers of the "conservative revolution" speak. However, despite this difference, Strauss believes that right-wing thinkers at least manage to focus on the need to overcome bourgeois society. It is evident that here Strauss risks confusing two plans of discourse: unless the recovery of premodern reason also constitutes the recovery of a premodern society (which is impossible, as well as undesirable), then the solution to the political problem of modernity must be found on the philosophical-political and not exclusively on the theoretical level.

Despite Strauss having previously underestimated the danger represented by Hitler, regarding which Klein warned him on 27 March 1933 (cf. Strauss and Klein 2001, 460–62; cf. also Strauss and Löwith 2001, 624–25), he did not show any indulgence towards Nazi Germany. This appears in a letter he addressed to Krüger on 17 July 1933, lamenting the "grave" inside which German politics, currently dominated by social hatred, had fallen (cf. Strauss and Krüger 2001, 430). Also in his lecture on *The Re-education of Axis Countries Concerning the Jews*, held on 7 November 1943 at the New School, during the annual Conference on Jewish Relations, Strauss accuses the Germans of having operated a politics of power, in which all means have been considered licit to realize the final target: Germany's worldwide supremacy. Therefore, the reeducation of the Germans concerning the condition of Jews has to be considered a part of a broader reorientation to the virtues of civil cohabitation and respect of human dignity (cf. Strauss 2007b). Such a general process is not possible inside schools alone, but also has to take place in streets, squares, markets and, before that, on the battle fields (where Strauss now was certain the Anglo-American bloc would be victorious). Moreover, such a reeducation has to confront some substantial problems on which success is not granted. Firstly, it is impossible to forget about the great weakness of the liberal-democratic tradition in Germany. Secondly, this process must proceed from inside the German people, through their own free choice, and it cannot be imposed by the victorious powers. The issue becomes even thornier, according to Strauss, if one moves the attention from the process of reeducation of Germans in general to that of Germans in respect to Jews. Strauss goes right to the point: since the Nazi regime has been the sole regime in the entire human history to find its only reason for existing in the degradation and humiliation of Jews (as demonstrated by the adjective "Aryan," which indicates the will to distinguish from Jews), then Germans—all Germans, not only Nazis—have to purify themselves from the horrors they committed in concentration camps, with acts of self-humiliation and compensation. Even such processes of reeducation and purification towards Jews, however, have to be the interest of German people alone, since Jews are not able to direct them.

However, where can Germans find a reference model for their behavior towards Jews? Also in this case, Strauss goes right to the point. His words are testament to his great independence in judgment and his intellectual freedom, given that he also presents the condition of Jews in the US as very problematic. Indeed, he asks: how can Germans reeducate themselves in regard to Jews if they observe Americans' behavior, which is in turn dominated by anti-Jewish feelings? Under certain aspects, there are German movements and intellectuals that express feelings regarding Jews that are even more favorable than those expressed in the US. It is the case with German Catholics, much more tolerant than American Catholics, who can therefore become an important engine for the reeducation of Germans in regards to Jews (much more than liberals, whose political and social importance has become insignificant). Antisemitism is diffused among German educational professionals, especially among high school and university teachers, as well as among Reformed pastors, following a long tradition, which favored the broad diffusion of anti-Jewish feelings by means of the works of figures like Adolf Stöcker. The hope, Strauss continued, lies in the fact that Germans have understood that radical anti-Judaism leads to radical anti-Christianism and that the horrors of Nazi neo-paganism have created the conditions for a reconciliation between Christians and Jews.

Strauss's observations on the critical condition of Jews in the US were not limited to this conference. In the 1950s and 1960s, Strauss had a dense correspondence with Willmoore Kendall, one of the main theorists of American conservatism, and a long-time member of the editorial board of the journal *National Review*. The attitudes of American right-wing politicians towards Jews and the State of Israel are among the numerous themes they touched upon in their correspondence.[7] On 19 November 1956, Strauss wrote Kendall a long letter, which later, thanks to Kendall's personal insistence (cf. Strauss and Kendall 2002, 192ff.), became an open letter to the journal, published on the first number of 1957. Strauss vigorously attacked some contributions that had appeared in the *National Review*, which focused on the criticism of the State of Israel. Strauss did not express surprise for the presence of a certain anti-Jewish feeling among right-wing Americans, but he noted how a journal that asserted itself as the expression of a conservative perspective should praise Israel for more than one reason in the age of the Cold War. Strauss's intention was twofold. On one side, defend Israel in its existence and honor. On the other side, try to demonstrate to conservatives that their alliance with Israel (and with Jews) would be completely normal, given the conservative (and not progressive) character of Jewish morality and of political Zionism:

> The first thing which strikes one in Israel is that the country is a Western country, which educates its many immigrants from the East in the ways of the West: Israel is the only country which as a country is an outpost of the West in the East . . . The spirit of the country as a whole can justly be described in these terms: heroic austerity supported by the nearness of biblical antiquity. A conservative, I take it, is a man who believes that "everything good is heritage" . . . [In Israel] the possibility of disastrous defeat or failure is obvious and always close. A conservative, I take it, is a man who despises vulgarity; but the argument, which is concerned exclusively with calculations or success, and is based on blindness to the nobility of the effort, is vulgar . . . Herzl was fundamentally a conservative man, guided in his Zionism by conservative considerations. The moral spine of the Jews was in danger of being broken by the so-called emancipation, which in many cases had alienated them from their heritage, and yet not given them anything more than merely formal equality; it had brought about a condition which has been called "external freedom and inner servitude"; political Zionism was the attempt to restore that inner freedom, that simple dignity, of which only people who remember their heritage and are loyal to their fate are capable. Political Zionism is problematic for obvious reasons. But I can never forget what it achieved as a moral force in an era of complete dissolution. It helped to stem the tide of "progressive" leveling of venerable, ancestral differences; it fulfilled a conservative function. (Strauss 1957d)

The Hermeneutics of Reticence

Ever since his work on Spinoza, Strauss was an attentive reader of classical texts. He dug inside the folds of those texts in search of implicit premises, covered aims, and unconscious contradictions. Along the years, this personal attention to detail increasingly developed. It also influenced the way Strauss wrote his essays, which progressively changed to resemble the medieval and late antiquity commentary. From the second half of the 1930s, most of Strauss's production is characterized by the contemporary presence of philosophical reflection, hermeneutical inquiry, and historical reconstruction, filtered by his anti-historicist polemics, which is based on the distinction between history and historicism. In many cases, Strauss seems to identify philosophical activity with the minute reconstruction of the structure of certain texts of the past, drawing lines of dialogues and family trees among philosophers, which allows the tracing of historiographical paths. In the meantime, his way of writing about history of philosophy is clearly founded on a specific conception of philosophical activity, intended as the search for truth. The earliest complete expression of the intertwinement between history and philosophy, philosophy and politics, esotericism and exoterism appears in his famous 1941 essay *Persecution and the Art of Writing*, which he had begun writing in 1939.

With this essay, Strauss meant to offer the methodological guidelines to read, interpret, and understand the texts of the past, directly opposing political society's prerogatives and philosophy's needs, against any historicist attempt to consider philosophical thought as a product of the spirit of a given time. There always is, in any age, a social, political, and religious power that limits the freedom of the few independent authors. Such limitation imposes on writers who do not yield to the flattery or the threats of authority to present their thought in an indirect way. This occurs in totalitarian or tyrannical societies, but also in societies that grant freedom of thought, especially due to conformism and the narcissistic desire of public honors and social recognition, which orients actions and thoughts of the majority of writers. According to Strauss, neither persecution nor conformism can avoid the existence and public expression of an independent thought, since heterodox authors elaborate a peculiar writing technique, which uses silences, repetitions, and contradictions to communicate the truth on fundamental issues exclusively *between the lines* (Strauss 1941a). The writing technique that provides the practical answer to the problems posed by persecution and conformism, which transforms *public* communication into *private* and vice versa, is a necessary form of defense adopted by philosophy. Naturally, the case of reticent writing easily applies to all the authors that experienced political or religious persecution in life, however, the reference of Strauss's interpretation goes well beyond the analysis of historical contingency, expanding in principle to all the authors of the past who accepted a distinction between esoteric and exoteric thought, leaving various aspects of their teaching implicit. The problem of reticence cannot be identified tout court with the problem of persecution: the fundamental role played by reticent writing in favor of philosophical thought is not lost even in the presence of liberal societies, in which reticent literature performs the task of responding to the problem of education and to avoid the risks of homologation.

Despite Strauss's insistence on the reticence of philosophical texts, which inevitably leads to a distinction between the "few" able to understand philosophical topics and the "many" who are excluded from them, his hermeneutics is not a theory of mystical or hermetic experience—as was Scholem's Kabbalah—and it is not even a universal theory of the hermeneutical experience—as was Gadamer's *Horizontverschmelzung*—but rather a rational research method, concrete and flexible, through which it becomes possible to read past texts.[8] The reticence of those texts is connected to a rational, anti-traditional, and anti-conformist conception of philosophical activity, which allows the interpretation of philosophical activity also as an *education to philosophy*. Limiting himself to providing a number of signs that lead to theoretical truth inside a discourse that is in other terms current, the philosopher is able to remedy to the essentially defective character of writing. The art of reticent writing provides the method to *say different things to different people*. The reader's attention, therefore, has to linger on dark passages, contradictions, repetitions, omissions, mistakes, and silences inside the text, with the aim of bringing to light the true design planned by the author. The purpose of these thematic and formal irregularities consists in dissimulating unconventional opinions. A reticent book contains two teachings: an edifying one, on the surface, and a philosophical one, which appears exclusively between the lines. The reader of a reticent writing can take a path that can allow him to ascend from common opinions to theoretical concepts and truths, but he can also remain connected to the world of imagination. Indeed, philosophy is a discourse of a *peculiar* genre, which requires the development of a gradual procedure of *introduction* to philosophy:

> Those to whom such books are truly addressed are, however, neither the unphilosophic majority nor the perfect philosopher as such, but the young men who might become philosophers: the potential philosophers are to be led step by step from the popular views which are indispensable for all practical and

political purposes to the truth which is merely and purely theoretical . . . All books of that kind owe their existence to the love of the mature philosopher for the puppies of his race, by whom he wants to be loved in turn: all exoteric books are "written speeches caused by love" . . . In Plato's *Banquet*, Alcibiades . . . compares Socrates and his speeches to certain sculptures which are very ugly from the outside, but within have most beautiful images of things divine. The works of the great writers of the past are very beautiful even from without. And yet their visible beauty is sheer ugliness, compared with the beauty of those hidden treasures which disclose themselves only after very long, never easy, but always pleasant work. This always difficult but always pleasant work is, I believe, what the philosophers had in mind when they recommended education. Education, they felt, is the only answer to the always pressing question, to the political question par excellence, of how to reconcile order which is not oppression with freedom which is not license. (Strauss 1941a, 503–4)

In Strauss's interpretation, the gradual, but necessary, introduction to philosophy is defined, as in the example of Greek classics, as a peculiar education to reading and writing, made possible by reticent writing. Philosophy is *liberal education* because it consists of the ascent from what is "first for us" to what is "first for nature" and therefore in the attempt to substitute opinions on things with knowledge of things. However, this substitution does not occur without danger, because opinions are the element on which the city lives. To avoid persecution and conformism, the philosophical work is written in a way that requires an interpretation. The true meaning of some terms is not always the literal meaning, even though it is not always possible to establish the meaning of a term without considering the context in which it appears. Each time we find, in minutely accurate texts, an unexpected turn, a simple mistake, a clear contradiction, a clear silence, we have to find, by means of a conjectural analysis, the reasons of such apparent irregularity.

A Changing Maimonides

The author that is most present in Strauss's intellectual biography, alongside Plato, is Maimonides: Strauss included him in his research from his writings in the 1920s to the ones in the 1960s (cf. Green 2013). Inside a general interpretative frame that does not experience radical changes, we can divide Strauss's reading of Maimonides into four different periods. In the first period, between 1924 and 1928, Maimonides—as a representative of a rational, but not atheist interpretation of the Bible—is the term of comparison for a critique of Spinoza's biblical science. In the second period, from 1929 to 1937, Strauss uses Maimonides's figure as a reference to analyze the theological-political problem, through which he identifies the presence of Platonic political philosophy—mediated by the *falasifa*—in the *Guide of the Perplexed*, in an interpretative perspective that moves Maimonides away from the world of faith towards skeptical rationalism. The third period begins in 1938, with a dense series of studies conducted when Strauss had just arrived in New York (cf. Strauss and Klein 2001, 545, 549–50, 553–54). It includes the works of the 1940s and 1950s, when Strauss reaches the complete formulation of his hermeneutical theory, through which he reads the relationship between philosophy, revelation, and politics inside the *Guide*. The fourth period coincides with the essays Strauss wrote in the 1960s. Strauss presents his writing by means of esoteric screens, often independent from the esotericism of the classical authors he deals with. His hermeneutics focuses in particular on the relationship between biblical exegesis and Greek classical philosophy (especially Aristotelian) inside the *Guide*.

The third phase of Strauss's studies on Maimonides, the beginning of which coincides with his arrival in New York, starts off with the elaboration of his theory of reticent writing, already outlined in its primary details between 1938 and 1939. Motivated by his hermeneutical questions, Strauss focuses his attention not only to the content of the text, but also to the *form* in which Maimonides wrote the *Guide of the Perplexed*. Already in *Philosophie und Gesetz* (1935), Strauss repeatedly points his attention to a number of passages in Maimonides's writing, which give way to suspects concerning the *caution* with which the author composed the *Guide*. However, only with the essay *The Literary Character of "The Guide of the Perplexed"* (1941, but written from 1938), does the new hermeneutical approach raise the problem of reticence as a *principle*. In this essay, Strauss's research essentially consists of testing a series of interpretative tools that enable him to penetrate the numerous esoteric screens of the *Guide*. Strauss's Maimonides is not the guardian of a *philosophia perennis*, nor the representative of an esoteric tradition only reserved for initiates. His teaching, founded on the use of speculative, i.e., rational, premises, is "secret" only because the purposes and necessities of philosophy do not coincide with those of political society, just like the search for truth does not coincide with the search for consent. Classical authors' esotericism (from Plato to Maimonides) is founded on the separation of the "many" from the "few," of the unaware from the learned, of the citizens from the philosophers. However, such separation is not rigidly established, and it is not determined by the fact of belonging, or not, to the dominating class. Also, politicians and aristocrats are among the "many," since their behavior is determined by opinion, by belief, and by values that characterize practical and not theoretical life.

Inside the *Guide of the Perplexed*, the Law presents two different levels of reading: a public one, for the community, and a secret one, destined for the learned, who in any case are not allowed to distinguish in public between theoretical truths and popular opinions. In his essay on Maimonides, Strauss intends to bring light to the *Guide*'s hidden plan. Its purpose is that of revealing the truth while concealing it and concealing it at the same time it manifests it. Acting with caution, Strauss's Maimonides moves in a space between oral and written teaching, between exoteric and esoteric doctrine, without trespassing the prohibition, imposed by the Law, of publicly communicating the secrets of the Torah. Outspoken in his criticism of the historicist tradition that claimed the primacy of the historical-social dimension on the individual one, Strauss's interpretation aims at understanding what can be defined the oral, i.e., private, teaching that hides inside the written and publicly visible teaching: "By the historical situation no historian understands the secret thoughts of an individual, but rather the obvious facts or opinions which, being common to a period, give that period its specific coloring" (Strauss 1941b, 52). The existence of a reticent literature implies the abandonment of any perspective of historical reconstruction determined and oriented according to idealistic, historicist, or sociological terms. There is no room for any *Zeitgeist* in the study of classical texts, which, far from being representative of a specific political society, actually constitute examples of (esoteric) opposition to political society.

Alongside the hermeneutical and methodological problems, in his essay on Maimonides Strauss also raises the question of the definition of the *Guide*'s topic, meaning the identification of the *science* to which this work pertains. The *Guide* is dedicated to the "true science of the Law" (*aggadah*), distinguished from the legal study of the Law (*halakah*). Indeed, the science of the Law has two branches: a practical one, which

Maimonides elaborates in his *Mishneh Torah*, dedicated to the legal and authoritative codification of actions prescribed or prohibited by the Law;[9] and a theoretical one, elaborated in the *Guide*, dedicated to the demonstration of the opinions and beliefs taught by the Law (with particular attention to the explanation of the Torah's secrets). In this sense one should understand the superiority of the *Guide of the Perplexed* over the *Mishneh Torah*: "The *Mishneh Torah* is primarily addressed to the general run of men, while the *Guide* is addressed to the small number of people who are able to understand by themselves" (Strauss 1941b, 91). The demonstration of the opinions and beliefs taught by the Law is superior to the legal codification of actions prescribed or prohibited by the Law just like the perfection of the soul is superior to the perfection of the body: "Wisdom is the demonstration of the opinions taught by the law. Now the *Guide* is devoted to such demonstration; hence the true science of the law . . . is identical with wisdom" (Strauss 1941b, 89). Moral virtue is an auxiliary means, a necessary but *not sufficient* condition to reach speculative virtue.[10] Wisdom is knowledge and intimate understanding of theoretical truth, which is greater in dignity than good deeds. In the *Guide*, Strauss's Maimonides asserts "*my* argument, which presents *my* opinion" as different from "*our* argument, which presents *our* opinion," enunciated in the *Mishneh Torah*. While in the first case Maimonides speaks in first person and demonstratively discusses the opinions and beliefs contained in the Law, in the second case he appears as the bearer of Jewish tradition, compiling a list of precepts and norms that are necessary to respect communitarian habits and shared practices. For this reason, in *The Literary Character of "The Guide of the Perplexed"* Strauss does not seem to change the background coordinates already identified in *Philosophie und Gesetz*: "The prophet's ascent to the highest knowledge is followed by his descent to the 'people of the earth,' i.e., to their government and instruction" (Strauss 1941b, 87). Moving his attention on the fact that political virtue is necessary, but incomplete by itself, Strauss concludes with the legitimization of the absolute superiority of philosophical life also in the context of revealed religion.

The Conflict Between Philosophy and City

Maimonides was not the only author that Strauss read again in the light of the new hermeneutical principles. Quite the opposite. Many authors he had already analyzed in the 1920s and 1930s (Plato, Hobbes, Spinoza) received renewed interpretative attention, including Al-Farabi. Strauss's attention to the relationship between esotericism and exoterism dates back to 1931 (cf. Strauss 1997a, 393–436), when he presented the issue in a lecture he gave, on 4 May, at the *Hochschule für die Wissenschaft des Judentums* in Berlin, and it is also very present in *Philosophie und Gesetz* (1935). However, at that time he did not relate the issue of pre-modern philosophers' reticence to their writing method, but rather with the theme of *double truth*, which concerns the difference between the "few" and the "many" in the government of political issues. A radical change occurred in Strauss's thought when, from the second half of the 1930s, he began a minute analysis of the *form* in which past texts are written, resulting in his idea of a "writing between the lines."

In the second phase (1937–1957) of his reading of Al-Farabi, Strauss considers the Islamic philosopher not so much as Maimonides's source, but rather as the interpreter of Plato, particularly highlighting the conflicting relationship between philosophy and the city (exemplified by Socrates's life) and shifting towards an interpretation of Al-Farabi as a skeptical thinker. In his essay *Farabi's Plato* (1945)—later partly included in the introduction to *Persecution and the Art of Writing* (1952)—Strauss notes that, inside the whole *De Platonis Philosophia*, there is not even one mention regarding the immortality of the soul. Al-Farabi implicitly refuses Plato's doctrine of the immortality of the soul, or rather he considers it as an exoteric doctrine, without stating it explicitly. Al-Farabi actually also entirely excludes the term "soul" from his summaries of Plato's *Phaedo* and *Republic*, implicitly asserting that the only true happiness is the one that can be found "in this world." Likewise, Al-Farabi—who pretends to use Plato as an "author/character," presenting himself just as the commentator of his writings—attributes an exclusively socio-political role to religion, which lacks any relevance for theoretical truth, which, in turn, constitutes philosophy's specific domain. According to Strauss, Al-Farabi can be so bold in expressing heterodox and "dangerous" truths in his *De Platonis Philosophia* because he does not present his personal point of view outspokenly, but he exposes someone else's perspective. As the commentator of Plato's writings, Al-Farabi is almost constrained to embrace a relatively orthodox doctrine on life after death. However, his silence on the immortality of the soul inside a treatise destined to present Plato's philosophy means that the assertions concerning the immortality of the soul that appear in his other writings should be judged as a prudent way to settle his own position with respect to the commonly accepted dogma. The deviation from the Greek philosopher's teaching proves that he considers belief in a happiness different from the happiness in this world or the faith in another life as completely wrong (Strauss 1945a, 371ff.).

Precisely due to the severe danger he faces as a philosopher, in his Platonic readings Al-Farabi avails himself of the specific immunity associated to the historian and the commentator, in order to assert, only inside his historical works (in which he simply appears as the exposer of positions held by other authors), heterodox theories on the *superiority* of philosophical speculation over religious speculation. Therefore, through Plato's figure, in the *De Platonis Philosophia* Al-Farabi asserts that revealed religion does not provide the true science of being, since this is the specific domain of philosophy. From his perspective, the secret one, the Islamic philosopher considers philosophy as *necessary and sufficient* to lead to *perfection* and *happiness*, while, from a public perspective, he expresses the opinion according to which philosophy, although able to lead to perfection, is insufficient alone to lead to happiness. However, the "supplement" to philosophy that Al-Farabi requires to achieve happiness is not religion (nor ethics), but rather politics, intended in the sense of Platonic politics. The perfection and happiness of the citizens is impossible outside the "other city," the perfect city. This does not concern philosophers since their happiness is also possible inside an imperfect city. The "other city" replaces the "other world," or, better, the "other city" lies between "this world" and the "other world," given that it is an earthly city, which however only exists "in words." Philosophy—and therefore happiness—does not require the institution of a perfect political community. However, in imperfect cities, which are effectively the existing cities, happiness can only be achieved by philosophers, while all others are excluded from it. According to Al-Farabi, the solution to this difficult relation between philosophy and the city is not the "ethical" one offered by Socrates—let alone the "religious" one offered by revelation—but rather the "political" one elaborated by Plato, which corrects Socrates's solution in a decisive point, avoiding its dangers:

> "The way of Socrates" is characterized by the emphasis on "the scientific investigation of justice and the virtues," whereas the art of Plato is meant to supply "the science of the essence of every being" and hence especially the science of the divine and of the natural things. The difference between the way of

Socrates and the way of Plato points back to the difference between the attitude of the two men toward the actual cities. The crucial difficulty was created by the political or social status of philosophy: in the nations and cities of Plato's time, there was no freedom of teaching and of investigation. Socrates was therefore confronted with the alternative, whether he should choose security and life, and thus conform with the false opinions and the wrong way of life of his fellow-citizens, or else non-conformity and death. Socrates chose non-conformity and death. Plato found a solution to the problem posed by the fate of Socrates, in founding the virtuous city in speech: only in that "other city" can man reach his perfection. Yet, according to Farabi, Plato "repeated" his account of the way of Socrates . . . The repetition amounts to a considerable modification of the first statement, or to a correction of the Socratic way. The Platonic way, as distinguished from the Socratic way, is a combination of the way of Socrates with the way of Thrasymachus; for the intransigent way of Socrates is appropriate only for the philosopher's dealing with the elite, whereas the way of Thrasymachus, which is both more and less exacting than the former, is appropriate for his dealings with the vulgar. What Farabi suggests is that by combining the way of Socrates with the way of Thrasymachus, Plato avoided the conflict with the vulgar and thus the fate of Socrates. Accordingly, the revolutionary quest for the other city ceased to be necessary: Plato substituted for it a more conservative way of action, namely, the gradual replacement of the accepted opinions by the truth or an approximation to the truth. (Strauss 1952d, 16–17)

Al-Farabi's Plato is far from reducing philosophy to the study of political things. He defines philosophy as the art of demonstration, meaning the theoretical art that provides science with the essence of all beings. The political dimension of Platonic philosophy, therefore, consists in the public form through which philosophy has appeared to the city by means of reticent writing, which allows the philosopher to avoid Socrates's destiny, the ultimate example of the conflict between philosophy and the city. Faced with this conflict, extremely dangerous for philosophy—which can be forbidden in the city—and for the philosopher—who can be persecuted—

Al-Farabi's Plato identifies a middle way that, thank to reticence, allows him not to betray philosophical activity and, at the same time, does not lead to open conflict with the city.

The relationship between the theoretical investigation on being and the reticence of philosophical texts is at the center also of the essay *How Farabi Read Plato's "Laws"* (1957), in which Strauss develops a minute analysis of internal repetitions and contradictions and more generally on the ambiguities of Al-Farabi's text. The problems are immediately evident: what is Al-Farabi's purpose? What guides the selection of the topics presented? Why does Al-Farabi limit himself to summarizing only the first nine books of Plato's *Laws*? The main question lies, once again, in the unavoidable difference between philosophy and city, that is, in the need for reticence in a context of danger and persecution that requires the drafting of deliberately obscure texts, which can only be deciphered through a careful study of stylistic details and content. According to Strauss, the great importance of Al-Farabi consists in having rewritten Plato's *Laws* taking into account the different political situation and the different religious context that were created with the affirmation of revealed religion understood as Law.

In this way, Al-Farabi presents the model of a *skeptical* philosophical research, both radical (on the level of the private "demythologization" of the political and religious community's shared opinions and beliefs) and moderate (on the level of public prudence concerning the philosopher's "political" action, which has to be cautious), able to defend philosophy's specific nature, its being a "foreign wisdom," or its *critical* character with respect to any constituted authority, to any normative habit, to any political myth, and to any socio-religious tradition. Only philosophy leads to happiness, in its purely and exclusively theoretical quest for truth. Precisely in this philosophy *lies* happiness (cf. also Strauss 1957a).

The Philosopher and the Tyrant

The variegated intellectual context at the New School, and in general in American universities, experienced a progressive growth of social sciences with a positivistic and behaviorist orientation, founded on a *value free* reading of social phenomena. Precisely in light of what happened in Europe in the first half of the twentieth century, Strauss judged such an approach fatal, considering it relativistic. Hence his notification—through the recovery of the categories of classical political philosophy—of the modern incapacity to understand the reach and meaning of modern tyranny: "Tyranny is a danger coeval with political life . . . When we were brought face to face with tyranny . . . our political science failed to recognize it" (Strauss 1991, 22–23). Due to social science's inability to read political phenomena in their reality, a return to classics becomes necessary. The categories of classical political philosophy have to be studied, by means of methods that avoid historicism, and then applied to the study of a tyranny—the modern one—that is very different from the ancient one. Indeed, unlike the ancient tyrannies, contemporary ones possess ideologies, science (or, better, a "peculiar" form of science), and technology:

> We are now brought face to face with a tyranny which holds out the threat of becoming, thanks to "the conquest of nature" and in particular of human nature, what no earlier tyranny ever became: perpetual and universal. Confronted by the appalling alternative that man, or human thought, must be collectivized either by one stroke and without mercy or else by slow and gentle processes, we are forced to wonder how we could escape from this dilemma . . . The manifest and deliberate collectivization of coordination of thought is being prepared in a hidden and frequently quite unconscious way by the spread of the teaching that all human thought is collective independently of any human effort directed to this end, because all human thought is historical. There seems to be no more appropriate way of combating this teaching than the study of history. (Strauss 1991, 27–28)

With such a methodological premise, Strauss undertakes the study of tyranny turning to a small, forgotten classic of Greek thought: Xenophon's *Hiero*, which narrates a brief dialogue between the tyrant Hiero and the poet Simonides, using Socratic rhetoric, which presents thoughts through indirect allusions and assertions. The purpose of Socratic rhetoric is the defense of philosophy and philosophers—shutting access to philosophy for those who do not possess the necessary spirit for it—while guiding young potential philosophers to philosophy, freeing them from the seductions that dominate common men. As he has already done in his 1939 essay on Xenophon, also in this occasion Strauss intends to analyze not only the limits of politics (a peculiar knowledge) from the perspective of philosophy (general knowledge), but also and especially the difference between the lives of the philosopher and the political man, beginning from the certainty that Xenophon is an author who applies the screens of reticence and that, therefore, the contents of the dialogue must be read in light of the dialogue's structure and action.

Xenophon did not outspokenly state his intentions in writing the *Hiero*. The work's thesis does not appear openly after just a first reading, even though the dialogue almost exclusively consists of the sentences pronounced by the two interlocutors. At a first look, it seems like the *Hiero* ends up suggesting that the life of a good tyrant is more desirable for the well-being of his subjects. However, what Xenophon meant with this peculiar conclusion is not clear, because we do not know the reasons that pushed Xenophon to present the teaching of positive tyranny under the form of a dialogue between a non-Athenian tyrant and a poet. The relationship between the two characters itself is ambiguous, just as Xenophon's almost complete silence inside the work is ambiguous. Indeed, in the absence of Xenophon's explicit declaration, we cannot identify Simonides as the character who speaks for the author. In Strauss's interpretation, the difficulty connected to the comprehension of the dialogue on tyranny is visible in the dialogue's *action*. Simonides's thesis is also ambiguous. It is aimed at a tyrant who has just declared that the best thing a tyrant can do is hang himself. But then how can we consider Simonides's thesis to be sincere? Xenophon presents the dialogical form as the only possible form through which a wise man can *publicly* communicate the teaching of benefic tyranny. Even more, since the earnestness of such a teaching seems to be put in doubt by the difficult practical actuation of the reforms proposed by Simonides to Hiero. Indeed, the practical advice that Simonides gives at the end of the dialogue, to which Hiero does not give an answer, are practically impossible to actuate in real political life, especially because it has never been possible, in the historical experience of political regimes, to put tyranny together with justice, freedom, and the citizens' well-being.

The conversation begins with a question posed by Simonides, who appears eager to learn from Hiero the difference between the life of the tyrant and that of a private citizen in regard to pleasure and pain. At the beginning of the dialogue, Simonides presents himself, explaining his purpose of learning something important, attributing wisdom and authority to Hiero, not only, as is obvious, in the matter of political life, but also in the matter of knowledge. However, Strauss notes that the argument used by Simonides to justify his question (the tyrant, but not the poet, has direct experience of the two forms of life) cannot be true, but only *likely*, because it disregards the role played by judgment in evaluating experienced facts. If anything, Simonides's question pertains to the kind of questions to which only the wise man can give a complete answer. Even more, Simonides's question should *already* have found an answer in a wise man. Despite this, Hiero considers Simonides's arguments very seriously, because he knows that the conversation occurs in an atmosphere of prudence in which neither of the two characters appears sincere. According to Strauss, a reason different from the desire to learn moves Simonides to question Hiero on this topic. Given that the dialogue ends with advice regarding the reform of tyranny, it is possible to suppose that Simonides's hidden purpose is that of reforming Hiero's art of government. Oriented by this hidden purpose, Simonides finds himself in a dangerous situation: since receiving criticism for one's shortcomings is never pleasant and often even humiliating, nobody is safe when he outspokenly contradicts a tyrant. Simonides's wisdom, therefore, appears in the creation of a situation in which Hiero, certain of the poet's practical wisdom, not only accepts his advice, but even explicitly requests it. Simonides reassures Hiero by dissimulating his wisdom, pushing the tyrant to admit spontaneously the miseries of his life, even with some self-satisfaction. Pushed by his suspicion regarding Simonides's real intentions, which remain unknown, Hiero goes as far as supporting a devastating argument. Against the poet, who assumes the popular opinion according to which the tyrant's life is preferable to the life of a private citizen, Hiero tries to demonstrate that the life of the tyrant is extremely unhappy, even inescapable. At this point, Simonides is able to create an *ironic* situation, which he can use to give "friendly" advice to Hiero.

Strauss's Xenophon hides behind the action of the dialogue, which proceeds in an uneven way between the tyrant and the poet. In the first part of Xenophon's text (I–II.5), we find a wise man who appears much less wise than we would expect and the severe accusation against tyranny contained in the second part (II.6–VI) is uttered by the tyrant himself. Simonides's assertions on tyranny's advantages, in terms of pleasure and honor, justify Hiero's suspicions on the poet's envy, to the point that they increase the tyrant's personal interest in insisting on the negative aspects of tyranny. Conversely, Simonides is not impressed by Hiero's strong reprimand against tyrannical life, centered on the immorality and injustice of tyrannical life. In the third part of the dialogue (VII), Hiero crumbles in front of the poet's shrewdness, which, especially by means of an insisted silence, forces him to a situation where he is unable to make any further moves. Simonides is not a courtly poet. He is able to reach a position from which he can advise a tyrant precisely because he masks himself as an unscrupulous man. Indeed, in the fourth and last part of the dialogue (VIII–XI), Simonides utters his advice on political virtue, in front of which Hiero has no answers to give. The dialogical procedure allows the tyrant to understand how far a wise man can go in his plot against power. It is not a case that Strauss sarcastically highlights how the political prudence to which Simonides urges the tyrant does not consist in the elimination of evil from tyranny, but simply in hiding it. The praise of benefic tyranny pronounced by Simonides, as well as Hiero's condemnation of tyrannical life, can only be occasional, or, better, *rhetorical*. After all, Hiero's silence in front of Simonides's advice at the end of the dialogue, besides being a sign of the difference that separates political and philosophical language, is also a clear sign of Hiero's scarce intention to follow Simonides's recommendations, since these are not applicable. Good tyranny is utopic because the poet's final promise is utopic: that the tyrant may be happy without being envied.

Chapter Six

Chicago (1949–1967)

The Arrival in Chicago

The years spent in New York were interspersed with moments of economic difficulty, especially at the beginning, and by the dramatic events that involved Strauss's family in Germany, due to Nazism, and in Egypt, for the premature deaths of his sister and brother-in-law. Despite this, Strauss's life proceeded with greater tranquility than in France or England. However, the context in New York was not the most suitable for his reserved character and conservative mentality. The consequence was that he did not establish any real friendships at the New School. Inclined to solitude and reflection, characterized by an irony considered coarse by his interlocutors, pedantic and annoyed by any form of public exposition, anxious and truly interested only in philosophical issues, clumsy in social relations and unfit for secular life (cf. Anastaplo 1976, 35), in New York Strauss led a rather retired life, made of didactical work and research, accompanied by some moments of vacation that the progressively improving economic condition allowed him to spend on the hills and mountains of Vermont together with his wife Miriam. Possibly also this socio-cultural context—alongside the obvious improvement in his *status* as university professor—contributed to pushing Strauss to apply for a chair in political science at the University of Chicago.

The Political Science chair at Chicago had remained vacant since Charles Merriam's retirement. Besides Strauss, Alessandro Passerin d'Entrèves and Alfred Cobban also applied for the position. In 1948, the university nominated a commission composed of Edward S. Shils,

Theodore Schultz, and Hans Morgenthau. During the summer of 1948, Strauss's application was recommended to Robert Maynard Hutchins by Michael Oakeshott, Ernest Barker, Mortimer Adler, and Richard H. Tawney. After his failed attempt in 1942, Tawney again intervened with Hutchins and with Nef (who preferred Passerin d'Entrèves), stressing the value of Strauss's latest publication on Xenophon and, more generally, the fact that the topic of tyranny was very current and perfectly fitting a political science chair. Thus, Tawney played a primary role in Strauss's professional life, given he favored his academic settlements—in Cambridge, New York, and Chicago—from 1934 to 1948. To Hutchins and Nef, Tawney showed a great appreciation for the methodological approach adopted by Strauss, who differentiated between historicism and historical research and who recovered classical themes of political science. Tawney also discussed these themes at length with Strauss himself inside their correspondence, contextualizing them in his critical analysis of the general history of modern culture. Despite their different perspectives (like Strauss, Tawney criticized liberalism, commercial society, and capitalism, but he was a Christian socialist), Tawney and Strauss shared a belief in the necessity of reopening the *querelle des anciens et des modernes*.[1] However, despite Tawney's intervention, the commission's job in Chicago proceeded slowly. Schultz—an economist—declared his discomfort in selecting a candidate pertaining to a disciplinary area different from his own. Morgenthau and Shils expressed their preference for Strauss, but knew that Leonard White, head of the Department of Political Science, and Nef, head of the Committee on Social Thought, did not share their position. Shils—president of the commission—decided to widen the range of action by addressing Hutchins in person, sending him a detailed and "objective" memorandum on the profiles of the three candidates, filtering his preference for Strauss. Shils's intention was clear: he wanted to reach his purpose of selecting Strauss without directly clashing with White and Nef, trying to do it through the most authoritative shelter, the university's chancellor. It turned out to be a winning move: Hutchins read the memorandum, easily understood the problems that troubled the commission, and decided to speak with Shils. Their dialogue was brief and decisive: Hutchins posed a direct question ("Who is the best of them?") and, after Shils answered, accepted without hesitation his recommendation ("All right, let's have Strauss").[2] This time, the result of Strauss's candidacy was positive. In the summer of 1948, the University of Chicago decided to hire him, and from January 1949, he became full professor in the Department of Political Science of the University of Chicago. It was an appointment that, for various reasons, marked a turn in Strauss's career. Firstly, the chair provided him with an academic and editorial visibility that had been unthinkable before, favoring his rise inside the narrow circle of the most influential voices of political philosophy in the US. Secondly, also thanks to the importance of the chair, he received numerous invitations for lectures and university courses in several American cities. Last but not least, for the first time he had the chance to teach actual university classes, educating—in almost twenty years of teaching in Chicago—hundreds of students in philosophy, political philosophy, and history of philosophy.

Life conditions in Chicago immediately improved. On 6 February 1949, Strauss wrote to Klein that, thanks to Hutchins's intervention, he was assigned to a magnificent apartment (cf. Strauss and Klein 2001, 596–97). After a provisional settlement in the university residence, Strauss lived for about six years at 1209 East 60th Street, to later move to 6019 South Ingleside Avenue, where he stayed for the following twelve years. Frequentations with his colleagues were not particularly developed, but not completely absent. Among the colleagues at the university, he was in good terms especially with Ludwig Bachhofer, Peter Heinrich von Blanckenhagen, Charles M. Hardin, Jerome G. Kerwin, and Charles Herman Pritchett (long-time director of the Department of Political Science). Moreover, Strauss showed a certain familiarity with David Grene, Friedrich A. von Hayek, Edward S. Shils, and Yves R. Simon. He also attended—sometimes as chairman—lectures delivered by foreign professors invited to Chicago, among whom were Raymond Aron, Mircea Eliade, Bertrand de Jouvenel, Bruno Leoni, Louis Massignon (whom Strauss encountered again after having met him in Paris), Arnaldo Momigliano, Karl Popper, Karl Reinhardt, Paul Ricoeur, and Arnold Toynbee. Particularly significant was the episode that concerned his introduction to Martin Buber's lecture, in January 1952, at the Hillel House in Chicago. In this occasion Strauss showed—besides his little consideration of Buber's work—his cutting irony, which caused him so many problems in his academic life. Seth Benardete narrated the episode in the following terms:

> Strauss began this way: "I have the great pleasure to introduce Martin Buber, who is probably the greatest Jewish thinker since Mmm. . . ." And after a long time it finally came out "Moses." Then he went on, "since Moses Mmm. . . ." Everybody thought—Maimonides, at least. But Strauss continued

"Mmm . . ." and at last "Mendelssohn." I flipped over the back of the chair. I thought it was the funniest thing I had ever heard. What happened was—you could see from Buber's face—when Strauss said "Moses," he blew up like a frog, and then he was slightly deflated when Strauss said "Moses Mmm . . ." and completely so by the end.[3]

Academic Life

In Chicago, Strauss held his first course on Rousseau—to very few students—between January and March 1949. Already in October 1949, Jerome G. Kerwin, chairman at the Charles R. Walgreen Foundation, invited him to give the prestigious Walgreen Lectures at the University of Chicago. The six lectures he delivered in this occasion were the origin of the essays (cf. Strauss 1950a; 1950b; 1951; 1952a; 1952e) that later resulted in *Natural Right and History* (1953), initially planned as a handbook on natural right. This would not be the only invitation Strauss received to deliver a series of Walgreen Lectures, given that in autumn 1953 he held four lectures on Machiavelli, which were the origin of the book *Thoughts on Machiavelli* (1958). In the 1950s—and until the mid-1960s—Strauss gave many lectures in different universities, research centers, foundations, and colleges (Amherst College, Divinity School in Chicago, American Society of Church History, American Historical Association, Virginia University, University of California in Davis, Volker Foundation, Relm Foundation, Institute of Jewish Theology, Hebrew Union College in Cincinnati, Jewish Theological Seminary in New York). At the Hillel House in Chicago, after the invitations of rabbis Maurice Pekarsky and Richard Winograd, he held numerous lectures in the years 1950–1963, including those on "Jerusalem and Athens" (October and November 1950), on "Progress or return?" (November 1952), on Heidegger's existentialism (February 1956), on "Freud, Moses, and monotheism" (in the spring of 1958), on Maimonides (February 7 and 14, 1960), on the meaning of Jewish identity (February 4, 1962), and on "Religion and commonweal" (January 27, 1963).[4] At the University College of the University of Chicago, for the adult education program and for the "Works of Mind Lecture Series," he held some lectures, including those on the Book of Genesis (January 25, 1957), on Plato's *Republic* (December 1958), on liberal education (June 6, 1959) (cf. Strauss, 1961b; 1962a; 1981a), on Hobbes's *Leviathan* (April 27, 1962), on Aristophanes's *Clouds*, and on

Lucretius's *De rerum natura*. His didactic and editorial success pushed the University of Chicago's board, in 1959, to award him the prestigious title of Robert Maynard Hutchins Distinguished Serving Professor at the University of Chicago. In the meantime, Strauss was visiting professor at the University of California in Berkeley (1953) and at St. John's College in Annapolis (1949, 1952, 1957, 1959), where his friend Klein taught. As visiting professor, invited by Scholem, Strauss spent an entire academic term at the Hebrew University of Jerusalem (cf. Strauss and Scholem 2001, 728ff.), where, between December 1954 and January 1955, he held the Judah L. Magnes Lectures, a selection from which became part of the essay *What Is Political Philosophy?* (cf. Strauss 1957c). During his journey to Israel, in the summer of 1954, Strauss visited some European cities (Paris, Geneva, and Zurich among others) and, invited by Gadamer, he visited the Heidelberg University (this was the only time that Strauss returned to Germany) to give a lecture on Socrates. Another appointment Strauss received as visiting professor, between June 1960 and July 1961, was from the Center for Advanced Study in Behavioral Sciences at Stanford University (a rather unconventional appointment, given the theoretical difference between his teaching and the disciplinary characters of this research center). Between 1950 and 1960, Strauss was also nominated fellow of the American Academy of Arts and Sciences and of the American Academy for Jewish Research, as well as a member of the executive committee of the Leo Baeck Institute in New York. In the 1960s, Strauss received honorary degrees from Dropsie College in Philadelphia (1963), from the Hebrew Union College in Cincinnati (1966), and from St. John's University in Annapolis (1969). The University of Hamburg, where he graduated in 1921, invited him to teach a course during the summer term of 1965, when he was also destined to receive an honorary degree, but Strauss could not travel to Germany in that occasion due to his own and his wife's bad health. Finally, Joseph Cropsey organized the publication of a *Festschrift* for his sixty-fifth birthday, entitled *Ancients and Moderns. Essays on the Tradition of Political Philosophy in Honor of Leo Strauss* (New York: Basic Books, 1964). The volume contains fifteen essays, written by friends, colleagues, and students (among whom were George Anastaplo, Seth Benardete, Peter H. von Blanckenhagen, Allan Bloom, Hilail Gildin, Jacob Klein, Alexandre Kojève, David Lowenthal, Muhsin Mahdi, and Hans Speier) on topics that cross the entire history of philosophy, from Sophocles to Plato, from Aristotle to emperor Julian, from Averroes to Shakespeare, from Hobbes to Swift, from Montesquieu to Stuart Mill.

The amount of work Strauss conducted in his years in Chicago is impressive. He held over eighty courses and seminars at the university, he was visiting professor in five research centers, published seven monographs and over thirty essays, delivered dozens of lectures in different locations, and edited a monumental *History of Political Philosophy* (cf. Strauss 1963b) together with Cropsey, who, from 1957, was his assistant in Chicago. Cropsey, whom Strauss had met at the New School, later became his successor as the chair in Chicago as well as the heir of the intellectual property of Strauss's work, which he held until 2008. The collective work on the *History of Political Philosophy*—planned already in 1960—featured twenty-six authors, for a total of over thirty monographic entries dedicated to the major thinkers of the past. Besides the obvious entries (from Plato to Hobbes, from Aristotle to Locke, from Burke to Marx, from Paine to Bentham, from Hegel to Tocqueville), it is important to note the presence of chapters dedicated to authors that can hardly be considered classics of political philosophy, such as Maimonides, Luther, Bacon, Descartes, Hume, Blackstone, and Nietzsche. In the first edition, Strauss authored the chapters on Plato and Marsilius of Padua, as well as the *Introduction*. In the second edition, published in 1972, Strauss also wrote the chapter on Machiavelli, which Warren Winiarski prepared in the first edition. Many of the authors involved in the editorial enterprise were his colleagues and students in Chicago or had been his colleagues at the New School. Among them: Laurence Berns, Walter Berns, Allan Bloom, Werner Dannhauser, Martin Diamond, Harry V. Jaffa, Ralph Lerner, Henry M. Magid, Muhsin Mahdi, Harvey Mansfield Jr., Stanley Rosen, Herbert J. Storing, and Howard B. White.

However, not everything turned out for the best. Alongside the fortunate developments of his academic career, in these years Strauss also experienced major health problems. In May 1956 he suffered from a severe coronary thrombosis, the consequences of which never faded, forcing him to a second long hospitalization in October 1965, as well as numerous briefer hospitalizations and medical check-ups. His heart problems were accompanied by other complications (asthma and pneumonia in particular), which became an almost continuous medical condition in the last fifteen years of his life. Poor health was also a problem for Strauss's wife Miriam. Already pestered by sickness and small accidents since the years they spent in England, her condition worsened in New York and continued to remain critical also in Chicago, due to a profound depression. At least, however, her periods of ill health were intermittent, and moments of crisis alternated with moments of better health, during which the Strauss family spent some days of vacation in the Michigan woods and on the Great Lakes.

Some problems also appeared in Strauss's professional life in Chicago (cf. Strauss and Klein 2001, 597). Despite the importance of his academic role, the editorial prestige of his publications, and the renowned authority of his intellectual stature, his academic relations did not lack problems, to the point that Strauss developed a feeling of intellectual isolation in respect to the academic environment, not only in Chicago, but also more generally in the US, as he confided to Willmoore Kendall in a letter dated 12 June 1958 (cf. Strauss and Kendall 2002, 200). Indeed, we must recall that, in Chicago, Strauss—the *philosopher* Strauss—did not teach in the Department of Philosophy, which refused to have him among his faculty, also due to Richard McKeon's stubborn opposition, nor did he teach in the Department of Classics. Strauss was well aware of this inconvenience. On 29 April 1953, for instance, he laconically wrote to Voegelin that he clearly saw how his critical interpretation of Locke—heir of Hobbes and not of Greek classics—was destined to severe criticism inside the Department of Philosophy in Chicago, where they taught an essential harmony between Locke and Aristotle (cf. Strauss and Voegelin 1993, 97). Strauss did not even enjoy particular sympathies inside the Department of Political Science, given his fierce critique of positivism. Although Chicago was not a stronghold of social sciences in an empirical or behavioral perspective like Stanford or Yale, also their political sciences were often studied with a "scientific," i.e., positivistic and neo-positivistic, orientation, which contrasted with Strauss's attention to the great books of the past. The same problem was true for Strauss's contribution to American philosophical or social science journals, which never invited him to be a member of their editorial boards. The effects of these academic "battles" are especially visible in his 1950s' monographs, in which he expressed in the form of a "doctrine" and, under certain aspects, of a "handbook" his critique of modern political philosophy, almost as if he wished to build a "system" he could oppose to dominating doctrines. With increasing evidence, Strauss's polemical target in these monographs is the social sciences with a behaviorist and analytical perspective that characterize the American cultural environment. His polemics against European historicism, existentialism, and positivism also grew increasingly evident. Inside the Department in Chicago, these polemics also turned into personal conflicts, sometimes accompanied by expressions of scorn that Strauss imprudently phrased during academic meetings. Probably also for these reasons—as well as for his introverted and distrustful character, dominated by traits that were often hardly comprehensible to his interlocutors—Strauss never became a member of the prestigious Committee on Social Thought at the University of Chicago, despite his good relationship with some of the members (among whom was David Grene) and despite the fact that, on some occasions, his seminars were part of the committee's didactic program. However, one further reason caused disappointment for Strauss: the difficulty he found in helping his graduates and doctorates to undertake an academic career, to the point that some of them had to present themselves to other American universities without emphasizing the fact that they had studied with Strauss, as he sadly admitted to Willmoore Kendall in a letter dated 3 February 1964 (cf. Strauss and Kendall 2002, 249–50).

Inside this wide and complex professional frame, right at the beginning of his appointment in Chicago, a further option opened for Strauss, announced to him by his friend Scholem in a long letter dated 20 January 1950. The possibility to teach at the Hebrew University of Jerusalem was again available, replacing Buber as chair of Sociology or Guttmann as chair of Jewish Philosophy. Strauss's answer was negative (cf. Strauss and Scholem 2001, 718ff.), for two reasons. Firstly, because he felt too tired to change his professional situation again (which would require a spoken and written fluency of modern Hebrew). Secondly, the health condition of his wife did not allow him to consider excessively adventurous prospects. Despite Strauss's profound respect for everything that Jerusalem represented, it is evident that an entirely lay university context actually remained more congenial to him than the Hebrew University. Scholem appeared to be rather annoyed by this refusal but did not miss out on asking Strauss for advice for the chair of Jewish Philosophy left by Guttmann, whose illness soon brought him to death. At this point a dense correspondence began, inside which several names were mentioned (Georges Vajda, Simon Rawidowicz, Alexander Altmann, Emil Fackenheim) and immediately discarded, until Strauss made his successful suggestion: Shlomo Pines, whom both he and Scholem had met in the late 1920s in Berlin (cf. Strauss and Scholem 2001, 722ff.). First-class erudite, and expert of over ten ancient and modern languages, Pines was shy, didactically not charming, and insensible to philosophical issues: for this reason the Hebrew University waited for two years—looking for better choices—before taking a final decision in his favor. However, the traits that made the Hebrew University most dubious about appointing

Pines were the same that instead convinced Strauss, who, few years later, entrusted him with the English translation of Maimonides's *Guide of the Perplexed*, which appeared in 1963.

University Courses

At first, Strauss's university courses were scarcely attended, but his audience progressively grew to crowd his classroom. It was made up, besides the students of the course, by listeners of various provenance—Catholic priests, officers of public administration, young politically engaged Jews—who registered to attend his classes officially. The variety of his programs, dedicated to classical works of philosophical-political thought, is impressive: Aristophanes, Thucydides, Plato (on single works such as the *Statesman, Gorgias, Republic, Laws, Symposium, Crito, Apology of Socrates, Meno,* and *Protagoras*), Xenophon, Aristotle (*Politics, Rhetoric,* and *Nicomachean Ethics*), Cicero, Marsilius of Padua, Thomas More, Machiavelli (*Discourses, The Prince*), Grotius, Harrington, Hobbes (*De cive* and *Leviathan*), Spinoza, Locke, Vico, Rousseau, Burke, Montesquieu, Kant, Hegel, Comte, Marx, Nietzsche (*Zarathustra, Beyond Good and Evil,* and *Genealogy of Morality*), Weber, and Collingwood, as well as courses on natural right, historicism, and the fundamental concepts of political philosophy.[5] The care with which Strauss prepared his lessons was obsessive: he even worked at night, filling page after page with his notes (Klein et al. 1974, 3). Strauss gave one or two courses for each quarter: the lessons took place in the afternoon, beginning at 3:30 p.m. on Tuesdays and Thursdays (the first course), and on Mondays and Wednesdays (the second course, when present). Generally, Strauss gave two books as readings for each quarter, advising his students to read the texts before they took the class. This request, made kindly, was the premise of a hard and severe exam, sometimes preceded by demanding seminars, during which students had to give presentations on single parts of the program. At the beginning of each course, Strauss made a general introduction to frame the topic, but almost immediately went on to read the passages he wished to comment and discuss in class, in a continuous production of connections inside texts and between different texts. At the end of the course, the students had to be able to read and comment on those texts in *detail*, even by evaluating their internal contradictions. To the students who intended to write their dissertation with him, Strauss recommended that they choose a classic, because spending time with a great author was the only sensible thing to do at university. In class, Strauss's lessons were dense, but not complex. One of the characteristic traits of his lessons was simplicity, accompanied by numerous examples taken from ordinary life and by the refusal to elaborate complex concepts to explain philosophical-political issues, which are actually easy to understand. This is a method that Strauss also used when presenting his interpretations of the classics in his books: "The problem inherent in the surface of things, and only in the surface of things, is the heart of things" (Strauss 1958b, 13).

The climate in which his lessons took place was serious, almost somber. He was a short man, and his voice was weak, to the point that, in the 1960s, it almost became a whisper, which necessarily required him to use a microphone in a class that was attended by twice the amount of students allowed (generally there were between fifty and sixty people in a classroom that could host thirty). Strauss did not refer to any histrionic or spectacular device, but rather with extreme composure and poise (cf. Dannhauser 1975, 638). Silence dominated the classroom and the words of classics spread into the air, creating an atmosphere filled with passions and intellectual images that raised numerous questions and lengthy discussions. The discussions continued also outside the classroom: first in Strauss's office, where a copy of Albrecht Dürer's *Feldhase* (1502) dominated, then on the road towards his house. The distinguishing trait of Strauss's lessons on ancient and modern classics consisted in being able to hold the general and complex frame of long-term history of philosophy together with a strong attention to the details of texts. In this way, students avoided both of the dangers that are often present in university classrooms—that of listening to generic and shallow notions and of losing focus on insignificant details—in order to achieve understanding of the nature of a single topic in the way it appears inside the broader picture of history of philosophy and, vice versa, to give life to the history of philosophy through the attention given to single details. Thanks to Strauss's reading of classics, his students could see the functions of single parts that make up the whole, while understanding the whole in light of the function of its single parts. In this context of seriousness and attention, there was also time for moments of irony and levity, caused by jokes made by Strauss—who possessed a subtle sense of humor—during class, as well as quotations from crime novels, which he read and watched on TV with an almost childlike passion. Such teaching method was even more emphasized during the seminars that Strauss held with graduate students working for their PhD: in each seminar he chose a text—during the 1950s he dedicated special attention to Xenophon's *Hiero*, Machiavelli's *Discourses*, and several Platonic dialogues, such as the *Republic, Euthyphro, Minos*, and *Theages*—which was read and commented in minute philological and philosophical detail to finally reach the reconstruction of the complete frame of the interventions made by the author.

With the passing of the years and the worsening of his state of health, Strauss's figure became even more fragile and diminished, due to general physical weakness. His stride became unstable, so much so that he had to use a walking stick and hold the arm of a student who helped him to sit at his desk. Other students—generally seniors and, primarily, Cropsey and Storing—took care, from 1954, of recording the lessons, which were also transcribed, but not reviewed by Strauss, who allowed their use just to a narrow and select number of people. Despite his bad health, the duration of his lessons did not decrease. Far from respecting the canonical ninety minutes, since the early 1950s Strauss held classes that lasted almost three hours, to the point that some student circulated a petition requesting him to respect timetables, allowing them to return home on time. Strauss did not decrease the length of his lessons, but publicly announced that students could leave the classroom whenever they preferred (cf. Anastaplo 1976).

Over the years, legends grew around Strauss's university lessons, increasing especially from the 1990s and reaching their apex when George W. Bush Jr. became president of the United States. During this presidency, Strauss came to be—wrongly—considered the icon of the neoconservative movement.[6] According to these legends, Strauss would have used his university lessons to identify, among the mass of students, the adepts he could "initiate" to his esoteric teaching: for the majority of students the lessons were incomprehensible or simply boring due to the meticulous insistence on insignificant details of classical texts, however, for the adepts of the sect, it was an "initiation rite," which they had to go through to reach the core of Strauss's teaching, constituted of Machiavellian contents hidden under an anti-Machiavellian cover. Essentially, Strauss was considered the—anti-democratic and anti-egalitarian—theorist of a politics of power devoted to the defense of the political and economic interests of the dominating elites. Aware of the impossibility of publicly supporting such a position, Strauss would have hidden it under esoteric screens. In public, he would have bitterly criticized it—therefore, the mentions of the best regime, of virtue, of the idea of good were only appearance for the ignorant and gullible mass—in order to communicate the truth of his teaching just to the narrow circle of "straussians." Therefore, Strauss was an even more cynical master of evil than Machiavelli, because he was lucidly aware that—to win—the Machiavellian contents had to be hidden under anti-Machiavellian covers.

Actually, it is easy to identify the reasons for the notoriety and for the appeal that his university lessons enjoyed. We can imagine a typical student who enrolled in a political science course at the University of Chicago: male, white, bourgeois, in his early twenties, wealthy or middle-class, coming from small towns of Illinois or Michigan, raised in a culturally traditionalist family, certain of the goodness of scientific knowledge (in the positivistic sense of the term), subject to social and family pressures concerning his future career, certainly not interested in the *Guide of the Perplexed* or the *Tractatus Theologico-Politicus*, but rather in learning the basic notions of American political institutions. Therefore, such a student did not enroll in the political science course at the University of Chicago because he knew that he could attend Strauss's courses, but because he reckoned it one of the most important universities—although not comparable to Yale, Harvard, or Stanford—which could lead to a career in public administration or in liberal professions. To such a student, Strauss read and commented on classical texts written in ancient and modern languages, highlighting obscure details, bringing unknown perspectives to light, and speaking about philosophical problems—the themes of friendship or virtue, of good or justice, of happiness, and tyranny—which answered the existential questions of his students, avoiding handbook schematizations and journalistic simplifications, but rather going into the texts' details and explaining *why* it is important *today* to study ancient and modern classics (cf. Lerner 1976). Once exposed to the "epiphanies" coming from Plato and Xenophon, from Machiavelli and Hobbes, this student—whom Strauss addressed with courtesy and kindness, but always maintaining a distance and with a cautious and prudent attitude—began to perceive with boredom and tiredness all those other teachings, whose purpose was to build logical systems in accordance with the data provided by experience, with the aim of expanding—in breadth but not in depth—knowledge (cf. Berns 1978). The awareness raised inside such student that many of the social theories learned up to that point did not answer fundamental questions of political philosophy and, more in general, of the human being ("How should we live? Which is the best life?"). It is very likely that these fundamental questions did not receive an answer from

Strauss's lessons either, but at least they raised the questions, igniting some small, intermittent light that allowed students to understand the nature of those problems, to which any one of us must try to find an answer: not simply by accepting what Strauss proposed, but through the dialogue we can establish with the classics, trying to understand from them. That same student, thus, understood that the books he believed he knew—be it the *Republic* or the *Leviathan*, the *Memorabilia* or the *Discourses*—still hid other worlds completely unknown to him, which he now craved to meet: he awaked his *eros* for *sophia* starting from the great books of the past, which are read not for a nostalgic or antiquarian inclination, but rather to understand the problems of the present. Indeed, Strauss was not interested in recovering the forms of daily or political life in Athens, but rather in asking, like the ancients, "Which is the best life?" and "How should we live?" Certainly, with the years passing and Strauss's increased notoriety, groups of students formed in his classes, wishing to "drink" from his spring, or looking for a new dogma; others participated because it was trendy to do so. However, all this occurred without Strauss encouraging similar "anti-philosophical" practices (cf. Dannhauser 1975, 640). Strauss aimed at teaching how to read classical books, to see their beauty and perfection, rediscovering the simplicity of marvel and the effort of study. This is the only possible way to understand which philosophical problems to identify and what to learn inside those ancient and modern texts, which contain a philosophical knowledge more advanced than the one available in the twentieth century. In brief: in his lessons Strauss promoted an experience of knowledge of good and beauty through the classics.

The philosophical, not political, perspective of his lessons is demonstrated by the fact that in his classroom Strauss was always extremely cautious and prudent. Only rarely did he express his own ideas on issues of public politics, as the time he asserted that, having to choose which economic resources to allocate to the Ministry of Health and to the Ministry of Education, he would prefer school, because education is more important than health (cf. Banfield 1991, 496), following the perspective that characterized him since *Philosophie und Gesetz*, according to which the "first" good is not the "supreme" good. He never dwelled on the positions of the two major American parties, just like he never published articles on newspapers or journals dedicated to the discussion of political issues. In his lessons, Strauss aimed at recovering the "natural" vision of political things, which stops far before personal ideology. Anyway, it is clear that the *citizen* Strauss had conservative political opinions—he voted for Barry Goldwater in 1964—but it is also clear that the perspective of his *philosophical thought* was completely *radical*, since it was critical towards any political ideology, that is against any opinion that pretended to be more than an opinion and, therefore, pretended to have the *status* of truth. In his being a philosopher and his profession as a philosophy professor, Strauss submitted any political position, including right-wing ones, to a critical, i.e., *philosophical*, analysis, as demonstrated by his public letter addressed to the editorial board of the conservative journal *National Review*, inside which he openly criticized the attitude of American right-wing politics towards the State of Israel (cf. Strauss 1957d).

Despite the latent enmity that surrounded his teaching, a consistent group of Strauss's disciples soon formed in Chicago, those who would later be called the "first generation straussians." From their memories we can even recover some details of Strauss's daily life, as well as an image of him. He was uninterested in figurative arts and music, attentive to literary classics, passionate for great book (towards which he showed a great literary sensitivity and a deep erudition), an enthusiastic reader of detective stories, which he also watched on TV, frugal with money, and unable to solve even the smallest technical or practical problems of daily life, such as changing a light bulb or the function of the air-conditioning (cf. Anastaplo 1974; Banfield 1991; Dannhauser 1975 and 2006; Deutsch and Murley 1999, XI–XV). Among his pupils there were—in addition to Joseph Cropsey, David Lowenthal, Henry M. Magid, Howard B. White, and Harry V. Jaffa, who had already been his students at the New School—George Anastaplo, Edward C. Banfield, Seth Benardete, Laurence Berns, Walter Berns, Allan Bloom, Richard Cox, Werner Dannhauser, Martin Diamond, Paul Eidelberg, Hilail Gildin, Victor Gourevitch, Ralph Lerner, Muhsin Mahdi, Aryeh L. Motzkin, Robert Osgood, Stanley Rosen, Herbert J. Storing. And more: Hadley Arkes, Sotirios A. Barber, David Bolotin, Christopher Bruell, Jeffrey Burnam, Charles Butterworth, Roger Masters, Thomas L. Pangle, Thomas S. Schrock, and others. However, it is completely wrong to think that there was one single solid front that associated all these thinkers, among whom we find liberals (Pangle) and conservatives (Anastaplo), democrats (Dannhauser) and republicans (W. Berns), religious (Arkes and Jaffa) and lay (Bloom), to testify to the philosophical, not political, inclination of Strauss's teaching. Therefore, it is rather simple to deny the existence of an organized and solid group of straussians that arrogantly occupied American politics, as Strauss in person announced: "You must know that while I may have a slight intellectual influence, I have no influence whatever in the field of politics, administration, and business" (Strauss and Kendall 2002, 219).

The distance between Strauss's thought and the left-wing political cultures was patent. However, Strauss did not adjust himself to the right-wing cultures either. Among the numerous critical points he raised with respect to American right-wing politics it is important to remember the Jewish question, but it is necessary to highlight another one in particular. On several occasions, Strauss asserted that the contemporary intellectual was a sophist versed in the construction of social consent. Naturally, the intellectual he had in mind—in 1960s' US—was especially the New Left intellectual that dominated in American university campuses, creating liberal trends and orthodoxies that had success through the diffusion on newspapers and televisions. However, from a typological and functional point of view, his use of the word as ideology and as an instrument for political battle, the left-wing American intellectual was not different from the right-wing American intellectual, because the latter used his thought in service of the great industrial and commercial organizations instead of proletariat, youth movements, and racial protests. Although with an opposite purpose, both intellectuals used philosophy in service of politics. Without being a progressive, nor a New Left intellectual, Strauss did not fail to see that contemporary society was characterized by consumerism, conformism, and mass culture, forms of social life determined by the capitalistic power system in which, paradoxically, subaltern classes contradict Marxist theories on the collapse of capitalism and on the revolutionary necessity of the working class, freely and spontaneously offering their consent in maintaining the income of great corporations in exchange for *panem et circenses*. Inside this system—with roles and functions of different importance—politicians and scientists, businessmen and technicians secured an organic alliance, able to make the "great organizations" more efficient, determining the *status quo* in which the society of mass consumption flourishes. Faced with the perspective of this reigning conformism, which appeared as the "good face" of the politics of power, the opposition of such mass society is only represented by some marginal categories, divided and reciprocally opposed, which do not identify with either of the two American parties, nor with dominating political opinions of American universities. A non-institutional political opposition (traditionalist and religious movements on the one hand, radical and anarchic ones on the other) and an "un-political" opposition, constituted by philosophers.

Faced with the choice between consent and opposition to the society of mass consumption, Strauss did not take sides with "the great organizations," but, instead, chose the "un-political" separation operated by the philosopher, as he declared—summarizing Nathan Glazer's paper—in the closing speech at a conference on the dialogue between Jews and Protestants held at the Divinity School of the University of Chicago in 1962:

> Through "the organizational revolution" of our age the gap between "the intellectuals," "the radical and liberal critics," on the one hand and the organizations "representing the status quo" has been closed or at least very much narrowed. The reason was that the intellectuals proved to possess "new techniques for making organizations more efficient" . . . The question which troubled Mr. Glazer was whether the society rendered possible by the co-operation of the scientists and the managers can be regarded as the good society . . . Mr. Glazer sees only one way out: "to improve the organizations" by setting up "the great organization" or "the big organization" or "the determining center of allocation" which is enabled to direct all other organizations because it "will have far more information and will make much better diagnoses" than anyone else can. Hence it will be "the good big society." Alongside it, Mr. Glazer predicted "there will be developing good small societies" . . . But he was not sure whether "the organization will be tolerant enough to let them be" nor whether "they will be clever enough to evade it." Faced with the grim prospect of universal philistinism, we are forced to wonder whether Judaism and Christianity belong on the side of the big organization or on that of the anarchists. I believe that Jews and Christians would have to choose anarchism or secession. (Strauss 1963d, 8)

Strauss gave his last lesson in Chicago, entitled *The Socratic Question*, on 1 December 1967, introduced by his student George Anastaplo. The venue that hosted the event, however, was not the main campus of the Department of Political Science, but the University College, where the conferences of the Basic Program of Liberal Education for Adults took place, in which Strauss—devoted to this mission since the 1920s, when he conducted didactic activity for adults appointed by the *Lehrhaus* and by the *Akademie*—took part for over a decade with lectures open for the public and lessons for educators, also inviting his students to do the same. The decision concerning the venue of this last lecture is descriptive of the climate in which Strauss lived his last years inside his department, especially after the end of Pritchett's direction in 1964. Never loved by his colleagues, but considered unassailable (for obvious reasons), in the moment of his decreasing ability of academic action (which had actually always been rather weak), he was abandoned and left alone also in the occasion that was supposed to be, if not a party, at least a moment of respect and thanks for the service made to the university. This event sadly concluded a path that, from its very start, had showed a persisting hostility from a good portion of the university and of the department towards Strauss. His solitary destiny—of an *émigré* permanently in exile—arrived at another sad station, one more in his life.

Germany in Chicago

Despite the fact that World War II and the Shoah constituted a point of no return in Strauss's opinion on Germany, it is clear that also in America he continued to work, *mutatis mutandis*, on the "German" issues, regarding the crisis of modernity, on which he had begun his research in the first decades of the twentieth century. The changes that characterized his intellectual biography—the passage from the belief that a return to pre-modern philosophy is impossible to the opposite belief, the turn from political radicalism to political conservatism, the passage from cultural conservatism to philosophical radicalism, the shift from political elitism to rational philosophical esotericism, the interpretative changes concerning authors such as Al-Farabi, Maimonides, Machiavelli, and Hobbes—testify to a continuously moving personality, but inside an interpretative and conceptual grid that remained substantially stable, determined by the years of education he received in Germany. Therefore, changes occurred inside a substantial continuity, in a philosophical path that remained compact and organically structured.

The persistence of the "German" issues is also testified by the continuity with which Strauss maintained his relationships and discussions with a number of German philosophers during the years he spent in the US. However, one figure in particular stands out for being absent from Strauss's correspondence and from the writings he produced while in Chicago: Hannah Arendt. Strauss and Arendt met in Berlin at the end of the 1920s, when they both frequented the *Staatsbibliothek*, however, no friendship or affection sparked between the two.[7] Quite the opposite. Arendt's offhanded ways and Strauss's peevish character made the right mix to result in reciprocal scorn and resentment, which remained vivid for the rest of their lives. The object of their contrast was the evaluation of the success of Nazism and of growing antisemitism. Unable to make political analysis adherent to reality and inclined to sympathize with right-wing and anti-bourgeois radicalism, the young Strauss was accused by Arendt—with sound reason—of not realizing the danger represented by Hitler. In Berlin, Arendt continued to speak critically of Strauss's political positions, defining them "nationalistic" in the negative sense of the term, even when, in 1933, Strauss was already in Paris (cf. Strauss and Klein 2001, 466). After these events Strauss maintained a complete silence on Arendt, which she substantially reciprocated. Things did not even change when, in the 1950s, they met again—maintaining a clear distance—at the University of Chicago. Strauss's considerations on recent German history had obviously changed and had determined his strongly rigid attitude towards contemporary Germany, which could not forget the horrors of the concentration camps remaining unpunished. However, this rigidity did not seem to justify the fact that, inside intellectual circles, Arendt spoke—this time mistakenly—of Strauss as someone harvesting the position of the Germans' "collective guilt." Therefore, it is not hard to believe Arendt when, in a letter addressed to Kurt Blumenfeld on 26 April 1956, she asserted that "after the lectures . . . I left Chicago (where Leo Strauss gladly expelled me)."[8] In a following letter, dated 31 July 1956,[9] Arendt's position was more nuanced: she continued to accuse Strauss of being a "Korinthenkacker," i.e., a pedantic man with a "closed" mentality, but she recognized that in the US he was fulfilling an important task—that of widening philosophical knowledge through the direct reading of texts—to the point that she was even personally proselytizing in his favor among students, despite completely disagreeing with Strauss's philosophical perspective, according to which everything had already been said by Aristotle. This less polemical vision of Strauss's work by Arendt had already appeared two years earlier in her correspondence with Karl Jaspers.[10] Jaspers had just finished reading *Die Religionskritik Spinozas* and asked Arendt if she knew the author, "an Orthodox Jew with a very rational mind." In her answer, Arendt informed Jaspers that Strauss currently was "a highly respected professor of political philosophy" in Chicago and that he had the gift of "a very sharp mind." After mentioning some of Strauss's most important works, Arendt warned Jaspers that Strauss was not an Orthodox Jew, but a "decidedly atheist" Orthodox Jew, and concluded asserting: "I don't like him." Jaspers was perplexed regarding the definition that Arendt gave of Strauss as an atheist and, in the following letter, asked how it could be possible that the author of a book clearly written by an Orthodox Jew in search for a justification for authority had become an atheist. Jaspers misunderstood Strauss's position, while Arendt offered interesting food for thought when she gave her—acceptable—definition of Strauss as a "decidedly atheist" Orthodox Jew. A definition on which also Scholem would have agreed.

During the years Strauss spent in Chicago, everything was absent but his relationships with Scholem, Löwith, and Gadamer. In Strauss's correspondence with Löwith, Krüger, and Klein in the 1930s, Gadamer's name continuously appears (cf. Strauss and Krüger 2001, 389, 393, 398, 422, 441–43, 447; Strauss and Klein 2001, 474, 485, 490, 494–97, 502, 528, 533), often with the instruction to extend his greetings to him, but the direct intellectual and personal relationship between the two was not comparable to the one Strauss maintained with Klein, Kojève, Scholem, and Löwith. Despite this, the communication between the two always remained active[11] and they regularly exchanged their respective publications (Gadamer especially appreciated *The Political Philosophy of Hobbes* and *Persecution and the Art of Writing*). Gadamer in person invited Strauss to deliver a lecture at Heidelberg University in 1954. It was the only time Strauss returned to Germany after 1932, in one of the European stops while traveling to Jerusalem. Moreover, between January and May 1962, Strauss played the role of "mediator" for an invitation—declined—that Gadamer made to Kojève to give a lecture at the *International Hegel Association* symposium that took place in Heidelberg in July 1962 (cf. Strauss and Kojève 1991, 305ff.). After 1962, the two friends repeatedly met in the US, always renewing their reciprocal esteem and courtesy (cf. Gadamer 1978, 1984). An important, though brief, epistolary exchange occurred between February and May 1961 and concerned their discussion on the book *Wahrheit und Methode* (1960). Strauss's debut was almost nostalgic, but immediately set out the distance that separated him from Gadamer:

> I am very grateful to you for having sent me your book and I am very glad that you have written it. It is an important work. As far as I know it is the most important work written by a Heideggerian . . . Reading it meant to me something

more than reading most other books. I was reminded of my youth in Germany, of Natorp's seminars, of many conversations, last but not least of our last conversation in Heidelberg in 1954. A certain community of "background" helped me in understanding your book to the extent to which I understood it. As I knew in advance, we have marched from that common ground in opposite directions. (Strauss and Gadamer 1978, 5)

According to Strauss, Heidegger's philosophical revolution allowed the emergence of Gadamer's hermeneutics, which developed in a post-historicist background, inside the problem of the "night of the world" thought precisely by Heidegger. However, in his letter dated 26 February 1961, Strauss asserted that Gadamer was stuck in modern relativism, exemplified by his conception of the "historicity of comprehension" and of *Wirkungsgeschichte*. Strauss reproached him for building an "all-embracing" hermeneutical theory, which remained in between historical determination and universal comprehension, i.e., between relativism and dogmatism. Strauss's hermeneutics, instead, was not a universal theory of "hermeneutic experience" like Gadamer's, but rather a rational research method, concrete and flexible, which aimed at rebuilding the original form of comprehension of the text. Against Gadamer, Strauss was certain of the invariably "occasional" character of any interpretation, which, however, does not preclude in principle the possibility to reach the true interpretation: "I have always seen that there remained in the text something of the utmost importance which I did not understand, i.e., that my understanding or my interpretation was very incomplete; I would hesitate to say however that no one can complete it or that the finiteness of man as man necessitates the impossibility of adequate or complete or *the* true understanding" (Strauss and Gadamer 1978, 6). According to Strauss, the interpreter has to ponder on his own historical and hermeneutical condition, but not with the purpose of understanding past thought in a way that is different from the way in which that same thought was able to understand itself. This is, instead, what Gadamer tends to do with the concept of *Horizontverschmelzung*. Gadamer's hermeneutical ontology cannot pretend to be "historical" because it is rooted in a specific historical world and in the meantime "universal" because it is the foundation of a general theory of the hermeneutical experience. On this point, according to Strauss, Gadamer follows Heidegger in refusing the possibility of a "natural" comprehension of the world, asserting the radical historicity of any form of comprehension and building a philosophy of history which lacks foundation.

The 1950s' Writings

Strauss's works from the 1950s constitute a particular case in his entire career for two reasons. Firstly, because he published two books—*Natural Right and History* (1953) and *What is Political Philosophy?* (1959)—with a didactic perspective, at times almost pedagogical. This differentiates them both from his initial monographs on Spinoza and Hobbes (which have the classical perspective of historical-philosophical works), and from his works from the 1940s and 1960s, in which Strauss often adopted the technique of writing between the lines which he found used in classical philosophical writings. Secondly, these writings constitute a particular case in Strauss's career because they were often addressed to the American public, confronting authors and problems proper to American culture.[12] So much that they were discussed on the prestigious journal *American Political Science Review*[13] and they also received attention from the American Catholic environment.[14] Naturally, there were exceptions to this definition of Strauss's writings from the 1950s: it is the case of the book *Thoughts on Machiavelli* (1958) and of the essays on Maimonides and Al-Farabi (cf. Strauss 1953c; 1957a), where Strauss's writing was addressed to the "young philosopher" that has to go through the work of excavation in the classics before he can reach the happiness of contemplative life.

In these years, Strauss's research substantially expanded in four directions: the criticism of modern political philosophy and the hermeneutics of reticence (which occupy most of his scientific production, with four books [cf. Strauss 1952d, 1953b, 1958b, 1959b] and approximately ten essays on modern classics and on social positivism), as well as the reflections on historicism and on the relationship between natural science and political philosophy in modernity. Precisely on this latter issue, Strauss also debated with his German colleague Helmut Kuhn when the German translation of *Natural Right and History* appeared (cf. Strauss 1978b). Modern dualism between non-finalistic science of nature and finalistic science of human life can only have immediate reflections on the conceptions and on the procedures of modern political philosophy, different from classical political philosophy since the latter is not based on a dualistic conception of nature. The problem resides in the contrast between two opposed forms of skepticism: the ancient-medieval one on one side, represented by the Socratic-Platonic tradition, and the modern one on the other side, with the path that goes from Descartes to Hegel through Hume and Kant, ending in the contemporary nihilism, patent in Nietzsche and Heidegger. In Strauss's interpretation, the distinction between scientific and natural image, based on the Cartesian parameter of *radical* doubt, leads to results opposite to those obtained by Socratic skepticism, aware that the search for wisdom requires the *dialectic* path of contradicting common opinions. In making the model of scientific comprehension independent from the model of natural perception, Cartesian skepticism is only a modern form of dogmatism: "The Cartesian-Hobbesian notion of a dogmatism based on skepticism is derivative from the co-existence of dogmatism and skepticism" (Strauss 1978b, 23). The new concept of nature cannot be the foundation of the new ideal of civilization, given that nature "free of purposes and values" cannot say anything on purposes and values. Modern science, in giving up any anthropomorphism, cannot contribute to the foundation of morality and politics.

These themes are already present in the first chapter of *Philosophie und Gesetz* and again in *Natural Right and History*, where we see the resurfacing of the idea that the task assumed by modern science resides in the substitution of the image of reality provided by common sense with the *scientific* image of reality. Therefore, the issue of natural right is not independent from the concrete availability of models of natural science. While classical natural right is connected, in Strauss's interpretation, to the existence of a teleological conception of the universe, according to which all natural beings have a natural purpose, comprehensible, in the case of human beings, through reason, modern natural right is not equally connected to the existence of a teleological conception of the universe, but rather to the existence of a modern *dualistic* conception of nature:

> Natural right in its classic form is connected with a teleological view of the universe. All natural beings have a natural end, a natural destiny, which determines what kind of operation is good for them. In the case of man, reason is required for discerning these operations: reason determines what is by nature right with ultimate regard to man's natural end. The teleological view of the universe, of which the teleological view of man forms a part, would seem to have been destroyed by modern natural science. From the point of view of Aristotle . . . the issue

between the mechanical and the teleological conception of the
universe is decided by the manner in which the problem of
the heavens, the heavenly bodies, and their motion is solved.
Now, in this respect . . . the issue seems to have been decided
in favor of the nonteleological conception of the universe. Two
opposite conclusions could be drawn from this momentous
decision. According to one, the nonteleological conception of
the universe must be followed up by a nonteleological conception of human life. But this "naturalistic" solution is exposed
to grave difficulties: it seems to be impossible to give an adequate account of human ends by conceiving of them merely
as posited by desires or impulses. Therefore, the alternative
solution has prevailed. This means that people were forced
to accept a fundamental, typically modern, dualism of a nonteleological natural science and a teleological science of man.
This is the position which the modern followers of Thomas
Aquinas, among others, are forced to take, a position which
presupposes a break with the comprehensive view of Aristotle
as well as that of Thomas Aquinas himself. The fundamental
dilemma, in whose grip we are, is caused by the victory of
modern natural science. (Strauss 1953b, 7–8)

In *Natural Right and History* and in *What is Political Philosophy?* Strauss also criticizes the positivistic deviation of social sciences, in an open polemic with Max Weber and with the behaviorist inclinations of American culture, which, in the turn of few decades, has abandoned any reference to natural right (cf. Strauss 1953b, 35ff.). The modern distinction between scientific knowledge and natural knowledge produces the idea of a social science that is able to account for judgments of value and can therefore produce an ethically neutral political philosophy (cf. Strauss 1959b, 16ff.): this position is founded on the belief that there is a radical difference between facts and evaluations and that only factual judgments fall inside the competence of social sciences. The outcome of this position is catastrophic: knowledge becomes an instrument at the service of any purpose, independently from the goodness or evil of the latter. Moreover, such social science is for its own nature conformist, because, in its theoretical construction, it cannot bend on the reference values of present society, which cannot be discussed. Thus, political philosophy loses its critical potential and its tension towards truth, to limit itself to an instrumental dimension, available for any power *here and now*. The conception of values as dependent from society implies their dependence from *history*: the "objective" answers of science gain their meaning from "subjective" questions. Therefore, science itself appears to be *historical*:

> One must conceive of the values embodied in a given social science as dependent on the society to which the social science in question belongs, i.e., on history. Not only is social science superseded by historical studies; social science itself proves to be "historical" . . . It is only at this point that we come face to face with the serious antagonist of political philosophy: historicism. After having reached its full growth historicism is distinguished from positivism by the following characteristics. (1) It abandons the distinction between facts and values, because every understanding, however theoretical, implies specific evaluations. (2) It denies the authoritative character of modern science, which appears as only one form among many of man's thinking orientation in the world. (3) It refuses to regard the historical process as fundamentally progressive, or as reasonable . . . Historicism rejects the question of the good society, that is to say, of *the* good society, because of the essentially historical character of society and of human thought. (Strauss 1959b, 26)

Historical comprehension becomes the foundation of empirical science of society and the categories for theoretical comprehension imply principles of evaluation that are historically determined: in this way, social positivism becomes historicism. The refusal of the idea of *good life* is a necessary consequence of the contrast between philosophical relativism and scientific absolutism: due to the essential historicity of human thought, philosophy leaves its spot to *Weltanschauungslehre*. However, in Strauss's interpretation, philosophy cannot exist without an absolute perspective, which does not change with the changing of history. For historicism and for social positivism, instead, there are several historical-cultural principles of good and right, which contradict each other and which cannot demonstrate their superiority or justify their foundation.

Strauss identifies Max Weber as the primary representative of a social positivism that progressively becomes historicism. However, Strauss's polemic against contemporary social science is not limited to the criticism of early-twentieth-century classics. It is especially in the essay *Relativism* (1961) that Strauss shows the contrast between relativism and dogmatism of contemporary political science. Target of his discussion here is the famous work by Isaiah Berlin on the two concepts of freedom (cf. Strauss 1961a). Strauss notes a basic contradiction: relativism, i.e., the assertion that all purposes are relative to the person that chooses, requires some sort of absolutism. Berlin's liberalism is based on a requirement of sacredness of the private sphere, which demands an absolute basis, but which however cannot have such a basis because it is founded on relative criteria. Indeed, Berlin cannot philosophically justify the absolute claim of a minimum private sphere, given that his argument concerns the "empirical selves," in which any claim is potentially and equally legitimate, included those that consider positive freedom central. According to Strauss, Berlin's position constituted an exemplary proof of the crisis of contemporary liberalism, which has abandoned its absolutist foundation—the connection between truth and politics attempted by Kant, for instance—to become entirely relativistic, following positivistic social science founded by Weber.

On the method of historical research Strauss published an important essay criticizing the historicist perspective, stemming from the analysis of Collingwood's book *The Idea of History* (1946) and critically intervened on the position supported by Eric A. Havelock (author of the book *The Liberal Temper in Greek Politics*, 1957), who, in his studies on Greek philosophy, attributes qualification of liberal thinkers to the sophists, almost as if they were supporters of democracy (in the way in which moderns conceive it). Against this "historicistically anti-historical" research method, Strauss reiterates the necessity to study the texts of the past without modern prejudice, in order to understand them in the way in which their authors understood them (cf. Strauss 1952c, 1959a), and he radically distinguishes between a form of scientific-narrative knowledge related to facts and ideas of the facts (historical-philosophical research) and a particular philosophical interpretation of historical knowledge (historicism). On this point, his polemic against modern philosophy becomes clear. He believes modern philosophy culpable of having made scholars forget the fundamental difference between philosophy and history, a classical antinomy (of Aristotelian origin) that has the merit of rendering visible the distinction between individual and universal, between what is essential and what is secondary, between what is permanent and what is transitory. The modern "confusion" between history and philosophy is due to the reformulation of the radically *historical* character of modern philosophy, in which the idea of the historical conditioning of any thought is embedded. Instead, always in these years, Strauss praised Isaac Husik's position for its "objective" intention in the study of medieval Jewish philosophy (cf. Strauss 1952b).

Such anti-historicist methodological perspective was an essential part of Strauss's studies on hermeneutics, which in this period featured the publication of the book *Persecution and the Art of Writing* (1952), where he collected a number of essays already published in the 1940s. Moreover, the book's introduction presents a brief rewriting of the 1945 essay on Al-Farabi, with the addition of a very important observation—unfortunately not developed—concerning the "sociology of philosophy" (cf. Strauss 1952d, 5–6). In these years, there was no interpretative change on reticent writing in respect to what Strauss had already elaborated in the 1940s and the only new specifically hermeneutical research was the one he made on Al-Farabi's *Compendium Legum Platonis* (cf. Strauss 1957a). However, in these years, Strauss grew even more convinced of the validity of what he had asserted, in principle, in his 1941 methodological essay, since he witnessed the persecution of McCarthyism, which—alongside the anti-Jewish feelings diffused in American culture—confirmed that freedom of thought and speech were not completely safeguarded even in liberal democracies. It was thus possible to ascertain once again that political life has prerogatives and demands that do not coincide with those proper to free thought.

However, it is clear that in the 1950s Strauss dedicated his greatest efforts to criticism of modern political philosophy and it is again to this topic that we have to turn our attention.

The Origins of Philosophy

Natural Right and History is known for its criticism of historicism (from the Historical School to Heidegger) and of social positivism (Max Weber), as well as for the opposition between classical natural right (namely Plato and Aristotle, as well as Cicero and Thomas Aquinas) and modern natural right (Hobbes, Locke, Rousseau, Burke). However, probably the most original contribution contained in this volume consists of the chapter dedicated to the origins of natural right and therefore of philosophy, which appears when the term "nature" is "invented." The discovery of "nature," which is a *distinctive* term inside the totality of phenomena, is the work of Greek philosophy and it is not traceable in other cultures (as, for instance, the Jewish one). Philosophy appears as the search for the "principles" of all things, of their origins as well of their criteria, and poses itself as the *alternative* explanation of traditional narratives on the origins and causes of phenomena. The birth of philosophy, therefore, equates the birth of a critical principle towards tradition, since *physis* is not *nomos*.

In the same way in which philosophy appears as the search for the "principles" of all things, political philosophy appears as the search for the "principles" of human and political things. In the perspective of the definition of the good political order, it presents itself as the critical analysis of the principle according to which good lies in tradition. The authority is put in doubt in the precise moment in which political philosophy abandons what is "ancestral" for what is "good in itself," distinguishing what is "first for us" from what is "first for nature." The discovery of nature—and therefore of the distinction between nature and convention—is the necessary condition for the formation of the idea of natural law, which is not made by human beings (nor by gods), but which, instead, poses the limits to the arbitrary aspects of the laws that can be instituted in human societies, prefiguring in this way a natural order (i.e., good and just) of individual and social life that is *different* from the traditional order, which, instead, finds its purpose in hiding natural order. Political life, therefore, exists before political philosophy and, later, *beside* political philosophy. Inside political life, "habit" plays a primary role:

> While every thing or every class of things has its custom or way, there is a particular custom or way which is of paramount importance: "our" way, the way of "us" living "here," the way of life of the independent group to which a man belongs. We may call it the "paramount" custom or way . . . The paramount way is the right path. Its rightness is guaranteed by its oldness . . . But not everything old everywhere is right. "Our" way is the right way because it is both old and "our own" or because it is both "home-bred and prescriptive." Just as "old and one's own" originally was identical with right or good, so "new and strange" originally stood for bad. The notion connecting "old" and "one's own" is "ancestral." Prephilosophic life is characterized by the primeval identification of the good with the ancestral . . . The identification of the good with the

ancestral leads to the view that the right way was established by gods or sons of gods or pupils of gods: the right way must be a divine law. (Strauss 1953b, 83–84)

From the perspective of "habit," the answer to the problems related to the "principles" of political things is evident even before their appearance and it is given by the moral authority of tradition, by the style of life of the community. Moreover, by means of the binding character of mythical narrations of origins, the identification of good with the ancestral form tends to disguise its origin as divine and, therefore, beyond any possible criticism. Political philosophy, instead, owes its anti-traditional character to the inflexible *indifference* towards such an authority. The philosopher must be able to contemplate the possibility that such binding perspectives are just *common opinions*. However, philosophy rests on the inflexible disregard of this habit: submitting political philosophy to any authority or tradition means transforming it into *ideology*, which is an apology of the social order in question. The refusal of the idea of natural right equates the *positive* assertion of any right and leads to a very dangerous path, which is, however, undertaken with levity by moderns, especially by Kelsen's legal positivism:

> To reject natural right is tantamount to saying that all right is positive right, and this means that what is right is determined exclusively by the legislators and the courts of the various countries. Now it is obviously meaningful, and sometimes even necessary, to speak of "unjust" laws or "unjust" decisions. In passing such judgments we imply that there is a standard of right and wrong independent of positive right and higher than positive right: a standard with reference to which we are able to judge of positive right. Many people today hold the view that the standard in question is in the best case nothing but the ideal adopted by our society or our "civilization" and embodied in its way of life or its institutions . . . If there is no standard higher than the ideal of our society, we are utterly unable to take a critical distance from that ideal . . . Our social science may make us very wise or clever as regards the means for any objectives we might choose. It admits being unable to help us in discriminating between legitimate and illegitimate, between just and unjust, objectives. Such a science is

instrumental ... According to our social science, we can be or become wise in all matters of secondary importance, but we have to be resigned to utter ignorance in the most important respect: we cannot have any knowledge regarding the ultimate principles of our choices, i.e., regarding their soundness or unsoundness; our ultimate principles have no other support than our arbitrary and hence blind preferences ... If our principles have no other support than our blind preferences, everything a man is willing to dare will be permissible. The contemporary rejection of natural right leads to nihilism—nay, it is identical with nihilism. (Strauss 1953b, 2–5)

To the nihilism in which the contemporary positivistic and historicist deviations result Strauss does not oppose an ontology or a metaphysics of natural right, but a dialectic. Human beings can try to know natural right, but they cannot "possess" it. The difference of opinions concerning natural right—i.e., concerning good and justice—not only do not exclude its existence, but rather constitutes its premise, because only by means of such diverse opinions is it possible to move towards the knowledge of a superior order (cf. Strauss 1953b, 93ff.). The existence of natural right does not request the effective consent of all societies on the principles of good and justice, as asserted, instead, by the conventionalism proper to sophists, epicureans, and skeptics (which is anyway different from modern "scientific" relativism) when it identifies good with pleasure. What human beings do and say is contradictory. Contradictory opinions on good and justice require a *dialectical* investigation through which it is possible to try to understand the nature of good and justice, starting precisely from these contradictions (cf. Strauss 1953b, 120ff.). Here is why Strauss's Plato operates a turn in matters, not so much towards the word itself, but rather towards the word seen in its contradictory dimension.

Machiavelli: Between Propaganda and Reticence

Following the complete elaboration of his hermeneutical theory, Strauss returned to the interpretation of some classical authors, on which he had previously brought his attention, resulting in the change of some of their traits. Hobbes was among the authors included in this revision. Indeed, in 1952 the reprint of the book *The Political Philosophy of Hobbes* appeared with a new preface by Strauss. He no longer identified the founder of modern political philosophy in Hobbes, but rather in Machiavelli:

> The immediate and perhaps sufficient cause of my error was inadequate reflection on the opening of Machiavelli's *Discorsi*. I had learned from Spinoza to appreciate the clarion call of the Fifteenth Chapter of the *Principe*. But I had been told by all authorities that the *magnum opus* of Machiavelli is not the *Principe*, but the *Discorsi*; and the *Discorsi* present themselves at first glance as an attempt to restore something lost or forgotten rather than as an attempt to open an entirely new vista. I did not consider the possibility that Machiavelli still exercised a kind of reserve which Hobbes disdained to exercise.[15]

It is an idea already formulated in July 1942, in the lecture *What Can We Learn from Political Theory?* held at the New School for Social Research, during which Strauss presented Machiavelli as a *philosopher* and founder of modern political philosophy (even if Hobbes remained the founder of the modern ideal of civilization in its bourgeois-capitalistic version). In *Natural Right and History* (1953), *Thoughts on Machiavelli* (1958), and *What is Political Philosophy?* (1959), Machiavelli appears as the discoverer of a New World of philosophy and politics, in which an idealistic conception of the nobility of political activity and an anti-idealistic conception of the misery of human nature blend together for the first time. Classical political science is guided by the question on the best way to live and culminates in the description of the best political order, the realization of which is not considered probable because it depends on chance. Machiavelli overturned this opinion—just like he did with Christian doctrine—asserting that the starting point is not "shall be" or virtue, but human being's effective life, which implicates a realistic analysis of political events and of the true purposes they pursue with their actions. Moreover, chance should be controlled in the limits of possible, in order to aim at an effective realization of political action in history.

Machiavelli did not only change the substance, but he also changed the *form* of philosophical-political teaching, as Strauss shows in *Thoughts on Machiavelli*. Precisely because he is a disarmed prophet, Machiavelli has no other hope for success except the one he finds in *propaganda*: "Machiavelli is the first philosopher who believes that the coincidence of philosophy and political power can be brought about by propaganda which wins over ever larger multitudes to the new modes and orders and thus transforms the thought of one or a few into the opinion of the public and therewith into public power" (Strauss 1958b, 173). Indeed, Machiavelli wrote with the perspective of provoking a change in the forms of political power, through a radical change of *modes* and *orders*, converting a number of political men that, sooner or later, were destined to create the conditions for a conversion of the masses. The Florentine secretary's enterprise is similar to that of the "new prince," whose work, essentially immoral because it is founded on an egoistic passion like the desire for glory, allows for the creation of the socio-political context inside which the concept of morality finds its sense and meaning. The term "new prince," however, is ambiguous. It can indicate the founder of a dynasty in an already established state, but it can also indicate the founder of an entirely new state, who, in turn, can imitate the modes and orders created by another prince or can be a radical innovator, creating new modes and orders, eventually even founding a new religion (cf. Strauss 1958b, 20ff., 74ff.). A real innovation, a total revolution, first of all requires a revolution concerning the ideas of good and evil. The foundation of a new moral is only possible in a context created by immorality. In this sense, the "new prince," who must not leave anything unchanged, the founder of an entirely new social order, the radical innovator, is Machiavelli in person. Through the image of the "new prince," Strauss's Machiavelli hopes for the advent and the diffusion of a new Decalogue, in harmony with the necessities that dominate human life. Indeed, political virtue does not consist in a compromise between charity and strictness, but in a wise *alternation* of humanity and inhumanity, of justice and injustice, of moral and immoral. It is the "middle way" between ambition and prudence, which allows the passage from goodness to cruelty and vice versa, based on necessities and circumstances and, especially, on what is most convenient. The "middle way" is the right way because honesty and goodness are appropriate in certain circumstances, while fraud and cruelty are appropriate in other ones.

According to Strauss, the *Discourses on the First Decade of Titus Livius* lack of an immediately perceivable plan. In the preface to the first book, Machiavelli informs us of having discovered new modes and orders taking paths never taken before. Just after this assertion, we learn that, surprisingly, the paths Machiavelli mentions are those of Antiquity. Therefore, given that his discovery is just a recovery, Machiavelli, far from being a radical innovator, is the restorer of forgotten Antiquity. At the same time, we can see the presence of numerous errors and evident contradictions in the structure of the *Discourses*, which are certainly not imputable to a defect in the knowledge and intelligence of the author. For instance, in more than one occasion Machiavelli discusses Florentine politics in regard to Pistoia and provides contradictory interpretations of it (cf. *Discourses*, II.21; II.25; III.27). It seems like Machiavelli is not interested in historical truth, given that he often changes historical data at his convenience, choosing examples that are not always exact nor true. Once he ascertains these problems, Strauss's main concern lies in the attempt to establish reading rules, on the basis of which the plan of the *Discourses* can become more accessible. Machiavelli, however, does not explicitly expose those rules and, therefore, the only way to grasp them consists in identifying the rules that Machiavelli adopted in his reading of the authors that were models for him, in this specific case Livy. The key to understanding the work can be the use, and the *lack* of use, that Machiavelli makes of Livy. The way in which he reads Livy can teach us a lot about his way of writing. Moreover, Machiavelli uses Livy in different ways: referring to a passage from Livy is different from quoting it, as well as referring a passage taken from Livy without explicitly saying so is different from referring to Livy in a generic way. As a philosopher, Machiavelli cannot follow Livy's historical proceeding, but he follows the substantial order of political issues. Furthermore, Machiavelli uses Livy in an arbitrary way, not quoting him in the first ten chapters, quoting him in the following five chapters and "forgetting" again to quote him in the other twenty-four chapters. Thus, Strauss can soon conclude that Livy is just one of Machiavelli's *characters* inside this work. Yet, the question remains: why did Machiavelli proceed in a way that is so hard to follow?

Machiavelli's rediscovery of the ancient modes and orders is dangerous because it implies that the virtue of the ancients be imitated by moderns, contradicting the truth and the precepts of Christian religion. The rehabilitation of ancient virtue implies a criticism of Christian virtue (cf. Strauss 1958b, 198ff.). Machiavelli challenges the modes and orders established by Christianity, going back to the authority of ancient Rome, to a tradition of civic religion (cf. Strauss 1958b, 92ff.). His plea is not directed to good as such, established through reason, but rather to a past antiquity considered authoritative. Indeed, Strauss's Machiavelli cannot begin to use Livy as an authority before he has established the authority of ancient Rome. However, it is clear that this praise of antiquity is only provisional. It has the precise purpose of providing a defense from the persecution of the Church, because the praise of ancient Roman religion implies the criticism of contemporary Roman religion. Machiavelli cannot criticize the authority of the Church without the support of an even higher authority. However, it is not possible to take the ancients' superiority for granted, because it has to be proved and legitimated. The identification of good with what is ancient highlights the difference between authority and reason. At this point, Strauss's Machiavelli stops believing in the identity of good and ancient and shifts his critical target forward. Once found in ancient Rome the authority able to protect him from the accusations of the Church, Livy becomes Machiavelli's "Bible," or rather his anti-Bible. Leaning on Livy's authority, Machiavelli starts exposing the defects of politics and of the Roman constitution. At this point, Livy becomes his only authority. The modes and orders of Rome are not the model *par excellence*: the Florentine secretary does not invite his reader to *imitate* the modes and orders of the past, he invites *innovation*. Therefore, Livy is quoted not only as a critic of the authority of the Church through the ancient counter-authority (Rome), but also as a critic of that same counter-authority. Strauss's interpretation of Machiavelli, however, does not end here. Slowly a doubt surfaces on Livy's own authority (cf. Strauss 1958b, 93–94, 136ff.). Machiavelli most relevantly notices that the events known through historical documents are objects of faith, not of reason. Machiavelli's criticism of Livy and of other authors of Antiquity opens the way to his criticism of authority as such. Only reason can obtain his consent. According to Strauss, Machiavelli is a revolutionary thinker. In using Livy as an anti-Bible, he implicitly substitutes biblical doctrine with Roman pagan theology as it is transmitted by Livy, while in the meantime he challenges the authority of ancient Rome and Livy. Facing the authority of the powers he attacks, Machiavelli depicts himself as a humble and vile being. However, as he personally taught, it is especially by means of fraud that one elevates oneself from such a condition. From this point of view, the Florentine secretary radically changes, not only the substance, but also the *form* of political teaching: the *Discourses* really trace new modes and orders.

The Three Waves of Modernity

In *What is Political Philosophy?*, Strauss puts his innovative interpretation of Machiavelli outlined in *Thoughts on Machiavelli* inside the broader picture of the history of political philosophy, from Socrates to Heidegger. He dedicates special attention to the genealogy of modernity, which unfolded in three "waves" (cf. Strauss 1959b, 40ff.). Indeed, according to Strauss, modernity is a *novum* that produces a clear fracture with respect to both classical philosophy and revealed religion, precisely due to the complete functionalization of nature to the human being's requirements and to his desire of omnipotence, of presenting himself as the absolute architect of his own history on a voluntary foundation that excludes any reference to a rationality other than the instrumental one. In this way, modern political philosophy—which is *historical* and *systemic*, differently from the classical one—obscures the difference between theory and praxis, first reducing praxis to theory (with Machiavelli and Hobbes), then reducing theory to praxis (with historicism). Thus, there is no continuity between pre-modern and modern: Machiavelli is a "Columbus," who discovers a new continent of ethics and politics.

The first wave of modernity is represented by Machiavelli, Hobbes, Spinoza, and Locke. In respect to the "dramatic" version of the fight for existence offered by Machiavelli and Hobbes, the liberal Locke declines the individualistic conception of natural right in a form that is more acceptable for bourgeois culture, without changing, for this reason, the anti-classical coordinates already formulated by Machiavelli, Hobbes, and Spinoza. Locke understands that, for his own good, the human being not only needs weapons, but he especially needs *property*. The desire of self-preservation changes into desire for property and the right of self-preservation becomes right of unlimited acquisition, thus providing the coordinates for Adam Smith and modern political economy: "The solution of the political problem by economic means is the most elegant solution, once one accepts Machiavelli's premise: economism is Machiavellianism come of age" (Strauss 1959b, 49). Indeed, if individuals only worry for their own well-being, it becomes clear that social and political harmony exclusively depend on a correct regulation and organization of economic transactions.

The second wave of modernity—at the origin of idealism, romanticism, and socialism—is constituted by the doctrines of Rousseau, Burke, Kant, Hegel, and Marx (Strauss 1959b, 50ff.). In Strauss's interpretation, despite his apparent return to the "pre-modern" morality of the *citoyen* (opposed to that proper to the *bourgeois*), Rousseau takes the decisive step in the criticism of classical natural right by elaborating the concept of "general will," which begins to delineate the process of *historicization* of modern philosophy. In Hobbes and Locke, natural right maintains its original state even inside civil society, which rises precisely to defend that right. Natural law remains the model of positive law, because the possibility to appeal to natural law—at least in theory—remains, in case natural right is in danger. Rousseau changes course, underlining the necessity that civil life be built with the purpose of making such an appeal completely unnecessary. A civil society built precisely following natural law automatically produces the right positive law, exemplified in the general will, which replaces natural right. However, if the ultimate standard of justice becomes general will, then no standard external to *will* constitutes the reference point for justice and for law. All that is popular will has to be considered sacred, independent from its rationality, given that it has freed itself from what transcends human reality.

The third wave of modernity begins with Nietzsche and develops from Weber to Heidegger (cf. Strauss 1959b, 54–55. Cf. also Strauss 1953b, 9–80). In the historical process, the human being experiences suffering and the abyss. Nature and eternity are by then two categories void of sense in front of an essentially irrational series of events, dominated by the will to power. The "philosophy of future," different from traditional theoretical philosophy, is both theoretical and practical, because it is the result of a *will*, not of knowledge. Given that the world is chaotic and senseless, any meaning has its origin in the will to power and human nature becomes a means of the will to power. The "philosopher of the future" ends the domination of chaos, of indifference, of the lack of sense. He is the first human being that consciously creates values based on the comprehension of the will to power. However, the doctrine of the will to power is not reality and it is not even a fact, because it is historical conscience, the relativistic result of Heidegger's historicism: "Modern thought reaches its culmination, its highest self-consciousness, in the most radical historicism, i.e., in explicitly condemning to oblivion the notion of eternity" (Strauss 1959b, 55).

At the end of this path, a profound doubt emerges towards the founding myths of modernity, in particular towards the sovereignty of the subject. Aware of the ambiguity of human freedom, Strauss re-evaluates an ethics of the *limit* contrary to the modern conception of the human being as the absolute master of nature and history. Of this modern conception, historicism after Nietzsche is the purest representative. Already Nietzsche, replacing *eros* with the will to power, affirms that truth is neither desirable nor vivifying, but mortal, and comes to consider that all meanings and all orders originate precisely in the will to power. With Heidegger, this relativistic historicism takes on even more radical tones. However, for Strauss, this historicist approach, which claims to have an anti-dogmatic character, is reversed into a new dogmatism, due to the progressive absolutization of historical consciousness. As a matter of fact, the historicist process transforms *eternal truth* into *historical truth*. In this way, there is the risk of depriving man of his "naturalness" in favor of his "historicity." For Strauss, therefore, it is necessary to reconstruct the elements of a philosophy capable of accounting for the human condition: philosophy must start from the beginning, that is, from the *zetetic skepticism* of Socrates, aiming at the restoration of a non-historical philosophy.

The End of History

The publication of *On Tyranny* (1948) did not go unnoticed to Voegelin and Kojève, both of whom consequently initiated a very significant debate with Strauss concerning tyranny and, more in general, modern political philosophy. On 14 January 1949, Voegelin addressed Strauss a letter (cf. Strauss and Voegelin 1993, 44), attaching a review he had written regarding *On Tyranny* and telling him he had been in contact with Waldemar Gurian, director of the *Review of Politics*, to publish it.[16] In the review—besides the book's merits, identified in the hermeneutical subtlety and in the criticism of contemporary social sciences—Voegelin stressed how Strauss lacked a concrete historical insight on the reasons that determine the advent of tyranny, given that in his book he limited the discussion only to "theoretical" aspects. Xenophon faces the problem of re-generating and stabilizing political order following the collapse of the constituted system, even resorting to forms of "Caesarism"; therefore, he faces a *practical* problem, not a "theoretical" one. Finally, in his book, Strauss analyzed tyranny with no concern of the fact that tyranny had radically changed in the modern world in respect to ancient Greece. Modern tyranny—just like all modern politics, product of the intrusion of biblical elements in the philosophical-political landscape—is "Christian-Western," not "Greek-pagan" and it contains messianic and apocalyptic elements mixed with forms of technology and secularization that have nothing to do with the tyranny that concerned Xenophon.

Voegelin's letter arrived while Strauss was moving from New York to Chicago and therefore the debate was not developed in the immediately following letters, since Strauss was busy with his relocation. However, Strauss anticipated his intention to answer to Voegelin's review with an article, in which he would also reply to the critical essay that Kojève promised to publish shortly (cf. Strauss and Voegelin 1993, 61, 69–72). The reply promised by Strauss arrived in 1954, published at the end of the French edition of *On Tyranny*,[17] which appeared from the editor Gallimard, promoted by Kojève, and with the help of Raymond Queneau's mediation (cf. Strauss and Kojève 1991, 240ff.). In his reply against Voegelin, Strauss protests the fact that Xenophon, in the *Hiero*, intends to deal with the historical problem of the regeneration of political order and denies that classics are unaware of the phenomenon of "Caesarism." Xenophon's intention is different. He wishes to reflect on the intrinsic limits of political life and on the contribution of philosophy to the definition of the *idea* of the best regime: "The classics could easily have elaborated a doctrine of Caesarism or of late kingship if they have wanted, but they did not want to do it" (Strauss 1991, 180), because distinguishing between Caesarism and tyranny can lead to the opening of Pandora's box, i.e., to the legitimation of authoritarian forms of power justified by a supposed historical necessity. Voegelin's insistence in disregarding Xenophon's real intention and in bending his works to the historical-political problems of the time in which he lived only repeats the big mistake made by contemporary historicism, which reads ancient and modern classics in light of our prejudice, according to which the historical and "common" sense of a work is more important than the work itself (in other words, the supposition according to which the ideas of the philosophers of the past are conditioned by the historical situation in which they lived). Strauss's reply, moreover, aims at refuting the idea—present also in Kojève's criticism—according to which contemporary tyranny is too different from ancient tyranny to be understood with the tools of classical philosophy. The difference, according to Strauss, is not the knowledge of political phenomena, but the philosophical eye with which we look at political problems: the possibility of the Caesarism and the possibility of the popularization of philosophy (or science) were known to the classics, but they rejected them as deleterious for human nature.

Solicited by Strauss already in August 1948 (cf. Strauss and Kojève 1991, 236ff.), Kojève opened the discussion concerning *On Tyranny* by writing a long critical essay in the spring and summer of 1949, which appeared in 1950.[18] Inside his essay, Kojève deals with the issue of the relationship between philosophy and politics, inserting the reference to *history* as it appears in Hegel's categories. Indeed, "it is not only Xenophon who is important in the book Strauss has devoted to him" (Strauss and Kojève 1991, 135), but the problem of the *fulfillment* of utopia. The philosopher that wishes to overcome the ideal and utopic dimension has to deal with the problem of responsibility of political action. Yet, in history, philosophers have limited themselves to providing advice to governors, without worrying about their unattainable character. However, despite such shortcoming, the philosophical lesson of universalism as a political ideal and the political idea of homogeneity (originated together with the Christian tradition of equality) has had concrete historical effects, currently being fulfilled in the universal and homogeneous State, a society without classes including the entire humanity. Precisely on this point, however, Kojève notes that Strauss denies this historical fulfillment of utopia.

Strauss's answer to Kojève, written in the summer of 1950, is very articulated and substantially focuses on three issues (cf. Strauss 1991, 177–212), which also appear in the correspondence between the two friends from 1950 to 1954: anthropology, history, and politics (cf. Strauss 1991, 186ff.). Concerning the anthropological aspect, Strauss agrees with Kojève that one's own realization constitutes the primary engine of the citizen's action. However, the citizen does not entirely coincide with the philosopher, or, better, he does not coincide with the classical philosopher, while he entirely coincides with the modern philosopher, who has fallen to the level of the ideologue and intellectual. Strauss blames Kojève, just like he had blamed Löwith (cf. Strauss and Löwith 1983, 106–8, 111–14), for confusing the Greek *philosopher* with the Greek *citizen*. Concerning the interpretation of the historical process, Strauss asserted that no opinion on history's *directionality* can be philosophically justified, be it a progressive one (which looks at the *future* as the apex of perfection) or a reactionary one (which looks at the *origin* as the place of lost perfection). History does not have a "destiny" nor a "meaning," because it has no immanent direction or necessary fulfillment.

Concerning the political issue, Strauss underlines the radical difference between the utopia of moderns and classics. Moderns aim at a planned and concrete fulfillment of political order through predictions and forms of social engineering that maintain the elimination of evil from history. For classics, the issue is that of finding the good and just natural order, which allows the outline of the best regime (*politeia*), the realization of which is however improbable, uncertain, and eventually rendered possible mostly by chance. Therefore, it is clear that, according to Strauss, the political problem cannot find a final solution in the way moderns deal with it. The secularization of eschatology in terms of a philosophy of history presupposes a "legal" approach in regard to the course of history, which does not have a philosophical justification. History is not the court of the world. Additionally, Kojève's historical dialectics presupposes the truth of the opinion he wants to prove. The meaning of the universal and homogeneous State, intended as the purpose of history, presupposes the truth of the assumption according to which the universal and homogeneous State is the right social order. History's purpose, however, is an issue reserved to religion and theology. Political philosophy does not deal with salvific expectations or secularized anticipations of the afterlife, in the certainty of their forthcoming accomplishment. A radical critic of ideas of progress and improvement towards perfection, Strauss strongly suspects any "messianic" and "activistic" perspective—including Kojève's—aimed at realizing universal happiness, or "paradise on earth." In Strauss's interpretation, only the convergence of two perspectives can make the universal and homogeneous State possible. On one side, technological progress must be considered necessary and sufficient for the satisfaction of the more specifically human abilities of human beings. On the other side, the distinction between wisdom and opinion must be abolished. However, far from being desirable, the convergence between these two perspectives would produce a dreadful human condition: the universal and homogeneous State is the State in which man loses his humanity, it is the State of Nietzsche's "last man." Perhaps the advent of the universal and homogeneous State will be inevitable; but, if so, the end of the history will be absolutely tragic.

In this direction the universal domination of technique favors the dislocation of political and economic power in an anonymous and non-transparent apparatus: the planning of forms of life, work, and thought proceeds through the "technical" re-elaboration of political ideologies, transformed in apparently a-political representations, beyond any possible conflict. Faced with such ideological, political, economic, and technical universally dominating apparatus, which presents itself as the guarantor of justice and freedom, i.e., as the best possible society, there only remains one question to ask: How to escape the oppression and the massification of universal tyranny? Indeed, under the face of universality and homogeneity, the political order outlined by Kojève, according to Strauss, hides the real modern essence of planetary tyranny. Without doubt, however, the advent of Kojève's secularized messianic project would mean the negation of the human being's humanity and the elimination of philosophy. Alongside the end of history, also the end of philosophy would reach its fulfillment:

> It seems reasonable to assume that only a few, if any, citizens of the universal and homogeneous state will be wise. But neither the wise men nor the philosophers will desire to rule . . . The Chief of the universal and homogeneous state, or the Universal and Final Tyrant will be an unwise man . . . To retain his power, he will be forced to suppress every activity which might lead people into doubt of the essential soundness of the universal and homogeneous state: he must suppress philosophy as an attempt to corrupt the young . . . The philosophers in their turn will be forced to defend themselves or the cause of philosophy . . . Everything seems to be a re-enactment of the age-old drama. But this time, the cause of philosophy is lost from the start. For the Final Tyrant presents himself as a philosopher, as the highest philosophic authority . . . He claims therefore that he persecutes not philosophy but false philosophies. The experience is not altogether new for philosophers. If philosophers were confronted with claims of this kind in former ages, philosophy went underground . . . And since there was no universal state in existence, the philosophers could escape to other countries if life became unbearable in the tyrant's dominions. From the Universal Tyrant however there is no escape. Thanks to the conquest of nature and to the completely unabashed substitution of suspicion and terror for law, the Universal and Final Tyrant has at his disposal practically unlimited means for ferreting out, and for extinguishing, the most modest efforts in the direction of thought. Kojève would seem to be right although for the wrong reason: the coming of the universal and homogeneous state will be the end of philosophy on earth. (Strauss 1991, 211)

The 1960s' Works

If the 1950s saw Strauss publish numerous works on modern political philosophy, the 1960s saw a marginalization of modern thinkers in his research, replaced by his studies on classical political philosophy and liberal education, especially the books *The City and Man* (1964), *Socrates and Aristophanes* (1966), and *Liberalism Ancient and Modern* (1968). This latter book contains a number of essays that had published in previous years and appeared when Strauss had already moved to Claremont Men's College (California). These studies on classical political philosophy are characterized by the precision with which Strauss usually read Greek classics and the "mimetic" disposition with which he began writing his works, following the example of medieval commentators. They later found further results in the early 1970s with the monographs on Plato and Xenophon, the last outcomes of Strauss's research path. However, Strauss's publications in the 1960s were not limited to his renewed interest for classical political philosophy and moved in different directions. The first edition of the monumental *History of Political Philosophy* appeared in 1963, edited with Cropsey. In the same year, his project to publish Maimonides's *Guide of the Perplexed*, in the English translation prepared by Shlomo Pines, came to a conclusion (for the University of Chicago Press). In 1965, his books on Spinoza and Hobbes were published again. His work on Hobbes appeared in Germany in its original German version (*Hobbes' politische Wissenschaft*, Luchterhand Verlag), while his work on Spinoza appeared in English translation (*Spinoza's Critique of Religion*, Schocken Books) accompanied by a long and important *Preface*, in which Strauss presents his intellectual biography in Weimar Germany. Moreover, in this decade, Strauss contributed—with three unpublished essays on Lucretius, Maimonides, and Mendelssohn—to the *Festschriften* in honor of three old friends (Karl Löwith, Gershom Scholem, and Gerhard Krüger: cf. Strauss 1962c; 1967c; 1967d). Furthermore, he published his review of two important books on Hobbes and modern natural law by Crawford B. Macpherson and Samuel I. Mintz[19] and presented a critical evaluation of a recent book dedicated to the discussion of Max Weber's position on the relationship between Calvinism and capitalism.[20] Finally, he also published writings against positivism, in which he expressed his critique of the main Anglophone supporters of social sciences, namely Isaiah Berlin and Sheldon Wolin (cf. Strauss 1961a; 1962b; 1963a; 1964b).

Strauss had been working at least from 1955 on the publication of the *Guide of the Perplexed* in English translation. The project experienced highs and lows due to both editorial and scientific reasons. Strauss wrote a long introduction to the translation, entrusted to Shlomo Pines, in which his hermeneutical tools find a decisive exposition, especially in regard to the use of biblical exegesis. Precisely with the purpose of understanding the structure and content of the *Guide*, as well as the reasons with which Maimonides thought his esoteric plan, Strauss's essay *How to Begin to Study "The Guide of the Perplexed"* (1963) is dedicated to the relationship between *biblical exegesis* and *philosophical speculation* in Maimonides's work. Through meticulous textual analysis, Strauss lingers on a number of key points of the *Guide* (among which include existence, God's unity and incorporeity, the theory of divine attributes, the characters of mosaic prophecy, and the difference between moral and theoretical life) and returns to the issue of the relationship between philosophy and the Law, accepting the *difference* between the public character of theological-political communication and the private character of the quest for philosophical truth. However, besides the philosophical analysis of the *Guide*'s structure and content, Strauss was interested in publishing an accurate translation of the work, not only from a philological and exegetical perspective, but also from a philosophical one. Precisely on this aspect a contrast between Strauss and Pines surfaced. Despite Pines and Strauss having met in Berlin already in the second half of the 1920s and despite Strauss, in 1950, having advised Scholem—with success—to appoint Pines as chair of Jewish Philosophy at the Hebrew University of Jerusalem, the few letters of their correspondence that we possess, exchanged in the years 1956–1959, reveal a strong reciprocal tension between the two, embracing different issues regarding the translation work: the syntax, the choice of English terms able to render crucial concepts, the kind of annotations to add to the text and, most importantly, the method of the translation (literal or interpretative?).[21] Such tension is also revealed by the fact that Strauss entrusted one of his students, Ralph Lerner, with the stylistic revision of the translation; a task that Lerner carried out regularly and for which he was also thanked in the book's *Acknowledgment*, signed by both Strauss and Pines. Among the different topics discussed in their correspondence, the one concerning the method of translation is certainly the most relevant. In a letter dated 10 September 1956, Pines offered the possibility to choose between two methods. The first, used by Ibn Tibbon (a contemporary of Maimonides, translator of the *Guide* into Jewish), aims at a literal translation, in order to preserve the esoteric character of the original text and provide the reader with the same reading experience of the original. Instead, the second method aims at the clarification and interpretation of the original text's meaning, which, in a literal translation, would risk becoming incomprehensible. Despite Pines's assertion that the second method appeared to him much more interesting for the translation work, the English edition is actually focused on the first method, much closer to Strauss's hermeneutical methodology.

In the 1960s, Strauss's attention decisively turned to the analysis of Greek classics, from Plato to Aristotle, from Aristophanes to Thucydides, with special attention to textual elements, which, in their *formal* aspect, determine the *content*'s structure. Rhetorical devices, dialogical exposition, the narrative's "dramatic" structure, the characters' actions, irony and dissimulation, argumentative contradictions, silences, repetitions: all this, for Strauss, represents a fundamental key to rediscovering the teachings of the Greek classics, focusing his attention on the dialectic relationship between political and philosophical life, symbolically represented by the life of Socrates. Working from a perspective that holds together comedy and tragedy, realism and utopia, conservatism and radicalism, Strauss believes that the Socratic interpretations offered by Plato, Xenophon, and Aristophanes agree upon the definition of the relationship between philosophy and politics and that they represent, although in different forms, the *stranger wisdom* of classical philosophy. In *Socrates and Aristophanes* Strauss stages the contrast that opposes philosophy and poetry. This was not the only occasion in which Strauss showed this opposition. In a university course given in the autumn 1959 on the *Symposium* he made the same operation, but, while the *Clouds* shows the attack of poetry against philosophy, the *Symposium* shows the attack of philosophy against poetry. The *Symposium* therefore constitutes Plato's answer to Aristophanes: "The *Symposium* is the dialogue of the conflict between philosophy and poetry where the poets are in a position to defend themselves. They cannot in the *Republic* and the *Laws*" (Strauss 2001b, 11). It is clear that the philosopher presented in Aristophanes's comedies has a lacking: unlike the poet (who, in this, is identical to the rhetorician and the political man), he is not able to persuade the citizens that fill city squares and, therefore, he is not able to carry out a direct political power. Despite this flaw on the part of the philosopher, Aristophanes expresses a sentiment which is midway between admiration and envy for Socrates, because the comic playwright knew that this lack is counterbalanced by a true advantage philosophy has over comedy: "The primary object of the comic poet's envy was not Socrates' wisdom but his sovereign contempt for that popular applause on which the dramatic poet necessarily depends, or Socrates' perfect freedom" (Strauss 1966, 5). In his being an author of comedies who induces a reflection on the relationship between wisdom and traditional justice, Aristophanes represents a long series of situations, Socratic and not, in which the affinity between philosophy, comedy, and "utopia" is clear, just like—according to Strauss—in Plato's and Xenophon's writings. Thus, Strauss concludes that there are no qualitatively significant differences between the images of Socrates offered by Aristophanes, Plato, and Xenophon. The classical philosopher, in adopting a *paradoxical*, i.e., "absurd" and "ridiculous," perspective is well aware of the "utopic," and therefore comical, character of the best regime, even if he is also aware that the presence of what is "ridiculous" does not exclude, but rather *dictates* the presence of what is "serious," i.e., right, good, and noble things. The ridiculous character of Aristophanes's Socrates, his moving the audience to laughter about philosophical utopias, concretely presents the idea according to which the realization of the just city is improbable, because it depends on chance. Political philosophy's task is not so much that of elaborating political models in order to reach their effective fulfillment, but rather that of playing as a model for regimes that exist in reality. The best regime is not a political regime in the strict sense of the term, because it actually does not exist or, better, it exists in words, not in facts. The case of the moderns (Machiavelli, Hobbes, and Rousseau in particular) is different, since they undertake a concrete and "serious" action of propaganda towards the progressive improvement of the political body, which requires the conversion of philosophy to a practical knowledge that can be used by power. Inside this will to power, the "somber seriousness" of the moderns is opposed to the "sober lightness" of the ancient, precisely because tragedy has replaced comedy.

Classical Political Philosophy and Liberal Education

In 1964, Strauss published the book *The City and Man*, which constitutes a revised and augmented version of the *Page Barbour Lectures* he had held at the University of Virginia in the spring of 1962 and which touches on the most important themes of Strauss's thought—reticent writing, criticism of contemporary social science, the relationship between philosophy and politics, the theological-political problem, the superiority of the ancient over the moderns, the crisis of modernity, the theme of education—analyzed through a close study of the works of Thucydides, Plato, and Aristotle. The reader of *The City and Man*, however, sees the volume begin with an introduction in which Strauss speaks of the twentieth-century world wars and of Soviet Russia, of the crisis of liberal West and of the Cold War, of communism and fascism, of Nagy, Spengler, and Marx. Then why does Strauss commit in the chapters that follow to a minute and contorted textual analysis of classics? Indeed, the book is dedicated to Aristotle's *Politics*, Plato's *Republic*, and to Thucydides's *History of the Peloponnesian War*. Strauss in person answers this question:

> It is not self-forgetting and pain-loving antiquarianism nor self-forgetting and intoxicating romanticism which induces us to turn with passionate interest, with unqualified willingness to learn, toward the political thought of classical antiquity. We are impelled to do so by the crisis of our time, the crisis of the West . . . The return to classical political philosophy is both necessary and tentative or experimental . . . We cannot reasonably expect that a fresh understanding of classical political philosophy will supply us with recipes for today's use. For the relative success of modern political philosophy has brought into being a kind of society wholly unknown to the classics, a kind of society to which the classical principles as stated and elaborated by the classics are not immediately applicable. Only we living today can possibly find a solution to the problems of today. But an adequate understanding of the principles as elaborated by the classics may be the indispensable starting point for an adequate analysis, to be achieved by us, of present-day society in its peculiar character, and for the wise application, to be achieved by us, of these principles to our tasks. (Strauss 1964a, 1, 11)

Strauss's return to Greek classics does not aim at the nostalgic recovery of a presumed "age of gold," nor at the restoration of anti-modern forms of political institutions. Such a return exclusively concerns the form of philosophical thought, clearly distinguished between ancient and modern: historical reflection is a necessary *means* to overcome the problems of modernity. Therefore, we cannot define Strauss's return to classical philosophy as a form of traditionalism characterized by a nostalgic desire of the origins, precisely because he was perfectly aware that an immediate recovery of the categories of classical political philosophy was impossible. Despite the necessity of such a recovery, it can only be an experimental one. Moreover, the recovery does not concern the actual solutions offered by classics (for instance, the theme of natural inequality), since they cannot be applied to the problems posed by modern societies. Rather, this recovery concerns the *forms* of classical philosophical-political thought. The first step in this direction consists in the definition of the way in which we read the classics. Here returns the theme of reticent writing, intended as a necessary defense adopted by philosophy against two different social phenomena: censure and conformism. Independently from the more or less liberal form of the political regime, according to Strauss "the philosopher and the non-philosophers cannot have genuinely common deliberations" (Strauss 1968c, 14). The radicalism of philosophical thought has to be accompanied by moderation of its public expression. Reticent writing represents the form with which philosophy appears to the city. The Platonic dialogue is the most representative example of philosophical communication and shows the connection that exists between the literary and the political question (Strauss 1964a, 51ff.).

Strauss's appeal to Greek classics connects to an *anti-traditional* and nonconformist conception of philosophy, refusing any theory concerning the necessary and immanent directionality of history, which leads to the realization of the best possible order. Indeed, throughout his entire cultural existence, Strauss—informed by the history of the twentieth century regarding the dangers connected to any attempt to saturate political experience and realize projects that lead to the "end of history"—was a strenuous opponent of any messianic movement that maintained to realize on earth the "final kingdom" of goodness and justice.[22] "I have never been a supporter of messianism and I never will be," he wrote to Scholem on 7 July 1973 (Strauss and Scholem 2001, 769–70).[23] Strauss's political philosophy avoids any messianic dimension and the anti-messianic perspective characterizes the political philosophy of Strauss's Plato. Assuming a perspective that is not commonly accepted and that could put the community's stability at risk, philosophy appears as a potentially "subversive" activity in regard to constituted order, but it does not offer itself as an alternative power. Instead, Strauss denies the possibility of a fulfillment *in facts* of the "utopic" regime described *in words* by Greek philosophers, especially by Plato in the *Republic*, and goes as far as drawing an anti-traditional image of Plato, interpreted not as the exponent of utopic thought, but rather of *political realism*. Far from being the philosophical-political work that outlines the characters of a utopic and truly just political order, for Strauss, the *Republic* is the demonstration of the *impossibility* of creating a just city (cf. Strauss 1964a, 116ff.). The just city can exist only "in words," precisely due to the natural antagonism between philosophical and political activity. Thus, it becomes clear that political conservatism finds its origin and justification in the necessity of the *body*, i.e., of the *private*, but not in those of *thought*, i.e., *public*:

> The just city is impossible. It is impossible because it is against nature. It is against nature that there should ever be a "cessation of evils," "for it is necessary that there should always be something opposed to the good, and evil necessarily wanders about the mortal nature and the region here." It is against nature that rhetoric should have the power ascribed to it: that it should be able to overcome the resistance rooted in men's love of their own and ultimately in the body; as Aristotle puts it, the soul can rule the body only despotically, not by persuasion; the *Republic* repeats, in order to overcome it, the error of the sophists regarding the power of speech. (Strauss 1964a, 127)

The nexus between hermeneutics and liberal education expresses this difference between philosophy and the city. Philosophy is a discourse that concerns the *particular*, which requires the refinement of a gradual procedure of *introduction* to philosophical discourse. In Strauss's interpretation, the gradual, but necessary, introduction to philosophy is defined as a particular education to reading and writing. Philosophy is *liberal education* in its highest sense, it is education to perfection, precisely because philosophy, in its being search of wisdom, is simultaneously *virtue* and *happiness*. Liberal education consists of the attentive study of the books left by great philosophers. This means acquiring awareness of the fact that the great thinkers do not say the same things on the most important topics. Even without being philosophers, it is possible to love philosophy, to listen to the dialogue between great philosophers by studying their books. However, this dialogue does not occur in absence of research. Indeed, all the great philosophers express themselves through monologues, even when they write dialogues. The scholar's task is that of trying to transform these monologues into dialogues. The scholar lives inside an "enchanted circle," protected by the work of philosophers who have dealt with issues without remaining in the shadow of any authority. In this sense, the great books reveal their full meaning, the one intended by their authors, only if one meditates on them "day and night" (cf. Strauss 1968c, 3–8).

This concept of liberal education does not have success in the modern world, where the term "education" implies a universal and popular education. In Strauss's interpretation, modern democracy, in its unrelenting trend to favor the development of mass culture, has not found a solution to the educational problem. What we call education today very often does not mean formation of the character, but rather instruction, training, and conditioning, which is a reduction of education to the leveling of consciences. Liberal education, however, would be necessary precisely to fight the limits of modern democracy, given that it appears unable to provide defenses against mass culture (cf. Strauss 1968c, 9ff.), while classical liberal education, in reminding us of the sense of human excellence, provides the antidote against conformism:

> Liberal education is the counterpoison to mass culture, to the corroding effects of mass culture, to its inherent tendency to produce nothing but "specialists without spirit or vision and voluptuaries without heart." Liberal education is the ladder by which we try to ascend from mass democracy to democracy as originally meant. Liberal education is the necessary endeavor to found an aristocracy within democratic mass society. Liberal education reminds those members of a mass democracy, who have ears to hear, of human greatness. (Strauss 1968c, 5)

Chapter Seven

Claremont and Annapolis (1968–1973)

The Last Years

At the end of 1967, having reached limits of age, Strauss left his teaching at the University of Chicago, which honored him with the title of emeritus professor, without however making any solid effort to retain him in service. As his senior student, Joseph Cropsey succeeded Strauss in his chair. Nevertheless, the discomfort that by then surrounded Strauss, due to the annoyance and distance showed to him by his colleagues, as well as the deterioration of his health,[1] induced him to leave Chicago. In January 1968, he moved to Claremont Men's College, in California, where he stayed until the spring of 1969. There he suffered a second heart attack in November 1968. Despite the worsening of his conditions, Strauss conducted his didactic activity, with courses on Plato's *Euthydemus* and on Aristotle's *Nicomachean Ethics*—attended also by Nathan Tarcov future director of the Leo Strauss Center—as well as some lectures, among which was one on Socrates delivered on 14 February 1968. However, independently from his health, the experience in Claremont—where he was invited thanks to Harry V. Jaffa—was disappointing, due to the rather low level of the students. Therefore, Strauss looked for another venue to spend the final years of his career.

Since 1938, Klein had been teaching at St. John's College in Annapolis (Maryland), one of the main centers for humanities in the US, which he directed between 1949 and 1958. Thanks to the administrative help provided by the director at that time, Robert A. Goldwin, he had no trouble organizing a long-term academic appointment for Strauss as "Scott

Buchanan Distinguished Scholar in Residence" (cf. Deutsch and Murley 1999, 31ff.). Between the 1940s and 1960s, Strauss had already taken part, on several occasion, in conferences and seminars at St. John's College and there he found a familiar atmosphere (cf. Strauss 1978a) that allowed him to write his last books on Xenophon and Plato, as well as numerous articles on Greek classics. In the autumn of 1969, Strauss moved to Annapolis, where he received an honorary degree and held some courses and seminars on Thucydides, Xenophon, Nietzsche's *Beyond Good and Evil*, Plato's *Laws*, and the relationship between Athens and Jerusalem, as well as a number of public lectures on Machiavelli and Socrates. Strauss fulfilled with a certain regularity his didactic obligations, but his lessons were shorter than the ones he used to hold in Chicago, and he tended to shorten the time dedicated to the discussion with students due to his weakness, which prevented him from working too long. Despite his poor health, as well as the shorter lessons and reduced discussion time, in Annapolis he found students passionate about his research, namely Ted A. Blanton, Jerrold R. Caplan, and Leon Kass. Strauss remained in Annapolis until his death, which occurred in the late afternoon of 18 October 1973, following pneumonia. He was buried in the cemetery of the Knesseth Israel Synagogue. A few days after his death, St. John's College organized, on 31 October, a public event in his memory, which featured four speakers—Jacob Klein, J. Winfree Smith, Ted A. Blanton, and Laurence Berns—whose words later appeared on the journal *The College* (cf. Klein et al. 1974). Other obituaries and commemorations appeared in other journals of political theory, philosophy, and Jewish culture, such as *Social Research, National Review, Political Theory, The University of Chicago Magazine, Interpretation, Commentary, Proceedings of the American Academy for Jewish Research, American Jewish Yearbook, The American Scholar, The Intercollegiate Review*, and *The Independent Journal of Philosophy*.[2] Strauss's death was not sudden: his health condition, already precarious for some time, rapidly worsened (concerning asthma and pneumonia, his prostate, and his spinal column), as he repeatedly wrote to Scholem (cf. Strauss and Scholem 2001, 757ff.).

Troubled by numerous practical problems—for instance, troubles in handwriting—and thousands of aches, Strauss did not give up on working. In the last years of his life, he continued to deal with modern philosophy—especially Machiavelli, Nietzsche, Cohen, and Husserl—and Greek classics. He published two important works on Xenophon (*Xenophon's Socratic Discourse*, 1970; *Xenophon's Socrates*, 1972) and a number of significant essays on Thucydides and Plato, as well as an important book on Plato's *Laws*, which, although already completed in the autumn of 1971, only appeared posthumously thanks to Cropsey in 1975 (*The Argument and the Action of Plato's "Laws,"* 1975). In these last years, Strauss also maintained his life-long interest for the issues of German philosophy, inside which he received his education and with which he confronted himself throughout his philosophical career. Besides the autobiographical testimony that Strauss gave, alongside Klein, to the students and the public of St. John's College on 30 January 1970 (cf. Strauss 1970d), these bonds are present in the last letters he exchanged with Löwith. In a letter he addressed to Löwith on 12 March 1970, Strauss debated some passages inside the essay his friend had published in the *Festschrift* for Heidegger's eightieth birthday. The essay deals with themes—the relationship between history and nature, the limits of historicism and the happiness of theoretical life—that recall a seminar discussion on Heidegger's *Sein und Zeit* (1927) that had taken place in a German university towards the end of the 1920s (cf. Strauss and Löwith 2001, 695–96). German issues are also present in Strauss's correspondence with Scholem, where some new interpretations of certain topics and figures also appear, such as Judaism's statute in German culture, the position held by Buber, Benjamin, and heterodox Marxism and, more in general, the considerations on the ambivalence of German thinkers and of *Deutschtum* (cf. Strauss and Scholem 2001, 757, 766). For Heidegger, Strauss had particularly severe words in a letter dated 7 July 1973, three months before his death (cf. Strauss and Scholem 2001, 770). His judgment was not new, since Strauss saw in Heidegger the union—which Strauss believed to be typical of much German culture—between a great theoretical ability and a worthless moral sensibility (cf. Strauss 1970d, 3; 1971, 2ff.; 1991, 250–52; Strauss and Löwith 2001, 673ff.):

> Heidegger became a Nazi in 1933. This was not due to a mere error of judgment on the part of a man who lived on great heights high above the lowland of politics. Everyone who had read his first great book and did not overlook the wood for the trees could see the kinship in temper and direction between Heidegger's thought and the Nazis. What was the practical, that is to say serious meaning of the contempt for reasonableness and the praise of resoluteness which permeated the work except to encourage that extremist movement? When Heidegger was rector of the University of Freiburg in 1933 he

delivered an official speech in which he identified himself with the movement which then swept Germany. (Strauss 1995a, 306)

Athens and Jerusalem

For Strauss, Jerusalem always represented the holy city. It was the seat and symbol of Judaism. Moreover, alongside Athens, is incarnated one of the two roots of Western culture (cf. Strauss 1967a). Strauss's deep admiration for Jerusalem clearly appears on numerous occasions, but it is especially outspoken in the opening passage of the essay *What Is Political Philosophy?*, which constitutes the re-elaboration of the lessons given at the Hebrew University of Jerusalem, hosted by Scholem, in the academic year 1954/1955:

> It is a great honor, and the same time a challenge to accept a task of particular difficulty, to be asked to speak about political philosophy in Jerusalem. In this city, and in this land, the theme of political philosophy—"the city of righteousness, the faithful city"—has been taken more seriously than anywhere else on earth. Nowhere else has the longing for justice and the just city filled the purest hearts and the loftiest souls with such zeal as on this sacred soil. I know all too well that I am utterly unable to convey to you what in the best possible case, in the case of any man, would be no more than a faint reproduction or a weak imitation of our prophets' vision. I shall even be compelled to lead you into a region where the dimmest recollection of that vision is on the point of vanishing altogether—where the Kingdom of God is derisively called an imagined principality—to say here nothing of the region which was never illumined by it. But while being compelled, or compelling myself, to wander far away from our sacred heritage, or to be silent about it, I shall not for a moment forget what Jerusalem stands for. (Strauss 1959b, 9–10)

Despite this deep admiration of the spiritual sphere represented by Jerusalem, Strauss's philosophical thought is not classifiable with labels such as "philosophy of religion" or "Jewish philosophy." Naturally, in more than one occasion, Strauss expressed himself in defense of the dignity of the

Jewish people and expressed a sincere feeling of veneration for the faith of his ancestors (cf. Strauss 1981a, 1994, 1997b, 2002b, 2012a). However, he always expressed this feeling of veneration in a way that was both passionate and rational, as an act of love and gratitude towards the Jewish tradition and community, not as a proof of an intimate participation in faith. A small yet significant episode in Strauss's intellectual biography can clarify his attitude towards Jewish tradition. At the beginning of his lecture *Why We Remain Jews*, held at the Hillel House in Chicago on 4 February 1962, Strauss publicly manifested his disappointment regarding the title itself of the lecture. Indeed, in the initial version of the title he had proposed for the lecture, the sentence ended with a question mark, as to acknowledge the possibility of abandoning Judaism: "When Rabbi Pekarsky first approached me and suggested this title, I was repelled by it, not to say shocked by it" (Strauss 1994, 43). However, the disappointment was not limited to this, since Strauss was unaware of a subtitle—*Can Jewish Faith and History Still Speak to Us?*—the existence of which he learned just few days before the lecture. Even in this case, he manifested his distance from the choice: "I could not with propriety speak on the theme of the subtitle because, after all, everyone is a specialist, and my specialty is social science rather than divinity" (Ibid.). The episode confirms that Strauss faithfully and loyally was, and remained, on the side of Jews. However, it also confirms that he could not entirely partake of the Jewish *faith*. Indeed, Judaism is not *religious conscience*, as any modern form of "Jewish philosophy" or "philosophy of religion" would claim, but a *revealed religion*, facing which it is necessary to show an unconditioned faith and obedience. A faith and an obedience that the *philosopher* Strauss—animated by *Socratic zetetic skepticism*—asserted he could not grant, because they rest on assumptions that the philosopher, as such, cannot make (cf. Strauss 1972b, XXIII).

Strauss dedicated two lectures to the relationship between philosophy and religion, entitled *Jerusalem and Athens* and respectively held on 13 and 15 March 1967 at New York City College. These represent the final formulation of his idea of the relationships between reason and revelation. He had already discussed the issue in previous lectures, such as two similar ones (*Jerusalem and Athens*, held at the New School in New York in 1946 and at the Hillel House of the University of Chicago in 1950 respectively), *Reason and Revelation* (1948, Hartford Theological Seminary), and *The Mutual Influence of Theology and Philosophy* (1952, Hillel House). Athens—i.e., classical Greek philosophy, especially Socratic-Platonic—does not only represent a model of knowledge able to distinguish between *doxa* and *sophia*, but also a *style of life* that unfolds in the domain of solitude and at the borders of the city. The philosopher, for his own nature, is a stranger at home: he lives inside the city without entirely identifying with the citizen. Philosophical life, however, is different from political life, as well as from religious life. Indeed, the first "chronological" question is *quid sit deus* ("what is god"), while the first "logical" question is the Socratic one ("what is it?"). From a theoretical perspective, the philosophical question precedes the religious (and political) one. Ideas are more important than gods, because research on gods is included inside the research on ideas. Philosophy cannot accept in principle the truth of revelation. However, since philosophy is not wisdom, but rather *search* for wisdom, it cannot exclude the possibility offered by Jerusalem, i.e., by revealed religion (cf. Strauss 1967a). Athens and Jerusalem, therefore, are bound to proceed side by side, without either of the two being able to mine the legitimacy and prestige of the other and without finding a union. The only great attempt made to unite the two, which occurred in Christianity, namely with the work of Thomas Aquinas, actually loses some fundamental characters of both Athens and Jerusalem.

Faced with this alternative, Strauss chose Athens, despite his deep and sincere affection towards Jewish tradition, as he announced to his friend Scholem in 1973. Strauss's perspective remained *skeptical*, and he proudly claimed for himself Averroes's motto in honor of philosophy as a style of life: *moriatur anima mea mortem philosophorum* (cf. Strauss and Scholem 2001, 768ff.). However, even if it is true that in the alternative between philosophy and religion Strauss chose philosophy, nevertheless, the idea of philosophy conceived by him is not the modern one, but rather the *zetetic* one proper to the classical world. It is a model of philosophy that, although able to unmask revealed religion's claim of truthfulness, is not however able to build an "absolute system of knowledge," but only to *stretch* towards knowledge:

> We must try to understand the difference between biblical wisdom and Greek wisdom. We see at once that each of the two claims to be true wisdom, thus denying to the other its claim to be wisdom in the strict and highest sense. According to the Bible, the beginning of wisdom is fear of the Lord; according to the Greek philosophers, the beginning of wisdom is wonder. We are thus compelled from the very beginning

to make a choice, to take a stand. Where then do we stand? We are confronted with the incompatible claims of Jerusalem and Athens to our allegiance. We are open to both and willing to listen to each. We ourselves are not wise but we wish to become wise. We are seekers for wisdom, *philosophoi*. By saying that we wish to hear first and then to act to decide, we have already decided in favor of Athens against Jerusalem. This seems to be necessary for all of us who cannot be orthodox. (Strauss 1967a, 4–5)

It is not possible to lead simultaneously a philosophical and a religious life, because there is no possibility to transcend the conflict between Athens and Jerusalem. The only necessary thing for the philosopher is contemplative life, for the Jew the only necessary thing is obedience to the Law. Both the philosopher and the prophet are interested in justice and rectitude; however, the orders they refer to are different: "The philosopher is the man who dedicates his life to the quest for knowledge of the good, of the idea of the good; what we would call moral virtue is only the condition or by-product of that quest. According to the prophets, however, there is no need for the quest for knowledge of the good" (Strauss 1967a, 27), because what is good was already revealed to them.

From Xenophon to Machiavelli

Strauss had been studying Xenophon since the second half of the 1930s, when he used the treatise on the constitution of the Lacedaemonians for an initial definition of his hermeneutics of reticence (cf. Strauss 1939). Indeed, although we can define Strauss's thought as a form of *Platonic political philosophy*, it would be misleading to underestimate the importance of Xenophon—and in particular of his Socratic writings—in Strauss's definition of the relationship between philosophical and political life. Indeed, precisely in this aspect lies the main difference between the use Strauss made of Xenophon and Plato. While he mostly used Plato to highlight that philosophy and politics diverge on the issue of knowledge (*episteme* vs. *doxa*), he recurred to Xenophon especially to underline the difference between philosophical and political life, i.e., between contemplative and practical life (cf. Strauss 1972a, 77ff.). Already in the book *On Tyranny* (1948) he offers a clear example of the superiority of philosophical life over political life. However, the works Strauss dedicated to Xenophon in the early 1970s are important examples of this interpretative perspective (cf. Strauss 1970a; 1972a; 1975b), which unwinds through Xenophon's main works in which Socrates plays the lead role: *Oeconomicus, Memorabilia, Apology of Socrates,* and *Symposium*. We know Socrates's thought thanks to Plato's dialogues, Aristophanes's *Clouds* and a number of passages from Aristotle. However, the primary source for our knowledge of Socrates's justice and prudence is Xenophon's work (cf. Strauss 1970a, 83–86). As he had already done with *On Tyranny,* also in these years Strauss meant to free Xenophon from the prejudice that had relegated him, during the modern age, to the role of rhetorician and mere author of chronicles, void of philosophical value, in order to bring him back to the level of philosopher *tout court*.

Each one of Xenophon's Socratic works treats a specific aspect of Socrates's thought and actions (the *Apology* treats the way he deliberated, the *Symposium* the way he acted, etc.). However, beyond such distinctions, Strauss identifies a contraposition between the philosopher and the political man (both the gentleman and the tyrant, the king and the citizen), which originates in a stretch that approaches, only for a theoretical and analytical purpose, the gentleman and the tyrant. If it is true that the gentleman, or the citizen who deals with the public matter without any regard to his personal interest, is clearly different from the tyrant or the monarch, it is also true that they, in their reciprocal diversity, possess a number of common traits, which make them different from the philosopher (cf. Strauss 1970a, 126ff., 159ff., 175ff.). Firstly, this difference resides in the different form of *eros* that animates the philosopher and the political man, which regards *theoria* in the first case, while in the second case it concerns *popular recognition* (not to mention the worst cases: unbridled personal economic interest, ambition, or desire of power). While the philosopher, guided by an erotic desire towards wisdom, wishes to be *admired* by a small minority, the political man wishes to be honored, i.e., *recognized,* by everyone. Secondly, the philosopher and the citizen can be friends—like Socrates and Critobulus in the *Oeconomicus*—but they possess two different natures and two different kinds of social obligations. The philosopher can be poor, because contemplative life does not require richness and, therefore, his social obligations exclusively consist in the respect of the law. The citizen, instead, has to think about incrementing his wealth and power as one of the main forms of honor and pleasure and, consequently, has to take up numerous daily occupations for this purpose, while the philosopher is completely free from them. Strauss embodies this difference in the relationship between Socrates and Ischomachus in the *Oeconomicus*: the latter sees pleasure where the former only sees trouble. Strauss's Xenophon perfectly knows the difference between the life of a political man that governs through the law and the life of a tyrant who governs without law. He also knows the difference between economy and chrematistics (that is, between a moderate and an immoderate desire of wealth). However, he also knows that, despite the differences, these forms of practical life (politics and economics) are similar to each other if confronted with philosophical life.

All this implies that the philosopher does not wish to govern. Indeed, Xenophon does not mention courage or military virtue in his enumerations of Socratic virtues (cf. Strauss 1972a, 78ff.). This is also because, strictly speaking, the philosopher is not part of the city. The only teachers that have a constitutive part in political society are priests. Moreover, the difference between the philosopher and the citizen resides in the fact that, while the citizen aims at obtaining riches, honor, and pleasure through the benevolence of his fellow citizens, who in turn benefit by him, the philosopher aims at the education of young potential philosophers (cf. Strauss 1972a, 55ff.). Socrates's teaching on philosophical life is a teaching on friendship (cf. Strauss 1972a, 43ff.), as well as happiness. This attempt of conversion to philosophical life is considered by the city as an attempt to "corrupt the youth," which leads the way to persecution. However, the philosopher cannot avoid it. The defense of philosophy goes through the attempt to convert young potential philosophers, whom the philosopher only finds inside the city, in an already political association, not in a state of nature. Persecution does not impede the philosopher's work, because philosophy and philosophical education are possible under any form of government. The philosopher's political action must aim at convincing the city that he is not an atheist, that he respects and honors the gods honored by the city, that he is not politically subversive, that he is a good citizen. However, such dissimulation—made possible by the ironical character of philosophical communication and by the praise of Socrates's prudence—is provisional, because the philosopher's destiny inside the city is always at risk, as Socrates's death demonstrates.

Socrates's figure is also present in the beginning of Strauss's entry on Machiavelli contained in the second edition of the *History of Political Philosophy* (cf. Strauss 1972c; cf. also Strauss 1970b). The question on which the writing is based is "what is virtue?" and the essay aims at establishing the clear difference that runs between classical and modern political philosophy. The answer given by the moderns—and by Machiavelli in particular—is the one that Strauss had already illustrated in *Natural Right and History* (1953) and in *What is Political Philosophy* (1959). Lowering the level of political purposes (from the search of the best government to the search of a realistic and stable government), Machiavelli identifies virtue with efficacy and usefulness, i.e., success. More precisely, according to Machiavelli virtuous is he who is able to wisely alternate—according to circumstances—virtue and vice, goodness and evil, morality and immorality, nobility and sordidness, gravity and levity. Being virtuous means knowing how to be good when it is useful to be so and knowing how to be cruel when useful. However, as a philosopher of politics, Machiavelli asks "what is virtue?" in the same way as Aristotle would have asked it, not how Gorgias and Protagoras would have. Anyway, Machiavelli provides an answer that represented the exact opposite of the one provided by Aristotle, not to mention the one provided by the Christian message. Living according to virtue, for the Florentine secretary, does not mean living with the aim of theoretical happiness, nor with the aim of morality and justice. Instead, living according to virtue corresponds to living with the aim of attaining the conditions of possibility of morality and justice, which reside in immorality and injustice: at the beginning there is the fear, not the love. From this perspective, the essay does not add anything substantial to what Strauss had already asserted in *Thoughts on Machiavelli* (1958).

Perhaps due to the influence of his recent studies on Xenophon, Strauss scrutinizes—already in the essay *Machiavelli and Classical Literature* (1970)—the relationship between Machiavelli and Xenophon, already outlined in *On Tyranny* (1948). He identifies a contact point between the two authors—who are very distant from each other and yet in some aspects very close—in their consideration of the relationships between politics and rhetoric. In the *Discorsi*, the writer that Machiavelli quotes most frequently, with the obvious exception of Livy, is Xenophon. But he quotes only two of Xenophon's writings, *Cyropaedia* and *Hiero*, without references to his Socratic writings, which are "suppressed" by Machiavelli. Then, there is a great moral and political difference between Xenophon and Machiavelli. But there is also an important point of contact between them. Machiavelli has often been compared to the sophists, but he does not believe in the omnipotence of the word, and he does not identify politics and rhetoric, just like Xenophon: for this important aspect, Machiavelli and Xenophon (as well as Socrates, Plato, and Aristotle) form a common front against the sophists. Machiavelli's admiration for Xenophon rested on his awareness—expressed in the *Cyropaedia*—that speech is not omnipotent and that human beings can be governed only through a mix of persuasion and coercion, of rhetoric and violence. However, Xenophon is not a Machiavellian thinker *avant la lettre*, because two moral poles coexist in him—in order of importance, Socrates and Cyrus—while in Machiavelli the Socratic pole does not play any role. Yet, Machiavelli is not a sophist, nor a simple political analyst, but an outright philosopher of politics. Despite the fact that the Florentine secretary radically criticizes the tradition of classical natural right, he shares with Socrates and Aristotle the idea that political philosophy must confront the issue of the just city. Differently from Socrates and Aristotle, however, Machiavelli refers to the just society from the perspective of an anthropological and political idea of *conventionalism*, based on a radical individualism, according to which the human being is not a social animal by nature. Therefore, Machiavelli supplies a synthesis between the two classical traditions, natural right and conventionalism. Such synthesis constitutes the new moral foundation of all modern political philosophy. Despite the evident mention of the authority of republican Rome—and of Livy—in the *Discourses* Machiavelli really creates "new modes and orders" (cf. Strauss 1970b, 9ff.).

Socrates, the Sophists, and the City

The sophists and the sophistry were not secondary discussion topics in Strauss's philosophical career—suffice it to think they were organically present already in *The Political Philosophy of Hobbes* (1936) and still present in *The City and Man* (1964)—and his last writings made no exception. The sophists are present not only in his works on Xenophon and Machiavelli, but also in the essay *On the "Euthydemus"* (1970), which constitutes the opening article of the first number of the journal *Interpretation. A Journal of Political Philosophy*, the hermeneutical and philosophical-political perspective of which was clearly determined by Strauss's teaching. The essay on the *Euthydemus* appears in the form of a punctual commentary of the Platonic dialogue, defined by Strauss as possibly the most frivolous and absurd work of the Platonic *corpus*, despite it having a structure similar to the *Crito*, perhaps the most sacred dialogue. This funny trait of the dialogue emerges especially at the beginning, after Socrates has told

Crito of having thought—the previous day, during a conversation with the brothers Euthydemus and Dionysodorus—of becoming a student of these two famous and excellent sophists. The only thing that has held Socrates back is the impossibility of paying the fee requested by the two brothers. Once the comical scene is over, Socrates goes on to tell Crito—who has already asked what kind of knowledge would receive a student of Euthydemus and Dionysodorus—about the dialogue that occurred the previous day. One of the themes that most frequently crossed the old Strauss's thought emerges here: the dialectic triangulation between philosophy, sophistry, and the city. It is not a new topic, given it already appears, in a more direct form, yet in a less erudite style, in the essay *On a New Interpretation of Plato's Political Philosophy* (1946). Indeed, Strauss identifies two polemical fronts, intimately intertwined in the structure of *Euthydemus*: the first and more traditional one is the contraposition of Socrates with the sophists, the second is the contraposition of Socrates and the sophists together with the city.

The dialogue, therefore, is divided into two parts. While in the first part an ironic Socrates refutes Euthydemus, in the second part Socrates defends Euthydemus from his opponents. Socrates is aware of the limits of Euthydemus's exclusively eristic knowledge, nevertheless he defends him because he identifies in sophistry an activity that is able to challenge common opinions, an activity that constitutes the first step towards philosophical research. At the beginning of the conversation with Socrates, the two sophists—in this aspect similar to the city—identify their power to "build" and "destroy" with words as a virtue, given that the eristic science they possess is the only actually possible and truly useful knowledge. Virtue only consists in the superiority in speaking and in the ability to refute any kind of argument, because knowledge in a strict sense—namely knowledge of the most important things—is impossible. In respect to this sophistic perspective, we know the position held by Socrates, who turns the conversation to the centrality of knowledge of any human activity. Knowledge is the greatest good. In fact, it is the only good under the guidance of which other goods—for instance freedom or richness—become such. Thus, if our happiness entirely depends on knowledge and if one can only attain virtue through learning, then philosophy is the only necessary thing. If the dialogue were to end here, there would be nothing new in respect to what we can read in other passages of the Platonic *corpus*. However, at this point, the second part of the dialogue begins, in which—according to Strauss—Socrates moves closer to the sophists, and the sophists to Socrates, in determining their common opposition to the city. Crito notices this harmony between philosophy and sophistry, telling his teacher and friend, as soon as Socrates has concluded his narration, about the disapproval he has heard in the city relatively to the improper character of the conversation between Socrates, Euthydemus, and Dionysodorus. At this point Socrates engages in a defense of the two brothers against the common opinion expressed by citizens. Socrates is not the sophists's mortal enemy, and the sophists are not his, to the point that Socrates defines Euthydemus's art as an introduction to philosophy, because it constitutes the ignition of the awareness concerning the radical difference between philosophy and politics.

In the Platonic association of sophistry and the city and in their distinction from philosophy, Strauss considers sophistry as a peculiar use of philosophy for non-philosophical purposes, made by men who are aware of the superiority of philosophy. The sophist cares about knowledge not because he loves it, but for the honor and power that he derives from it, or from the semblance of it. It is clear that, in this sense, all citizens are sophists, at least in their intentions (cf. Strauss 1970c). However, the sophist is not identical to the citizen. The doubt that the sophist promotes, in principle, towards common sense makes him suspicious to the eyes of the citizen, who, from this perspective, makes an outright identification of the sophist with the philosopher. While in a certain sense the sophist is the philosopher's opponent, in another and more decisive sense, the citizen is the philosopher's true opponent, while in this perspective the sophist is his "friend." Indeed, philosophy's greatest enemy, "the greatest sophist" is the multitude gathered in a city assembly. According to Strauss's Plato, there are two equally fundamental mistakes, which are diametrically opposite to philosophy, as well the one to the other: sophistry and the populace's ignorance. The reciprocal opposition of these two mistakes leaves the philosopher in the conditions to fight the one by means of the other and vice versa. Against the sophists's contempt for common sense, the philosopher appeals to the search for truth, which can be initiated by common sense. Against the popular satisfaction for common sense's self-sufficiency, the philosopher uses the sophists's doubt to mine common sense's authority (cf. Strauss 1946).

Reading Plato's "Laws"

The book on Plato's *Laws* not only represents the completion of Strauss's long studies on Greek classics, but also an ideal spiritual testament. Indeed, his book *The Argument and the Action of Plato's "Laws"* (1975)—published posthumously by Joseph Cropsey—incarnates the maximum expression of the theological-political question that always accompanied his research. Moreover, this book concludes the philosophical path inaugurated by Strauss with his "change of orientation." His "change of orientation" occurred due to the reading—at the *Staatsbibliothek* in Berlin in 1929—of the passage by Avicenna on the *Laws* that Strauss decided to use as an *exergo* in his last book: "The treatment of prophecy and the Divine law is contained . . . in the *Laws*." Together with Maimonides, Plato is the most relevant author in Strauss's bibliography.[3] Among the Platonic writings, the *Laws* is the one Strauss considered the most important to understand political things. He asserted this since the 1930s and even officially declared it in a lecture at the Hebrew University of Jerusalem in 1954: "The character of classical political philosophy appears with the greatest clarity from Plato's *Laws*, which is his political work *par excellence*" (Strauss 1959b, 29). Strauss's Plato is not the philosopher whose teaching we know through the Neo-Platonic tradition, nor the theorist of metaphysics whose teaching—according to the philosophers of crisis, from Nietzsche to Heidegger—is at the root of modern nihilism. Instead, Strauss's Plato is the philosopher of the dialectics, of Socratic rhetoric, of reticent writings and, especially, of the theological-political problem. Strauss reads his work through the interpretative key elaborated by Al-Farabi and as the reference model for a radical critique of the modern inaugurated by Machiavelli and Hobbes.

Besides the issue of its theological-political content, Strauss's book on the *Laws* is also characterized by a marked *formal* originality of the argumentative structure and writing. Using the model proposed by Al-Farabi in his *Compendium Legum Platonis*, Strauss "re-wrote" Plato's *Laws* using a writing method that was far from the traditional form of the essay or treatise (a fact that is made evident also by the total absence of footnotes and the almost complete absence of references to secondary bibliography). Strauss retraced Plato's text almost line by line and inserted his reflections as a reader in dialogue with the text, questioning its contradictions and obscurities, posing questions, problems, and solutions more explicitly (but not entirely explicitly) than they appear in Plato's writing. The key to understand Strauss's work, therefore, is the use and lack of use that he makes of Plato's text. The reader of Strauss's book has a double task. First, he must read Strauss's text for itself. Then he should read Strauss's text again confronting it with Plato's *Laws*, in order to verify the variations that exist between the original and its copy, trying to understand the theoretical reasons behind these variations, inside a writing based on the models of "repetition" and "imitation."

The problematic relationship between philosophy and the city does not only concern the style of philosophical writing, but also the contents of the Platonic dialogue. The *Republic* discusses the problematic nature of political things, given that, indicating the essential limits of the actual city, it asserts the impossibility of the just city. However, if the best regime is impossible (or hardly achievable), is the "second best" regime also impossible? This would be the best possible regime founded on good (although not perfect) laws, which is the only one truly achievable in the actual city. According to Strauss, the task of answering this question is delegated to the *Laws*, which, in the traditional order of Platonic dialogues, follows the *Minos*, the only dialogue in which Socrates explicitly poses the question "what is the law?" The Socratic question is ambiguous, because, at least initially, it does not distinguish between practical and theoretical aspect. One cannot know the kind and quality of the law to which he is subject without having at least an idea on the nature of the law as such. There are two alternative and complementary conceptions of the law. On one side, the law is clearly the judgment of the city on the city's business and therefore it is not *physis*, but *nomos*. On the other side, in its reaching for truth on political things, the law aims to a higher judgment than the simple judgment of the city:

> In the traditional order of the Platonic dialogues the *Laws* is preceded by the *Minos*, the only Platonic dialogue in which Socrates raises the question "What is the law?" It appears that not all laws are good or, at any rate equally good. The Cretan laws were given by Minos, who was not only a son of Zeus but the only hero educated by Zeus . . . We are thus led to believe that the Cretan laws, and next to them the Spartan laws, are the best laws. Minos was indeed regarded by the Athenians as savage and unjust, but for no other reason than that Minos had waged victorious war against Athens. The best legislator was an enemy of Athens. The most ancient good legislator was the most ancient enemy of Athens. The quest for the best laws seems to compel the Athenians to transcend the laws of Athens and to become the pupils of an enemy of Athens—to act in a way which could appear to be unpatriotic. (Strauss 1975a, 1)

In the *Laws* the role usually reserved to Socrates is played by an elderly and unknown Athenian stranger, who speaks of laws, constitutions, and regimes with other two old men with a long political experience, the Cretan Clinias and the Spartan Megillos, while the three are walking from the city of Cnossos to Zeus's cave on the isle of Crete. After the beginning, dedicated to the analysis of Cretan laws, especially to the analysis of their both ancient and divine origin, the topic of the conversation moves to the definition of a good constitution, in the perspective of the foundation of an actual city—a task entrusted to Clinias. The Athenian stranger—who is not Socrates, but who could be Socrates, if Socrates had fled Athens—focuses his attention, with great prudence, on the statute of Cretan and Spartan laws, critically investigating their origin, antiquity, and value. He claims he moves (as a stranger) in the spaces allowed by those laws, without incurring in any sort of violation concerning the transgression of traditional habits consecrated by the cities' protecting divinities. However, it is clear that the Athenian stranger does not aim at safeguarding, though critically, the authority of ancient laws, but rather at indicating new ones, in order to make the political institutions effectively better. The Athenian stranger—the political philosopher who has political knowledge—becomes the teacher of the future legislators. However, what he proposes can become suspicious to the eyes of his two interlocutors, both because it is *innovative* and because it is *foreign*. The Athenian stranger is thoughtful about acting in a way that is comprehensible and respectable in front of Clinias and Megillos, introducing the topic of Athenian banquets, and of drinking wine, so as to take on the role of the Athenian patriot defending Athenian institution in an Athenian way (and not the role of the philosopher). The topic of drinking wine and regulated drunkenness covers most part of the first two books of the *Laws*. The Athenian stranger asserts that drinking wine during well-administered banquets consists in a form of public education, or *phronesis*, which allows both the moderation of audacity (especially in the young) and the recovery of political imagination (especially in the old). According to Strauss, this Platonic device makes a decisive political fact visible: Clinias and Megillos, the two elderly citizens obedient to laws and loyal to their city suffer from a constitutive fault, which originates from their piety and from their respect of habits, which make them opponents of any change. Their virtue, the respect of laws, becomes a fault if current laws are bad or insufficient. Therefore, virtue is not limited to obedience to the laws, just like justice is not limited to the respect of traditional justice (as demonstrated by the opposition of Socrates and Cephalus in the *Republic*). Allowing the overcoming of unconditioned deference to the laws, the narration on the Athenian banquets, that is on drinking wine in a regulated way, creates a "transgressive" effect on the two interlocutors, to the point that it makes them inclined to hear not a political, but a philosophical, criticism of their political institutions.

Only after having specified that the purpose of political life, different from philosophical life, consists in the education of the citizen to virtue and after having shown the inadequacy of Spartan and Cretan legislations, the Athenian stranger, explicitly requested by Clinias, turns his attention to the concrete structure of a new legislation. The dialogue's attention moves to the geographical and demographical composition of the community, to the various administrative offices, to the magistrate's offices, to the military structures, to ministers, practices of economic life, punishments against public and private crimes. From the fourth book of the *Laws*, the Athenian stranger does no longer speak as a teacher of future legislators, but rather as the adviser of an actual legislator, here and now. In particular, he underlines that wisdom is not a sufficient title to govern. The best political order presupposes an equal presence of wisdom and consent, coercion and persuasion, *sophia* and *doxa*, *phronesis* and *logos*, *nomos* and *physis*. Still, precisely this "political" engagement of the Athenian stranger highlights, although between the lines, that philosophy is different from the city, just as *physis* is different from *nomos*, nature from law. Nature is eternal and unchanging, while laws and habits change from city to city, in an arbitrary way. If such arbitrariness does not want to turn into license or abuse, the effectively existing laws in the city must confront natural law, which is not created by neither men nor gods, but which, presenting "what is," indicates the limits of arbitrariness and shows the possibility of a good and just political order.

In the Athenian's narration, criminal legislation must dedicate broad space to the issue of impiety and atheism, to the negation of the existence of the gods of the city and of providence. To demonstrate the radically impious character of atheism (politically destabilizing and socially dangerous) one must keep in mind that good laws have as a purpose that of inducing citizens to love justice and flee injustice through an equal distribution of rewards and pains sanctioned by gods: legislation cannot avoid theology. Obedience to the laws of the city and veneration of the gods are therefore the same thing because justice and piety indicate the space of the citizen's legitimate action, circumscribed by legality and patriotism. From a theological-political perspective, impiety and anarchy are identical. Clearly, it is not a theology that concerns dogmas of faith, but a theology that—as a religion—has a direct incidence on the city, inside which the conflicts between different ethical-political systems, which imply different and opposing conceptions of justice, turn into conflicts between different "divine" authorities. Divinities—today we would say myths and political ideologies—are guarantors and supporters of what is right in different political associations.

Philosophy cannot follow the city—i.e., the union of politics and religion—on this field. Philosophizing finds its reason to be in the distinction between what is "first for us" and what is "first in itself" or "for nature." The difference between *nomos* and *physis* shows the distance between philosophical understanding and theological-political understanding of the city. Naturally, this does not mean that the requirements of the city should be postponed to the requirements of philosophy. Instead, the city comes before philosophy, the truths of which cannot be *sic et simpliciter* realized in the city and, therefore, must be expressed in public with prudence and moderation. What is right does not necessarily coincide with what is useful. Given that moral virtue can lead to political ruin, it is necessary to distinguish between what is desirable in itself and what is possible in a given circumstance. Notwithstanding the "chronological" primacy of politics, philosophy is superior to the city, because its virtue is theoretical, proper to contemplative life, while the virtue of the city is practical, or moral, and is oriented to what is convenient. These two styles of life—theological-political life and philosophical life—coexist inside the city. The philosopher forcedly has to elaborate strategies to preserve both freedom to philosophize and the possibility to live peacefully inside the city, respecting the requirements of political life. If it wants to maintain the stability and dignity of its order, political life forcedly has to promote practices of justice that are able to diffuse consent and well-being among the citizens. According to Strauss, both these styles of life must confront the issue of education, which is certainly education to virtue, but in two different ways. The virtue of the perfect human being is not the virtue of the perfect citizen. In both cases, it is a question of deciding which life is right for the human being. A life intended as different from pleasant life, although not completely separated from it. However, the difference is visible in the different concepts of *goodness*, *virtue*, and *truth*, which, for philosophical life—as opposed to theological-political life—must be universal ("first in itself" or "for nature") and cannot be valid just here and now ("first for us"). Thus, can there be a common purpose for philosophy and the city? The discussion on virtue is one of the central passages of the twelfth and last books of the *Laws*, where the Athenian stranger confronts the problem of the organization of a Nocturnal Council, which constitutes the city institution in which the tension between philosophy and politics shows the impossibility of a final solution:

> The Athenian adumbrates the fundamental difficulty regarding the Nocturnal Council: are all its members men each of whom can acquire within his soul science of the subjects in question? Are its members potential or actual philosophers? A glance at Kleinias is sufficient to make one see the pertinence of the question. The heterogeneous composition of the Council makes it impossible to give a simple answer . . . "This being so, what ought to be done, stranger?," Kleinias asks most appropriately. The Athenian begins his reply by pointing out how dangerous their undertaking is: the attempt to establish the Nocturnal Council may lead to total victory or total defeat for their attempt to found a city; if the attempt to establish the Nocturnal Council fails, the whole enterprise fails . . . If this divine council comes into being, we must hand the city over to it . . . The members of the divine Council must be carefully selected, properly educated, and, after the completion of their education, settled in the akropolis of the country; then they will be guardians the like of whom we have never seen before in our lives in regard to excellence of guardianship. Megillos, who has not said a word for a long time, is so much impressed by the glorious prospect which the Athenian has conjured up that he turns to "dear Kleinias" with unusual liveliness and tells him that one must either abandon the settlement of the city or not let the Athenian stranger go: he must be made a participant in the settlement of the city by means of beseeching and contrivances of all kinds. Kleinias fully agrees but adds that Megillos too must help. With Megillos' "I shall help" the dialogue ends. The Athenian "naturally" does not respond. (Strauss 1975a, 185–86)

Once reached the end of the *Laws* we must return to the beginning of the *Republic*. Once reached the end of the *Republic* we must return to the beginning of the *Laws*. Indeed, the city of the *Laws*, which has to be founded "in facts," needs the city of the *Republic*, founded "in words," but just in a partial and moderate way. Likewise, the city of the *Republic*, which does not exist, constitutes the comparison for any consideration on the city of the *Laws*, which aims at actually existing. Therefore, politics needs philosophy and vice versa. However, politics and philosophy are not the same thing. The philosopher is always a stranger, even at home, because he interprets the *thaumazein* as a quest for knowledge, not as an original wisdom (be it revealed or traditional). Precisely in its being a necessary and sufficient condition for happiness, philosophy—intended as "stranger wisdom"—chronologically follows politics, but it is superior to it. The perfection of the human being consists in the "science of the being of all things," in the level of theoretical knowledge represented by philosophy, not in the imaginative one, of lower level, represented by politics or religion, which takes shape in the "science of the ways of life." Thus intended, philosophy consists in the search for truth on being, animated by the belief that only such a research makes life worth living. Because contemplative life is superior to practical life, just like the philosopher is superior to the citizen and philosophy is superior to religion and politics.

Notes

Chapter One

1. Among the 1928–1932 writings, in which this "change of orientation" is most emphasized, there is the essay *Die geistige Lage der Gegenwart* (February 1932: cf. Strauss 1997a, 441–64).

2. This was due to a strong criticism of the authoritarian, mystical, and "pagan" tendencies of the *Blau-Weiss* led by Walter Moses: cf. Strauss 1923a.

3. Cf. Strauss, 1923a; 1923b; 1923c; 1923d; 1924a; 1924b; 1924e; 1924f; 1925a; 1925b; 1925c; 1928; 1929a.

4. Strauss radically criticized Buber also in his mature age, especially with regard to religious subjectivism (cf. Strauss 1965, 9ff.). For other severe assertions made by Strauss against Buber cf. Strauss and Scholem 2001, 740ff., 751ff.

5. A criticism similar to the one he moved against Buber is the one Strauss moved to the Zionist association in Frankfurt led by Ernst Simon, Leo Löwenthal, Erich Fromm, Fritz Goitein, and Erich Michaelis, who, in their refusal of the fascist tendencies of the *Blau-Weiss*, limited themselves to replacing the authoritarian rhetoric of the *Blau-Weiss* with a humanitarian rhetoric. Cf. Strauss 1923a.

6. In his maturity Strauss declared that the term "antisemitism" was obscene, to the point that it should be abolished and substituted with "hate towards Jews": cf. Strauss 1994, 52–53.

7. Cf. Hans Weinberg, "Zionismus und Religion," *Der jüdische Student*, no. 1–2 (1925): 8–15.

8. Cf. Max Joseph, "Zur atheistischen Ideologie des Zionismus," *Der jüdische Student*, no. 6–7 (1928): 8–18; Max Joseph, "Ist die Religion wirklich eine Illusion?," *Der jüdische Student*, no. 8 (1928): 6–17; Max Joseph, "Wissenschaft und Religion," *Der jüdische Student*, no. 5 (1929): 15–22.

9. Strauss already made these observations, in terms very similar to those used in 1962, in his 1923 essay *Anmerkung zur Diskussion über "Zionismus und Antisemitismus"* (cf. Strauss 1923b) and he also expressed them in a conference held at the Hillel House in Chicago on 4 February 1962 (cf. Strauss 1994).

10. Cf. Hermann Cohen, "Ein ungedruckter Vortrag Hermann Cohens über Spinozas Verhältnis zum Judentum eingeleitet von Franz Rosenzweig [1910]," in *Festgabe zum zehnjährigen Bestehen der Akademie für die Wissenschaft des Judentums (1919–1929)* (Berlin: Akademie Verlag, 1929), 42–68; Hermann Cohen, "Spinoza über Staat und Religion, Judentum und Christentum [1915]," in Hermann Cohen, *Jüdische Schriften*, vol. III (Berlin: Schwetschke, 1924), 290–372.

Chapter Two

1. Cf. Rosenzweig's letter to Cohen entitled *Zeit ist's. Gedanken über das jüdische Bildungsproblem des Augenblicks* (January 1917): Franz Rosenzweig, *Zweistromland* (Dordrecht: Nijhoff, 1984), 461–81; cf. also Hermann Cohen, "Zur Begründung einer Akademie für die Wissenschaft des Judentums," *Neue Jüdische Monatshefte*, March 10, 1918.
2. Cf. David N. Myers, "The Fall and Rise of Jewish Historicism. The Evolution of the 'Akademie für die Wissenschaft des Judentums,' " *Hebrew Union College Annual* (1992): 107–44.
3. Cf. Moses Mendelssohn, *Gesammelte Schriften: Jubiläumsausgabe*, vol. I: *Schriften zur Philosophie und Ästhetik I* (Berlin: Akademie-Verlag, 1929); vol. II: *Schriften zur Philosophie und Ästhetik II* (Berlin: Akademie-Verlag, 1931); vol. III.1: *Schriften zur Philosophie und Ästhetik III.1* (Berlin: Akademie-Verlag, 1932); vol. VII: *Schriften zum Judentum I*, Berlin 1930; vol. XI: *Briefwechsel I: 1754–1762* (Berlin: Akademie-Verlag, 1932); vol. XIV: *Hebräische Schriften I* (Breslau: Akademie-Verlag, 1938); vol. XVI: *Hebräische Schriften–Briefwechsel III* (Berlin: Akademie-Verlag, 1929). The direction of the edition was entrusted to Ismar Elbogen (for works on Judaism and the translations from the Bible), Julius Guttmann (for writings on philosophy and aesthetics) and Eugen Mittwoch (for Jewish studies writings), while the editors of each section of the volumes were Fritz Bamberger, Haim Borodianski, Simon Rawidowicz, Bruno Strauss, and Leo Strauss. To rebuild the difficult editorial history of the edition of Mendelssohn's writings, which, after an interruption in 1938, only picked up again in 1971 in Stuttgart edited by Alexander Altmann for Frommann, cf. the editor's note to the first volume of the new edition of Mendelssohn's *Gesammelte Schriften* (*Schriften zur Philosophie und Ästhetik I*, Stuttgart: Frommann, 1971, V–VIII).
4. The *Akademie* contributed to the publication of almost thirty books, among which it is worth mentioning the works of Chanoch Albeck (*Untersuchungen über die Redaktion der Mischna*, Berlin: Schwetschke, 1923; *Untersuchungen über die halakischen Midraschim*, Berlin: Akademie-Verlag, 1927), Arthur Spanier (*Die Toseftaperiode in der tannaitischen Literatur*, Berlin: Schwetschke, 1922; *Die massoretischen Akzente*, Berlin: Akademie-Verlag, 1927), Selma Stern (*Der preussische Staat und die Juden*, Berlin: Schwetschke, 1925, 2 voll.), Jacob Gordon (*Der Ich-Begriff bei Hegel, bei*

Cohen und in der südwestdeutschen Schule hinsichtlich der Kategorienlehre untersucht, Hamburg: Hanewacker, 1926), and Fritz Baer (*Das Protokollbuch der Landjudenschaft des Herzogtums Kleve*, Berlin: Schwetschke, 1922).

    5. Cf. Heinrich Meier, "Vorwort zur zweiten Auflage," in Strauss 1996d, XV–XX.

    6. Cf. Gerhard Krüger, "Besprechung von 'Die Religionskritik Spinozas als Grundlage seiner Bibelwissenschaft,'" *Deutsche Literaturzeitung* LI (1931): 2407–12.

    7. Schmitt worked in various phases on Strauss's book on Spinoza. Besides the mention he made of it in his *Der Leviathan in der Staatslehre des Thomas Hobbes* (1938), this note that Löwith addressed to Strauss on 28 June 1956 testifies to it: "Dear Strauss, in our Department library was not present your 1930 book on Spinoza. We have ordered it from an antiquarian catalogue and we have noticed that it is Carl Schmitt's copy with many annotations! A stamp indicates that the book was evidently confiscated by the US authorities in 1945 with its entire library. On the first page Schmitt reported by hand: 1st meeting: Spring 1932; 2nd meeting: Summer 1937; 3rd meeting (1st new meeting): July 1945" (Strauss and Löwith 2001, 683).

    8. Cf. Strauss 2012b. In the 1960s, Strauss published an essay on Mendelssohn that derived from the work he had done in the 1930s for the publication of Mendelssohn's *opera omnia*: cf. Strauss, 1962c. The rest of the texts Strauss wrote in the 1930s on two other works by Mendelssohn appeared after Strauss's death: cf. Strauss 1974b.

    9. For the *Akademie* Strauss prepared a German translation of Gersonides's work, which was never published: cf. Leo Strauss Papers, box 6, folder 2, Special Collections Research Center, University of Chicago Library.

    10. On biblical science's impossibility to refute Jewish faith Strauss had already written in his 1925 essay *Biblische Geschichte und Wissenschaft*, in which he explicitly opposed orthodoxy and enlightenment.

    11. The essay *Die geistige Lage der Gegenwart*, written in February 1932, but not published (cf. Strauss 1997a, 441–64), constitutes a clear representation of Strauss's—chronological and theoretical—path, since he dealt with the spiritual situation of the present, stemming off from the Jewish issue, moving on to the opposition of orthodoxy and Enlightenment, and ending with the *philosophical* opposition of the ancient and modern.

    12. Cf. Strauss's review of Ebbinghaus's book *Über die Fortschritte der Metaphysik*, *Deutsche Literaturzeitung* LI (1931): 2451–53.

    13. Obviously, Schmitt broke off his relationship with Strauss in 1933. The latter did not realize the radical change of the situation. Indeed, on 9 October 1933, Strauss asked Klein if he knew the reason why Schmitt was not answering his letters! Almost with affection for such a naive friend, on 12 October Klein warned him about Schmitt's situation. Evidently Strauss did not grasp this warning, since Klein, on 21 October, explicitly invited him to stop addressing letters to Schmitt

and, a year later, advised him to maintain an absolute silence both on Schmitt and his followers (cf. Strauss and Klein 2001, 474, 477, 481, 525).

14. Cf. Carlo Altini, "Hobbes in der Weimarer Republik. Carl Schmitt, Leo Strauss und die Krise der modernen Welt," *Hobbes Studies* XIX (2006): 3–30.

Chapter Three

1. Cf. Leo Strauss Papers, box 3, folder 8, Special Collections Research Center, University of Chicago Library: correspondence between Strauss and the Rockefeller Foundation. It is worth noting that Koyré had reviewed Strauss's book on Spinoza: cf. "Compte-rendu de *Die Religionskritik Spinozas*," *Revue d'histoire et de philosophie religieuses* XI (1931): 443–49.

2. Cf. Strauss 1988, 132; Strauss and Klein 2001, 457; Strauss and Krüger 2001, 408, 426.

3. A lot of material and documents concerning Hobbes from the early 1930s is present in his archive: cf. Leo Strauss Papers, box 14, folders 13–15; box 15, folders 1–11, Special Collections Research Center, University of Chicago Library.

4. The book Strauss reviewed is Zbigniew Lubienski, *Die Grundlagen des ethisch-politischen Systems von Hobbes* (München: Reinhardt, 1932). Kojève (whose name did not appear in the publication) translated Strauss's typewritten review from German into French.

5. To his interpretation of the Law intended as an all-embracing system that requires obedience, Strauss later found confirmation in Isaac Husik's position: cf. Strauss 1952b.

6. The fact that Strauss reproduced almost word-for-word entire passages from the *Introduction* to *Philosophie und Gesetz* regarding the modernity in his 1962 *Preface* to the English translation of the book on Spinoza, demonstrates the persistence, besides the obvious changes in details, of this general position: cf. Strauss 1965, 28ff.

7. The earliest among Strauss's texts that contain the issue of esotericism/elitism is *Cohen und Maimuni*, an unpublished manuscript of a lecture he held in early May 1931 at the *Hochschule für die Wissenschaft des Judentums* in Berlin: cf. Strauss 1997a, 393–436.

8. Despite the contrasts, Strauss's relationship with Guttmann always remained open. A testimony lies in their correspondence: cf. Leo Strauss Papers, box 1, folder 14, Special Collections Research Center, University of Chicago Library.

9. Cf. *The Correspondence of Walter Benjamin and Gershom Scholem: 1932–1940* (Cambridge: Harvard University Press, 1992).

10. Cf. Julius Guttmann, "Philosophie der Religion oder Philosophie des Gesetzes?," *Proceedings of the Israel Academy of Sciences and Humanities*, no. 6 (1976): 146–73.

Chapter Four

1. "I saw Downing Street, the seat of the greatest power of the world—much, much smaller than the Wilhelmstrasse" (Strauss and Kojève 1991, 223).

2. Cf. Leo Strauss Papers, box 3, folder 14, Special Collections Research Center, University of Chicago Library: letters by Tawney dated 23.3.1934, 1.5.1934, and 26.6.1934.

3. Cf. Leo Strauss Papers, box 4, folder 1, Special Collections Research Center, University of Chicago Library.

4. Cf. Leo Strauss Papers, box 3, folder 14, Special Collections Research Center, University of Chicago Library: letters by Tawney dated 26.6.1934, 20.2.1936, and 5.7.1936. Cf. John U. Nef Papers, box 42, folder 20, Special Collections Research Center, University of Chicago Library: letter by Tawney dated 17.3. 1942.

5. In Strauss's archive we can find the manuscript, entitled *Essayes*, which he copied and the photographs of Hobbes's manuscripts preserved in Chatsworth and at the British Museum, as well as the book proposal Strauss submitted to Cambridge University Press. Cf. Leo Strauss Papers, box 15, folders 5–9, Special Collections Research Center, University of Chicago Library.

6. The caution that English academic authorities forced on Strauss's writing was wrong and unjust. Indeed, in 1995, his proposal was confirmed, since Hobbes was identified as the author of the collection of essays *Horae subsecivae* and therefore of the *Essayes*. Cf. *Three Discourses. A Critical Modern Edition of Newly Identified Work of the Young Hobbes*, edited by Noel B. Reynolds and Arlene W. Saxonhouse (Chicago: University of Chicago Press, 1995).

7. Cf. Max Ascoli, "Book Review of *The Political Philosophy of Hobbes*," *Social Research* IV (1937): 127–30; Carl Badger, "Book Review of *The Political Philosophy of Hobbes*," *Australian Quarterly* IX, no. 3 (1937): 113–15; Hymen Ezra Cohen, "Book Review of *The Political Philosophy of Hobbes*," *American Academy of Political and Social Science*, no. 191 (1937): 252–54; Paul Léon, "Compte-rendu de *The Political Philosophy of Hobbes*," *Archives de philosophie du droit et de sociologie juridique*, no. 1–2 (1937): 220–22; Gordon Brett, "Book Review of *The Political Philosophy of Hobbes*," *University of Toronto Law Journal* (1937/1938): 459–60; George Edward Catlin, "Book Review of *The Political Philosophy of Hobbes*," *Political Science Quarterly* LIII (1938): 447–48; Alphonse de Waelhens, "Compte-rendu de *The Political Philosophy of Hobbes*," *Revue néoscholastique de philosophie* (1938): 458–61.

8. Cf. Michael Oakeshott, "Dr. Strauss on Hobbes," *Politica* II, no. 8 (1937): 364–80; also in Michael Oakeshott, *Hobbes on Civil Association* (Oxford: Blackwell, 1975): 132–49.

9. Cf. Georges Vajda, "Compte-rendu de *Philosophie und Gesetz*," *Revue des études juives* C (1935): 80–82; Shlomo Pines, "Compte-rendu de *Philosophie und Gesetz*," *Recherches philosophiques* V (1936): 504–7. The volume is also reviewed by

Ludwig Feuchtwanger: "Besprechung von *Philosophie und Gesetz,*" *Jüdische Rundschau* XXIX, no. 9 (1935): 7.

10. In the second half of the 1930s, Strauss published three important essays on Maimonides and Al-Farabi: cf. Strauss 1936a; Strauss 1936b; Strauss 1937a.

11. Cf. Strauss 1937b. Here Strauss marks the differences between Maimonides and Abravanel both on the hermeneutical and political level. Indeed, in respect to Maimonides, Abravanel does not make any use of esoteric writing, nor does he value the problem of esotericism in considering the divine law or the relationship between philosophy and revelation. Moreover, Strauss criticizes Abravanel's messianic and utopic doctrines—influenced by Christian scholastics—to conclude, almost in an ironic tone in respect to the essay's title, that his rationalism is more anti-philosophical than philosophical and that his practical orientation is more anti-political than political.

12. On Al-Farabi's skepticism cf. Strauss 1936b, 98–99 and 105–6, where Strauss—returning to the political character of the prophetical revelation—underlines the Islamic philosopher's lack of interest for the use of quotations from the Qur'an inside his works and for the identification of a concordance between the doctrines of revelation and the truths of philosophy. The books written by Al-Farabi are therefore not "Islamic," but philosophical.

Chapter Five

1. Cf. *Encounters and Reflections. Conversations with Seth Benardete*, edited by Ronna Burger (Chicago: University of Chicago Press, 2002): 34ff.

2. Cf. Strauss, 1939; 1986. Cf. also Strauss's review of the edition prepared by Moses Hyamson of Maimonides's *Mishneh Torah, Review of Religion* III, no. 4 (1939): 448–56.

3. Cf. Eric Voegelin, "Book Review of *On Tyranny,*" *Review of Politics* II (1949): 241–44; Leo Strauss, *Restatement on Xenophon's "Hiero,"* in Strauss 1959b, 95–104.

4. Cf. Leo Strauss Papers, box 1, folder 4, Special Collections Research Center, University of Chicago Library: letter by Ernest Barker dated 23 September 1945.

5. For the complete list of courses taught by Strauss at the New School cf. Strauss 2018a, 6ff., 285ff.

6. Cf. John U. Nef Papers, box 42, folder 21, Special Collections Research Center, University of Chicago Library: letters by Tawney dated 17.3.1942 and 22.3.1942.

7. On the difficult social position of American Jews and on the persisting discriminations inside a liberal society cf. Strauss 1994: 45–49.

8. Cf. the letter addressed by Strauss to Gadamer on 26.2.1961 (Strauss and Gadamer 1978).

9. On Maimonides's reticent writing and on the existence of two public images of this author (Maimonides the halakhist and Maimonides the philosopher) and on the difference between *Mishneh Torah* and the *Guide of the Perplexed*, Strauss already wrote two years before, reviewing an edition of the *Mishneh Torah* by Moses Hyamson (*Review of Religion* III, no. 4 [1939]: 448–56), where he asserts that this work—despite being addressed "to all men" and therefore exoteric—should still be read through the distinction between esoteric and exoteric.

10. The superiority of speculative life on moral life is a typical trait of Strauss's thought regarding all pre-modern philosophy. On this superiority, in very similar terms to the ones he used for the *Guide*, Strauss also wrote about Yehuda ha-Levi's *Kuzari*: cf. Strauss 1943.

Chapter Six

1. Cf. Leo Strauss Papers, box 3, folder 14, Special Collections Research Center, University of Chicago Library: letters by Tawney dated 7.1.1949, 31.3.1949, 10.7.1950, 19.7.1950, and 10.4.1951.

2. Cf. Edward S. Shils, "Robert Maynard Hutchins, 1899–1977," in *Remembering the University of Chicago*, edited by Edward S. Shils, 185–96. Chicago: University of Chicago Press, 1991.

3. *Encounters and Reflections. Conversations with Seth Benardete*, edited by Ronna Burger (Chicago: University of Chicago Press, 2002): 48.

4. Cf. Strauss, 1979; 1981b; 1994; 1995a; 1997b; 2013; 2018c; 2021. Cf. also the page dedicated to the recordings of his lectures on the *Leo Strauss Center* website: https://leostrausscenter.uchicago.edu/occasional-lectures.

5. For the complete list of courses held by Strauss in Chicago cf. George Anastaplo, *Leo Strauss at the University of Chicago*, in Deutsch and Murley 1999, 3–30. Cf. also the page dedicated to his course in the *Leo Strauss Center* website: https://leostrausscenter.uchicago.edu/audio-transcripts/courses-audio-transcripts.

6. Cf. John G.A. Pocock, "Prophet and Inquisitor: or, a Church Built upon Bayonets Cannot Stand," *Political Theory* III (1975): 385–401; Myles F. Burnyeat, "Sphinx Without a Secret," *The New York Review of Books*, May 30, 1985, 30–36; Shadia B. Drury, *The Political Ideas of Leo Strauss* (New York: St. Martin's Press, 1987, 2005²); Gordon S. Wood, "The Fundamentalists and the Constitution,": *The New York Review of Books* XXXV, no. 2, February 2, 1988, 33–40; Stephen Holmes, "Truths for Philosophers Alone?," *The Times Literary Supplement*, December 1–7, 1989, 1319–24; Brent Staples, "Undemocratic Vistas," *New York Times*, November 28, 1994, 16; Shadia B. Drury, *Leo Strauss and the American Right* (London: MacMillan, 1997); Anne Norton, *Leo Strauss and the Politics of American Empire* (New Haven: Yale University Press, 2004); Nicholas Xenos, *Cloaked in Virtue. Unveiling Leo Strauss*

and the Rhetoric of American Foreign Policy (New York: Routledge, 2008); Aggie Hirst, *Leo Strauss and the Invasion of Iraq* (London: Routledge, 2013).

7. Cf. Elisabeth Young-Bruehl, *Hannah Arendt. For Love of the World* (New Haven: Yale University Press, 1982): 98.

8. Cf. Hannah Arendt und Karl Blumenfeld, *". . . in keinem Besitz verwurzelt." Die Korrespondenz*, herausgegeben von Ingeborg Nordmann und Iris Pilling (Hamburg: Rotbuch Verlag, 1995), 141.

9. Cf. ibid., 149–50.

10. Cf. Hannah Arendt and Karl Jaspers, *Correspondence 1926–1969*, edited by Lotte Köhler and Hans Saner (New York: Harcourt Brace Jovanovich, 1992): letters dated 14 May 1954 (Jaspers to Arendt), 24 July 1954 (Arendt to Jaspers), and 29 August 1954 (Jaspers to Arendt).

11. Cf. their correspondence, that is preserved among the Leo Strauss Papers, box 1, folder 14, Special Collections Research Center, University of Chicago Library.

12. Cf. Strauss 1953a; 1956b. The "American" destination of his arguments continued in some 1960s essays: cf. Strauss 1962a; 1962b; 1963a.

13. Besides the review of John W. Gough, "John Locke's Political Philosophy," *American Political Science Review* XLIV, no. 3 (1950): 767–70, cf. Strauss 1957b; 1958a.

14. Cf. the review of Yves R. Simon, "Philosophy of Democratic Government," *New Scholasticism* XXVI, no. 3 (1952): 379–83.

15. "Preface to the American Edition," in Leo Strauss, *The Political Philosophy of Hobbes* (Chicago: University of Chicago Press, 1952): XV–XVI.

16. Cf. Eric Voegelin, "Book Review of *On Tyranny*," *Review of Politics* II (1949): 241–44.

17. Cf. "Mise au point," in Leo Strauss, *De la tyrannie*, traduit par Hélène Kern (Paris: Gallimard, 1954): 283–344. The English original appeared under the title "Restatement on Xenophon's *Hiero*," in Leo Strauss, *What Is Political Philosophy?* (Glencoe: Free Press, 1959): 95–133.

18. Cf. Alexandre Kojève, "L'action politique des philosophes," *Critique*, no. 41 (1950): 46–55; no. 42: 138–55.

19. Cf. book review of Macpherson's *The Political Theory of Possessive Individualism* (*Southwestern Social Science Quarterly* XLV, no. 1 (1964): 69–70) and book review of Mintz's *The Hunting of Leviathan*, *Modern Philology* LXII (1965): 251.

20. Cf. "Comment on W.S. Hudson, *The Weber Thesis Reexamined*," *Church History* XXX, no. 1 (1961): 100–2.

21. Cf. Joel Kraemer and Josef Stern, "Shlomo Pines on the Translation of Maimonides' *Guide of the Perplexed*," *Journal of Jewish Thought and Philosophy* VIII (1998): 13–24.

22. In his correspondence with Scholem, Strauss severely expressed himself about a renowned supporter of apocalypticism, Jacob Taubes. Scholem expressed himself in the same way, possibly even more severely. These criticisms were also

due to personal reasons, as well as theoretical ones: cf. Strauss and Scholem 2001, 727–28, 735–36.

23. For Strauss's criticism of messianism—and of the idea of progress—cf. Strauss 1981b.

Chapter Seven

1. Since 2 June 1967, Strauss wrote to Willmoore Kendall that he was impatient to move to Claremont, because the climate there (and, hopefully, the moral and political atmosphere) appeared more convenient for his health: cf. Strauss and Kendall 2002, 257.

2. Cf. Berns et al. 1973; Anastaplo 1974; Bloom 1974; Himmelfarb 1974; Schaefer 1974; White 1974; Altmann 1975; Cropsey 1975; Dannhauser 1975; Lerner 1976; Berns 1978.

3. A particularly relevant trace of Plato's centrality in Strauss's thought appears, as well as in his numerous publications, in the long list of courses and seminars on the Greek philosopher that Strauss held in Chicago: cf. Deutsch and Murley 1999.

Bibliography

Leo Strauss's Writings

1921. *Das Erkenntnisproblem in der philosophischen Lehre Fr. H. Jacobis.* Dissertation, Hamburg.
1923a. "Antwort auf das Prinzipielle Wort der Frankfurter." *Jüdische Rundschau* XXVIII, no. 9: 45–46.
1923b. "Anmerkung zur Diskussion über Zionismus und Antisemitismus." *Jüdische Rundschau* XXVIII, no. 8x3–84: 501–2.
1923c. "Das Heilige." *Der Jude* VII, no. 4: 240–42.
1923d. "Der Zionismus bei Nordau." *Der Jude* VII, no. 10–11: 657–60.
1924a. "Paul de Lagarde." *Der Jude* VIII, no. 1: 8–15.
1924b. "Soziologische Geschichtsschreibung?" *Der Jude* VIII, no. 3: 190–92.
1924c. "Cohens Analyse der Bibelwissenschaft Spinozas." *Der Jude* VIII, no. 5–6: 295–314.
1924d. "Zur Auseinandersetzung mit der europäischen Wissenschaft." *Der Jude* VIII, no. 10: 613–17.
1924e. "Zionismus und Orthodoxie." *Jüdische Rundschau* XXIX: 302.
1924f. "Quellen des Zionismus." *Jüdische Rundschau* XXIX, no. 77–78: 558; no. 79: 566.
1925a. "Ecclesia militans." *Jüdische Rundschau* XXX, no. 36: 334.
1925b. "Biblische Geschichte und Wissenschaft." *Jüdische Rundschau* XXX, no. 88: 744–45.
1925c. "Bemerkung zu der Weinbergschen Kritik." *Der jüdische Student* XXII, no. 1–2: 15–18.
1926. "Zur Bibelwissenschaft Spinozas und seiner Vorläufer." *Korrespondenzblatt des Vereins zur Gründung und Erhaltung einer Akademie für die Wissenschaft des Judentums* VII: 1–22.
1928. "Die Zukunft einer Illusion." *Der jüdische Student* XXV, no. 4: 16–22.
1929a. "Zur Ideologie des politischen Zionismus." *Der jüdische Student* XXVI, no. 5: 22–27.

1929b. "Franz Rosenzweig und die Akademie für die Wissenschaft des Judentums." *Jüdische Wochenzeitung für Kassel, Hessen und Waldeck* VI, no. 49, 13.12.1929: 2.
1930. *Die Religionskritik Spinozas als Grundlage seiner Bibelwissenschaft. Untersuchungen zu Spinozas Theologisch-politischem Traktat*. Berlin: Akademie-Verlag.
1931a. "Introduction." In *Pope ein Metaphysiker!; Sendschreiben an den Herrn Magister Lessing in Leipzig; Kommentar zu den "Termini der Logik" des Moses ben Maimon; Abhandlung über die Evidenz*; in Moses Mendelssohn, *Gesammelte Schriften: Jubiläumsausgabe*, vol. II: *Schriften zur Philosophie und Ästhetik II*, XV–XXIII; XLI; XLV–LIII; 379–96; 408–11; 416–28. Berlin, Akademie-Verlag.
1931b. "Book Review of Julius Ebbinghaus, *Über die Fortschritte der Metaphysik*." *Deutsche Literaturzeitung* LI: 2451–53.
1932a. "Introduction." In *Phädon; Abhandlung von der Unkörperlichkeit der menschlichen Seele; Über einen schriftlichen Aufsatz des Herrn de Luc; Die Seele*; in Moses Mendelssohn, *Gesammelte Schriften: Jubiläumsausgabe*. Berlin: Akademie-Verlag, vol. III, t. I: *Schriften zur Philosophie und Ästhetik III.1*, XIII–XLI: 391–437.
1932b. "Anmerkungen zu Carl Schmitt *Der Begriff des Politischen*." *Archiv für Sozialwissenschaft und Sozialpolitik* LXVII, no. 6: 732–49.
1932c. "Das Testament Spinozas." *Bayerische Israelitische Gemeindezeitung* VIII, no. 21: 322–26.
1933. "Quelques remarques sur la science politique de Hobbes." *Recherches Philosophiques* II: 609–22.
1934. "Maimunis Lehre von der Prophetie und ihre Quellen." *Le Monde Oriental* XXVIII: 99–139.
1935. *Philosophie und Gesetz. Beiträge zum Verständnis Maimunis und seiner Vorläufer*. Berlin: Schocken Verlag. Translated by Eve Adler, *Philosophy and Law. Contributions to the Understanding of Maimonides and his Predecessors*. Albany: State University of New York Press, 1995.
1936a. "Quelques remarques sur la science politique de Maimonide et de Farabi." *Revue des Etudes Juives* C: 1–37.
1936b. "Eine vermisste Schrift Farabis." *Monatsschrift für Geschichte und Wissenschaft des Judentums* LXXX, no. 1: 96–106.
1936c. *The Political Philosophy of Hobbes. Its Basis and Its Genesis*. Translated by Elsa M. Sinclair. Oxford: Clarendon Press.
1937a. "Der Ort der Vorsehungslehre nach der Ansicht Maimunis." *Monatsschrift für Geschichte und Wissenschaft des Judentums* LXXXI, no. 1: 93–105.
1937b. "On Abravanel's Philosophical Tendency and Political Teaching." In *Isaac Abravanel. Six Lectures*, edited by John B. Trend and Herbert Loewe, 93–129. Cambridge: Cambridge University Press.
1939. "The Spirit of Sparta or the Taste of Xenophon." *Social Research* VI, no. 4: 502–36.
1941a. "Persecution and the Art of Writing." *Social Research* VIII, no. 4: 488–504.
1941b. "The Literary Character of *The Guide of the Perplexed*." In *Essays on Maimon-*

ides, edited by Salo Wittmayer Baron, 37–91. New York: Columbia University Press.

1943. "The Law of Reason in the *Kuzari*." *Proceedings of the American Academy for Jewish Research* XIII: 47–96.

1945a. "Farabi's Plato." In *Louis Ginzberg Jubilee Volume*, edited by Salo Wittmayer Baron, 357–93. New York: American Academy for Jewish Research.

1945b. "On Classical Political Philosophy." *Social Research* XII, no. 1: 98–117.

1946. "On a New Interpretation of Plato's Political Philosophy." *Social Research* XIII, no. 3: 326–67.

1947. "On the Intention of Rousseau." *Social Research* XIV, no. 4: 455–87.

1948a. "How to Study Spinoza's *Theologico-Political Treatise*." *Proceedings of the American Academy for Jewish Research* XVII: 69–131.

1948b (1963²). *On Tyranny. An Interpretation of Xenophon's "Hiero."* New York: Political Science Classics.

1949. "Political Philosophy and History." *Journal of the History of Ideas* X, no. 1: 30–50.

1950a. "On the Spirit of Hobbes' Political Philosophy." *Revue Internationale de Philosophie* IV, no. 14: 405–31.

1950b. "Natural Right and the Historical Approach." *Review of Politics* XII, no. 4: 422–42.

1951. "The Social Science of Max Weber." *Measure* II, no. 2: 204–30.

1952a. "The Origin of the Idea of Natural Right." *Social Research*, XIX, no. 1: 23–60.

1952b. "On Husik's Work in Medieval Jewish Philosophy." In Isaac Husik, *Philosophical Essays: Ancient, Medieval and Modern*, edited by Milton C. Nahm and Leo Strauss, VII–XLI. Oxford: Basil Blackwell.

1952c. "On Collingwood's Philosophy of History." *Review of Metaphysics* V, no. 4: 559–86.

1952d. *Persecution and the Art of Writing*. Glencoe: Free Press.

1952e. "On Locke's Doctrine of Natural Right." *Philosophical Review* LXI, no. 4: 475–502.

1953a. "Walker's Machiavelli." *Review of Metaphysics* VI, no. 3: 437–46.

1953b. *Natural Right and History*. Chicago: University of Chicago Press.

1953c. "Maimonides' Statement on Political Science." *Proceedings of the American Academy for Jewish Research* XXII: 115–30.

1954a. "On a Forgotten Kind of Writing." *Chicago Review* VIII, no. 1: 64–75.

1954b. "Les fondements de la philosophie politique de Hobbes." *Critique* X, no. 83: 338–62.

1956a. "Kurt Riezler, 1882–1955." *Social Research* XXIII, no. 1: 3–34.

1956b. "Social Science and Humanism." In *The State of the Social Sciences*, edited by Leonard D. White, 415–25. Chicago: University of Chicago Press.

1957a. "How Farabi Read Plato's *Laws*." In *Mélanges Louis Massignon*, vol. III, 319–44. Damas: Institut Français de Damas.

1957b. "Machiavelli's Intention: *The Prince*." *American Political Science Review* LI, no. 1: 13–40.

1957c. "What is Political Philosophy?" *Journal of Politics* XIX, no. 3: 343–68.
1957d. "The State of Israel." *National Review* III, no. 1: 23.
1958a. "Locke's Doctrine of Natural Law." *American Political Science Review* LII, no. 2: 490–501.
1958b. *Thoughts on Machiavelli*. Glencoe: Free Press.
1959a. "The Liberalism of Classical Political Philosophy." *Review of Metaphysics* XII, no. 3: 390–439.
1959b. *What is Political Philosophy? And Other Studies*. Glencoe: Free Press.
1961a. "Relativism." In *Relativism and the Study of Man*, edited by Helmut Schoeck, and James W. Wiggins, 135–57. Princeton: Van Nostrand.
1961b. "What is Liberal Education?" In *Education for Public Responsibility*, edited by C. Scott Fletcher. New York: Norton.
1962a. "Liberal Education and Responsibility." In *Education. The Challenge Ahead*, edited by C. Scott Fletcher, 49–70. New York: Norton.
1962b. "An Epilogue." In *Essays on the Scientific Study of Politics*, edited by Herbert J. Storing, 307–27. New York: Holt-Rinehart & Winston.
1962c. "Zu Mendelssohns *Sache Gottes oder die gerettete Vorsehung*." In *Einsichten. Gerhard Krüger zum 60. Geburtstag*, herausgegeben von Klaus Oehler und Richard Schaeffler, 361–75. Frankfurt a/M: Klostermann.
1963a. "Replies to Schaar and Wolin." *American Political Science Review* LVII, no. 1: 152–55.
1963b (1972²). *History of Political Philosophy*, edited by Leo Strauss and Joseph Cropsey. Chicago: Rand McNally.
1963c. "How to Begin to Study *The Guide of the Perplexed*." In Maimonides, *The Guide of the Perplexed*, XI–LVI. Translated by Shlomo Pines. Chicago: University of Chicago Press.
1963d. "Perspectives on the Good Society." *Criterion* II, no. 3: 1–8.
1964a. *The City and Man*. Chicago: Rand McNally.
1964b. "The Crisis of Our Time." In *The Predicament of Modern Politics*, edited by Harold J. Spaeth, 41–54. Detroit: University of Detroit Press.
1964c. "The Crisis of Political Philosophy." In *The Predicament of Modern Politics*, edited by Harold J. Spaeth, 91–103. Detroit: University of Detroit Press.
1965. "Preface to the English Translation." In L. Strauss, *Spinoza's Critique of Religion*, 1–31. New York: Schocken Books.
1966. *Socrates and Aristophanes*. New York: Basic Books.
1967a. *Jerusalem and Athens. Some Preliminary Reflections*. New York: The City College.
1967b. "John Locke as 'Authoritarian.'" *Intercollegiate Review* IV, no. 1: 46–48.
1967c. "A Note on Lucretius." In *Natur und Geschichte. Karl Löwith zum 70. Geburtstag*, herausgegeben von Hermann Braun und Manfred Riedel, 322–32. Stuttgart: Kohlhammer Verlag.
1967d. "Notes on Maimonides' *Book of Knowledge*." In *Studies in Mysticism and Religion Presented to Gershom Scholem on His Seventieth Birthday*, edited by

Ephraim Elimelech Urbach, Raphael Jehudah Zwi Werblowsky, and Chaim Wirszubski, 269–83. Jerusalem: Magnes Press and Hebrew University.
1968a. "Natural Law." In *International Encyclopaedia of the Social Sciences*, vol. II, 80–90. London: MacMillan.
1968b. "Greek Historians." *Review of Metaphysics* XXI, no. 4: 656–66.
1968c. *Liberalism Ancient and Modern*. New York: Basic Books.
1970a. *Xenophon's Socratic Discourse. An Interpretation of the "Oeconomicus."* Ithaca: Cornell University Press.
1970b. "Machiavelli and Classical Literature." *Review of National Literatures* I, no. 1: 7–25.
1970c. "On the *Euthydemus*." *Interpretation* I, no. 1: 1–20.
1970d. "A Giving of Accounts." with Jacob Klein. *The College* XXII, no. 1: 1–5.
1971. "Philosophy as Rigorous Science and Political Philosophy." *Interpretation* II, no. 1: 1–9.
1972a. *Xenophon's Socrates*. Ithaca: Cornell University Press.
1972b. "Introductory Essay." In Hermann Cohen, *Religion of Reason out of the Sources of Judaism*, XXIII–XXXVIII. New York: Frederick Ungar.
1972c. "Niccolò Machiavelli." In *History of Political Philosophy*, edited by Leo Strauss and Joseph Cropsey, 271–92. Chicago: Rand McNally.
1973. "Note on the Plan of Nietzsche's *Beyond Good and Evil*." *Interpretation* III, no. 2–3: 97–113.
1974a. "Preliminary Observations on the Gods in Thucydides' Work." *Interpretation* IV, 1974, no. 1: 1–16.
1974b. "Einleitungen zu Morgenstunden"; "An die Freunde Lessings." In Moses Mendelssohn, *Gesammelte Schriften: Jubiläumsausgabe*, vol. III, t. II: *Schriften zur Philosophie und Ästhetik III.2*, herausgegeben von Alexander Altmann, XI–XCV; 277–342. Stuttgart: Frommann Verlag.
1975a. *The Argument and the Action of Plato's "Laws,"* edited by Joseph Cropsey. Chicago: University of Chicago Press.
1975b. "Xenophon's Anabasis." Edited by Joseph Cropsey. *Interpretation* V, no. 3: 117–47.
1976. "On Plato's *Apology of Socrates* and *Crito*." In *Essays in Honor of Jacob Klein*, edited by Samuel S. Kutler et al., 155–70. Annapolis: St. John's College.
1978a. "An Unspoken Prologue to a Public Lecture at St. John's College." *Interpretation* VII, no. 3: 1–3.
1978b. "Letter to Helmut Kuhn." *The Independent Journal of Philosophy* II: 23–26.
1979. "The Mutual Influence of Theology and Philosophy." Edited by Aryeh Leo Motzkin. *The Independent Journal of Philosophy* III: 111–18.
1981a. *On the Interpretation of "Genesis."* Edited by Nicolas Ruwet. *L'Homme*, XXI, no. 1: 5–20.
1981b. "Progress or Return? The Contemporary Crisis in Western Civilization." *Modern Judaism* I, no. 1: 17–45.

1983. *Studies in Platonic Political Philosophy*, edited by Joseph Cropsey and Thomas L. Pangle. Chicago: University of Chicago Press.
1986. "Exoteric Teaching." Edited by Kenneth Hart Green. *Interpretation* XIV, 1986, no. 1: 51–59.
1988. "Drei Briefe an Carl Schmitt." In Heinrich Meier, *Carl Schmitt, Leo Strauss und "Der Begriff des Politischen,"* 129–39. Stuttgart: Metzler.
1989. *The Rebirth of Classical Political Rationalism. An Introduction to the Thought of Leo Strauss*, edited by Thomas L. Pangle. Chicago: University of Chicago Press.
1991 (2000²). *On Tyranny*, edited by Victor Gourevitch and Michael S. Roth. New York: Free Press.
1994. "Why We Remain Jews. Can Jewish Faith and History Still Speak to Us?" In *Leo Strauss. Political Philosopher and Jewish Thinker*, edited by Kenneth L. Deutsch and Walter Nicgorski, 43–79. Lanham: Rowman & Littlefield.
1995a. "Existentialism." Edited by David Bolotin and Christopher Bruell. *Interpretation* XXII, n. 3: 301–20.
1995b. "The Problem of Socrates." Edited by David Bolotin and Christopher Bruell. *Interpretation* XXII, n. 3: 321–38.
1996a. "An Untitled Lecture on Plato's *Euthyphron*." Edited by David Bolotin and Christopher Bruell. *Interpretation* XXIV, no. 1: 3–23.
1996b. "The Origins of Political Science and the Problem of Socrates." Edited by David Bolotin and Christopher Bruell. *Interpretation* XXIII, no. 2: 127–207.
1996c. "How to Study Medieval Philosophy." Edited by David Bolotin and Christopher Bruell. *Interpretation* XXIII, no. 3: 319–38.
1996d (2001²) (2008³). *Gesammelte Schriften. Band I: Die Religionskritik Spinozas und zugehörige Schriften*, herausgegeben von Heinrich Meier. Stuttgart: Metzler Verlag.
1997a (2013²). *Gesammelte Schriften. Band II: Philosophie und Gesetz–Frühe Schriften*, herausgegeben von Heinrich Meier. Stuttgart: Metzler Verlag.
1997b. *Jewish Philosophy and the Crisis of Modernity*, edited by Kenneth Hart Green. Albany: State University of New York Press.
1999. "German Nihilism." Edited by David Janssens and Daniel Tanguay. *Interpretation* XXVI, no. 3: 353–78.
2001a (2008²). *Gesammelte Schriften. Band III: Hobbes' politische Wissenschaft und zugehörige Schriften–Briefe*, herausgegeben von Heinrich Meier. Stuttgart: Metzler Verlag.
2001b. *On Plato's "Symposium,"* edited by Seth Benardete. Chicago: University of Chicago Press.
2002a. "Vieles Gewaltige gibt es, doch nichts ist gewaltiger als der Mensch." In *475 Jahre Gymnasium Philippinum. Zukunft braucht Erfahrung: eine Festschrift*, herausgegeben von Erdmute Johanna Pickerodt-Uthleb, 123–26. Marburg: Gymnasium Philippinum.

2002b. *The Early Writings (1921–1932)*, edited by Michael Zank. Albany: State University of New York Press.

2006a. "The Living Issues of German Postwar Philosophy." In Heinrich Meier, *Leo Strauss and the Theologico-Political Problem*, 115–39. Cambridge: Cambridge University Press.

2006b. "Reason and Revelation." In Heinrich Meier, *Leo Strauss and the Theologico-Political Problem*, 141–80. Cambridge: Cambridge University Press.

2007a. "What Can We Learn From Political Theory?" Edited by Nathan Tarcov. *Review of Politics* LXIX: 515–29.

2007b. "The Re-Education of Axis Countries Concerning the Jews." Edited by Nathan Tarcov. *Review of Politics* LXIX: 530–38.

2008a. "Restatement." Edited by Emmanuel Patard. *Interpretation* XXXVI, no. 1: 29–78.

2008b. "Supplement to the Strauss-Kojève Correspondence." Edited by Emmanuel Patard. *Interpretation* XXXVI, no. 1: 79–100.

2012a. "More Early Writings by Leo Strauss from the *Jüdische Wochenzeitung für Kassel, Hessen und Waldeck* (1925–1928)." Edited by Thomas Meyer and Michael Zank. *Interpretation* XXXIX, no. 2: 109–38.

2012b. *Leo Strauss on Moses Mendelssohn*, edited by Martin D. Yaffe. Chicago: University of Chicago Press.

2013. *Leo Strauss on Maimonides. The Complete Writings*, edited by Kenneth Hart Green. Chicago: University of Chicago Press.

2014a. "Leo Strauss on Social and Natural Science. Two Previously Unpublished Papers." Edited by José A. Colen and Svetozar Minkov. *Review of Politics* LXXVI: 619–33.

2014b. "Lecture Notes for *Persecution and the Art of Writing*." Edited by Hannes Kerber. In *Reorentation. Leo Strauss in the 1930s*, edited by Martin D. Yaffe and Richard S. Ruderman, 293–304. New York: Palgrave MacMillan.

2017a. *Leo Strauss on Modern Political Science. Two Previously Unpublished Manuscripts*, edited by Svetozar Minkov and Rasoul Namazi. *Review of Politics* LXXIX: 413–25.

2017b. *Leo Strauss on Nietzsche's "Thus spoke Zarathustra,"* edited by Richard L. Velkley. Chicago: University of Chicago Press.

2017c. "Leo Strauss on Machiavelli's *The Prince* and the *Discourses*. A Recently Discovered Lecture." Edited by Rasoul Namazi. *Interpretation* XLIII, no. 3: 431–59.

2018a. *Toward "Natural Right and History." Lectures and Essays by Leo Strauss, 1937–1946*, edited by José A. Colen and Svetozar Minkov. Chicago: University of Chicago Press.

2018b. *Leo Strauss on Political Philosophy. Responding to the Challenge of Positivism and Historicism*, edited by Catherine H. Zuckert. Chicago: University of Chicago Press.

2018c. "Leo Strauss on Thomas Hobbes and Plato. Two Previously Unpublished Lectures." Edited by Rasoul Namazi. *Perspectives on Political Science*: 1–18.

2019. *Leo Strauss on Hegel*, edited by Paul Franco. Chicago: University of Chicago Press.

2021. "Religion and the Commonweal in the Tradition of Political Philosophy. An Unpublished Lecture by Leo Strauss." Edited by Svetozar Minkov and Rasoul Namazi. *American Political Thought* X: 86–120.

2022. *Leo Strauss on Plato's "Protagoras,"* edited by Robert C. Bartlett. Chicago: University of Chicago Press.

Correspondences

Strauss, Leo, and Hans-Georg Gadamer. 1978. "Correspondence Concerning *Wahrheit und Methode.*" *The Independent Journal of Philosophy* II: 5–12.

Strauss, Leo, and Karl Löwith. 1983. "Correspondence Concerning Modernity." *The Independent Journal of Philosophy* IV: 105–19.

Strauss, Leo, and Karl Löwith. 1988. "Correspondence." *The Independent Journal of Philosophy* V–VI: 177–92.

Strauss, Leo, and Alexandre Kojève. 1991. *The Strauss–Kojève Correspondence*. In Leo Strauss, *On Tyranny*, edited by Victor Gourevitch and Michael S. Roth, 213–325. New York: Free Press.

Strauss, Leo, and Eric Voegelin. 1993. "The Correspondence between Leo Strauss and Eric Voegelin (1934–1964)." In *Faith and Political Philosophy*, edited by Peter Emberley and Barry Cooper. University Park: Pennsylvania State University Press (II edition: Columbia: University of Missouri Press, 2004).

Strauss, Leo, and Jacob Klein. 2001. "Korrespondenz Leo Strauss–Jacob Klein." In Leo Strauss, *Gesammelte Schriften. Band III: Hobbes' politische Wissenschaft*, op. cit., 455–605.

Strauss, Leo, and Gerhard Krüger. 2001. "Korrespondenz Leo Strauss–Gerhard Krüger." In Leo Strauss, *Gesammelte Schriften. Band III*, op. cit., 377–454.

Strauss, Leo, and Karl Löwith. 2001. "Korrespondenz Leo Strauss–Karl Löwith." In Leo Strauss, *Gesammelte Schriften. Band III*, op. cit., 607–97.

Strauss, Leo, and Gershom Scholem. 2001. "Korrespondenz Leo Strauss–Gershom Scholem." In Leo Strauss, *Gesammelte Schriften. Band III*, op. cit., 699–772.

Strauss, Leo, and Willmoore Kendall. 2002. "Correspondence." In *Willmoore Kendall. Maverick of American Conservatives*, edited by John A. Murley and John E. Alvis, 191–261. Lanham: Lexington Books.

Critical Literature

Altini, Carlo. 2000. *Leo Strauss. Linguaggio del potere e linguaggio della filosofia*. Bologna: Il Mulino.

Altini, Carlo. 2001. "Leo Strauss y el 'canon occidental.' La historia de la filosofía como modelo hermenéutico para la filosofía política." *Res Publica* IV, no. 8: 9–34.

Altini, Carlo. 2006a. "Hobbes in der Weimarer Republik. Carl Schmitt, Leo Strauss und die Krise der modernen Welt." *Hobbes Studies* XIX: 3–30.

Altini, Carlo. 2006b. "Beyond Historicism. Collingwood, Strauss, Momigliano." *Interpretation* XXXIV, no. 1: 47–66.

Altini, Carlo. 2014. "Leo Strauss between Politics, Philosophy and Judaism." *History of European Ideas* XL: 437–49.

Altini, Carlo. 2016. "Philosophy and History of Philosophy." In *Leo Strauss, Philosopher*, edited by Antonio Lastra and Josep Monserrat Molas, 15–42. Albany: State University of New York Press.

Altini, Carlo. 2018. "Kabbalah contra Philosophy. Politics, Religion and Hermeneutics in Gershom Scholem and Leo Strauss." In *Issues of Interpretation. Texts, Images, Rites*, edited by Carlo Altini, Philippe Hoffmann, and Jörg Rüpke, 243–52. Stuttgart: Franz Steiner Verlag.

Altini, Carlo. 2019. "Tra gli antichi e i moderni. Qabbalah e filosofia in Gershom Scholem e Leo Strauss." *Rivista di storia della filosofia* LXXIV: 59–85.

Altini, Carlo. 2021. *Una filosofia in esilio. Vita e pensiero di Leo Strauss*. Roma: Carocci.

Altini, Carlo. 2022. "Entre Atenas y Jerusalén. El problema teológico-político en Leo Strauss." In *¿Atenas y Jerusalén? Política, filosofía y religión desde 1945*, edited by Jorge Del Palacio Martín and Guillermo Graíno Ferrer, 44–61. Madrid: Editorial Tecnos.

Altmann, Alexander. 1975. "Leo Strauss (1899–1973)." *Proceedings of the American Academy for Jewish Research* XLI–XLII: XXXIII–XXXVI.

Anastaplo, George. 1974. "On Leo Strauss. A Yahrzeit Remembrance." *The University of Chicago Magazine* 67: 30–38.

Banfield, Edward C. 1991. "Leo Strauss." In *Remembering the University of Chicago*, edited by Edward S. Shils, 490–501. Chicago: University of Chicago Press.

Batnitzky, Leora Faye. 2006. *Leo Strauss and Emmanuel Lévinas. Philosophy and the Politics of Revelation*. Cambridge: Cambridge University Press.

Berns, Laurence. 1978. "Leo Strauss: 1899–1973." *The Independent Journal of Philosophy* II: 1–3.

Berns, Walter, Herbert J. Storing, Werner Dannhauser, and Harry V. Jaffa. 1973. "The Achievement of Leo Strauss." *National Review* XXV: 1347–57.

Bernstein, Jeffrey A. 2015. *Leo Strauss on the Borders of Judaism, Philosophy and History*. Albany: State University of New York Press.

Bloom, Allan. 1974. "Leo Strauss: September 20, 1899–October 18, 1973." *Political Theory* II: 372–92.

Bluhm, Harald. 2002. *Die Ordnung der Ordnung. Das politische Philosophieren von Leo Strauss*. Berlin: Akademie-Verlag.

Bolotin, David. 1994. "Leo Strauss and Classical Political Philosophy." *Interpretation* XXII, no. 1: 129–42.

Brague, Rémi. 1998. "Athens, Jerusalem, Mecca. Leo Strauss's 'Muslim' Understanding of Greek Philosophy." *Poetics Today* XIX: 235–59.

Burns, Timothy W., ed. 2015. *Brill's Companion to Leo Strauss's Writings on Classical Political Thought*. Leiden: Brill.

Burns, Timothy W., and Bryan-Paul Frost, eds. 2016. *Philosophy, History, and Tyranny. Reexamining the Debate between Leo Strauss and Alexandre Kojève*. Albany: State University of New York Press.

Burns, Timothy W., and James Connelly, eds. 2010. *The Legacy of Leo Strauss*. Exeter: Imprint Academic.

Ciccarelli, Pierpaolo. 2018. *Leo Strauss tra Husserl e Heidegger. Filosofia pratica e fenomenologia*. Pisa: Edizioni ETS.

Colen José A., and Svetozar Minkov. 2018. "Introduction." In Leo Strauss, *Toward "Natural Right and History." Lectures and Essays by Leo Strauss, 1937–1946*, edited by José A. Colen and Svetozar Minkov, 1–22. Chicago: University of Chicago Press.

Cropsey, Joseph, ed. 1964. *Ancients and Moderns. Essays on the Tradition of Political Philosophy in Honor of Leo Strauss*. New York: Basic Books.

Cropsey, Joseph. 1975. "Leo Strauss. A Bibliography and Memorial, 1899–1973." *Interpretation* V: 133–47.

Cubeddu, Raimondo. 1983. *Leo Strauss e la filosofia politica moderna*. Napoli: Edizioni Scientifiche Italiane.

Dannhauser, Werner J. 1975. "Leo Strauss. Becoming Naive Again." *The American Scholar* XLIV: 636–42.

Dannhauser, Werner J. 2006. *Leo Strauss in His Letters*. In *Enlightening Revolutions. Essays in Honor of Ralph Lerner*, edited by Svetozar Minkov and Stéphane Douard, 355–61. Lanham: Lexington Books.

Deutsch, Kenneth L., and John A. Murley, eds. 1999. *Leo Strauss, the Straussians and the American Regime*. Lanham: Rowman & Littlefield.

Deutsch, Kenneth L., and Walter Nicgorski, eds. 1994. *Leo Strauss. Political Philosopher and Jewish Thinker*. Lanham: Rowman & Littlefield.

Deutsch, Kenneth L., and Walter Soffer, eds. 1987. *The Crisis of Liberal Democracy. A Straussian Perspective*. Albany: State University of New York Press.

Drury, Shadia B. 1987 (2005²). *The Political Ideas of Leo Strauss*. New York: St. Martin's Press.

Drury, Shadia B. 1997. *Leo Strauss and the American Right*. London: MacMillan.

D'Souza, Dinesh. 1987. "The Legacy of Leo Strauss." *Policy Review* no. 40: 36–43.

East John P. 1977. "Leo Strauss and American Conservatism." *Modern Age* XXI: 2–19.

Fackenheim, Emil L. 1985. "Leo Strauss and Modern Judaism." *Claremont Review of Books* IV, no. 4: 21–23.

Fackenheim, Emil L. 1996. "Jewish Philosophy and the Academy." In *Jewish Philosophy and the Academy*, edited by Emil L. Fackenheim and Raphael Jospe, 23–47. London: Associated University Presses.

Fussi, Alessandra. 2012. *La città nell'anima. Leo Strauss lettore di Platone e Senofonte*. Pisa: Edizioni ETS.
Gadamer, Hans-Georg. 1978. "Recollections of Leo Strauss. An Interview with Hans-Georg Gadamer." *The Newsletter* (Politics Department, University of Dallas) II: 4–7.
Gadamer, Hans-Georg. 1984. "Gadamer on Strauss. An Interview (conducted and edited by Ernest L. Fortin)." *Interpretation* XII: 1–13.
Gourevitch, Victor. 1968. "Philosophy and Politics." *Review of Metaphysics* XXII: 58–84 and 281–328.
Graf Kielmansegg, Peter, Horst Mewes, and Elisabeth Glaser-Schmidt, eds. 1995. *Hannah Arendt and Leo Strauss. German Émigrés and American Political Thought after World War II*. Washington: German Historical Institute and Cambridge University Press.
Green, Kenneth Hart. 1993. *Jew and Philosopher. The Return to Maimonides in the Jewish Thought of Leo Strauss*. Albany: State University of New York Press.
Green, Kenneth Hart. 2013. *Leo Strauss and the Rediscovery of Maimonides*. Chicago: University of Chicago Press.
Green, Simon J. D. 1995. "The Tawney-Strauss Connection. On Historicism and Values in the History of Political Ideas." *Journal of Modern History* LXVII: 255–77.
Gunnell, John G. 1991. "Strauss before Straussianism. Reason, Revelation and Nature." *Review of Politics* LIII, no. 1: 53–74.
Himmelfarb, Milton. 1974. "On Leo Strauss." *Commentary* no. 58: 60–66.
Jaffa, Harry V. 1975. "Leo Strauss: 1899–1973." In Harry V. Jaffa, *The Conditions of Freedom*, 1–5. Baltimore: Johns Hopkins University Press.
Jaffa, Harry V., ed. 2012. *Crisis of the Strauss Divided. Essays on Leo Strauss and Straussianism, East and West*. Lanham: Rowman & Littlefield.
Jaffro, Laurent, Benoît Frydman, Emmanuel Cattin, and Alain Petit, editors. 2001. *Leo Strauss. Art d'écrire, politique, philosophie*. Paris: Vrin.
Janssens, David. 2008. *Between Athens and Jerusalem. Philosophy, Prophecy and Politics in Leo Strauss's Early Thought*. Albany: State University of New York Press.
Kartheininger, Markus. 2006. *Heterogenität. Politische Philosophie im Frühwerk von Leo Strauss*. München: Fink.
Kinzel, Till. 2002. *Platonische Kulturkritik in Amerika*. Berlin: Duncker & Humblot.
Klein, Jacob, Winfree J. Smith, Ted A. Blanton, and Laurence Berns. 1974. "Memorials to Leo Strauss." *The College* XXV: 1–5.
Lampert, Laurence. 1996. *The Enduring Importance of Leo Strauss*. Chicago: University of Chicago Press.
Lastra, Antonio. 2000. *La naturaleza de la filosofía política. Un ensayo sobre Leo Strauss*. Murcia: Res Publica.
Lastra, Antonio, and Josep Monserrat Molas, eds. 2016. *Leo Strauss, Philosopher. European Vistas*. Albany: State University of New York Press.

Lerner, Ralph. 1976. "Leo Strauss (1899–1973)." *American Jewish Yearbook* LXXVI: 91–97.
Malherbe, Michel. 1989. "Leo Strauss, Hobbes et la nature humaine." *Revue de Métaphysique et de Morale* XCIV: 353–67.
Manent, Pierre. 1989. "Strauss et Nietzsche." *Revue de Métaphysique et de Morale* XCIV: 337–45.
Meier, Heinrich. 1988 (1998²). *Carl Schmitt, Leo Strauss und "Der Begriff des Politischen." Zu einem Dialog unter Abwesenden*. Stuttgart: Metzler.
Meier, Heinrich. 1996. *Die Denkbewegung von Leo Strauss. Die Geschichte der Philosophie und die Intention des Philosophen*. Stuttgart: Metzler.
Meier, Heinrich. 2006. *Leo Strauss and the Theologico-Political Problem*. Cambridge: Cambridge University Press.
Merle, Jean-Christophe. 1993. "Leo Strauss et l'idéalisme allemand." *Cahiers de Philosophie Politique et Juridique de l'Université de Caen* no. 23: 137–63.
Minkov, Svetozar. 2016. *Leo Strauss on Science*. Albany: State University of New York Press.
Momigliano, Arnaldo. 1967. "Ermeneutica e pensiero politico classico in Leo Strauss." *Rivista storica italiana* LXXIX 1164–72.
Monserrat, Molas Josep. 2001. "Arte de escribir y filosofía." *Caracteres literarios* IV, no. 5: 11–27.
Murley, John A., ed. 2005. *Leo Strauss and His Legacy. A Bibliography*. Lanham: Lexington Books.
Namazi, Rasoul. 2022. *Leo Strauss and Islamic Political Thought*. Cambridge: Cambridge University Press.
Novak, David, ed. 1996. *Leo Strauss and Judaism. Jerusalem and Athens Critically Revisited*. Lanham: Rowman & Littlefield.
Orr, Susan. 1995. *Jerusalem and Athens. Reason and Revelation in the Work of Leo Strauss*. Lanham: Rowman & Littlefield.
Pangle, Thomas L. 2006. *Leo Strauss. An Introduction to His Thought and Intellectual Legacy*. Baltimore: Johns Hopkins University Press.
Pangle, Thomas L., and Nathan Tarcov. 1987. "Epilogue. Leo Strauss and the History of Political Philosophy." In *History of Political Philosophy*, edited by Leo Strauss and Joseph Cropsey. Chicago: University of Chicago Press.
Parens, Joshua. 2016. *Leo Strauss and the Recovery of Medieval Political Philosophy*. Rochester: University of Rochester Press.
Pelluchon, Corine. 2005. *Leo Strauss: une autre raison, d'autres lumières. Essai sur la crise de la rationalité contemporaine*. Paris: Vrin.
Schaefer, David L. 1974. "The Legacy of Leo Strauss. A Bibliographic Introduction." *The Intercollegiate Review* IX, no. 3: 139–48.
Schröder, Winfried. 2015. *Reading between the Lines. Leo Strauss and the History of Early Modern Philosophy*. Berlin: de Gruyter.
Sfez, Gérald. 2007. *Leo Strauss, foi et raison*. Paris: Beauchesne.

Sheppard, Eugene R. 2006. *Leo Strauss and the Politics of Exile. The Making of a Political Philosopher*. Waltham: Brandeis University Press.

Smith, Steven B. 2006. *Reading Leo Strauss. Politics, Philosophy, Judaism*. Chicago: University of Chicago Press.

Smith, Steven B., ed. 2009. *The Cambridge Companion to Leo Strauss*. Cambridge: Cambridge University Press.

Sorensen, Kim A. 2006. *Discourses on Strauss. Revelation and Reason in Leo Strauss and His Critical Study of Machiavelli*. Notre Dame: University of Notre Dame Press.

Steiner, Stephan. 2013. *Weimar in Amerika. Leo Strauss' Politische Philosophie*. Tübingen: Mohr Siebeck.

Tamer, Georges. 2001. *Islamische Philosophie und die Krise der Moderne. Das Verhältnis von Leo Strauss zu Alfarabi, Avicenna und Averroes*. Leiden: Brill.

Tanguay, Daniel. 2003 (2005²). *Leo Strauss. Une biographie intellectuelle*. Paris: Grasset.

Tarcov, Nathan. 1991. "On a Certain Critique of 'Straussianism.'" *Review of Politics* LIII, no. 1: 3–18.

Taylor, Simon W. 2017. "Between Philosophy and Judaism. Leo Strauss's Skeptical Engagement with Zionism." *Journal of the History of Ideas* LXXVIII: 95–116.

Udoff, Alan, ed. 1991. *Leo Strauss's Thought. Toward a Critical Engagement*. Boulder: Lynne Rienner Publishers.

Velkley, Richard L. 2011. *Heidegger, Strauss and the Premises of Philosophy*. Chicago: University of Chicago Press.

Weichert, Ulrike. 2013. *Von der Geschichte zur Natur. Die politische Hermeneutik von Leo Strauss*. Berlin: Duncker & Humblot.

White, Howard B. 1974. "Leo Strauss: 1899–1973." *Social Research* XLI: 3–4.

Wussow, Philipp von. 2020. *The Philosophy of Leo Strauss*. Albany: State University of New York Press.

Yaffe, Martin D. 1992. *Autonomy, Community, Authority. Hermann Cohen, Carl Schmitt, Leo Strauss*. In *Autonomy and Judaism*, edited by Daniel H. Frank, 143–60. Albany: State University of New York Press.

Yaffe, Martin D., and Richard S. Ruderman, eds. 2014. *Reorientation. Leo Strauss in the 1930s*. New York: Palgrave Macmillan.

Zank, Michael. 2002. "Introduction." In Leo Strauss, *The Early Writings (1921–1932)*, edited by Michael Zank, 3–49. Albany: State University of New York Press.

Zuckert, Catherine H., and Michael P. Zuckert. 2006. *The Truth about Leo Strauss. Political Philosophy and American Democracy*. Chicago: University of Chicago Press.

Zuckert, Catherine H., and Michael P. Zuckert. 2014. *Leo Strauss and the Problem of Political Philosophy*. Chicago: University of Chicago Press.

Index

Abravanel, Isaac, 19, 47, 109, 111, 220
Adler, Cyrus, 87
Adler, Mortimer, 115, 148
Akademie für die Wissenschaft des Judentums, 19, 30, 41–42, 45, 216
Albeck, Chanoch, 216
Albo, Joseph, 19
Alcibiades, 135
Al-Farabi, 3, 5, 8, 46–48, 53, 66, 72, 77, 95, 109–112, 116, 119–121, 124, 139–142, 163, 167, 172, 208, 220
Alienation, 38–39, 54, 97, 129
Al-Razi, 47, 53
Altini, Carlo, 218
Altmann, Alexander, 154, 216, 223
Anastaplo, George, 157, 160, 162, 221, 223
Ancient and Medieval Rationalism, 47–48, 54, 57, 75–76, 82–84, 93–96, 109, 116, 136
Ancient Greek Philosophy, 5–8, 48, 55, 100–102, 108–112, 117–118, 138–146, 172–174, 189–194, 201–214
Antimodernism, 2, 6, 12–13, 16–17, 58, 93–94, 128–130
Antisemitism, 12, 15, 20, 27, 130–132
Arendt, Hannah, 163–165, 222
Aristophanes, 66, 150, 155, 189–190, 202

Aristotle, 18–19, 38, 67, 75, 79–80, 90, 98–101, 109, 111, 115–116, 124–125, 151–153, 155, 164, 168–169, 172, 189–191, 193, 195, 202, 204–205
Arkes, Hadley, 160
Aron, Raymond, 67, 149
Asch, Solomon, 125
Ascoli, Max, 219
Assimilationism, 15, 20–21, 23, 28–29, 32–36, 43, 46
Athenian Stranger, 210–211, 213
Austen, Jane, 85
Averroes (Ibn-Rushd), 44, 46–49, 53, 66, 68, 72–73, 77, 109–110, 151, 200
Avicenna (Ibn Sina), 46–48, 53, 66, 72–74, 77, 109–110, 208

Bachhofer, Ludwig, 149
Bacon, Francis, 91, 98, 152
Badger, Carl, 219
Baeck, Leo, 41, 151
Baer, Fritz, 43, 81, 93, 217
Bakunin, Mikhail, 62
Bamberger, Fritz, 43, 86, 216
Baneth, David Hartwig, 81
Banfield, Edward C., 14, 159–160
Barber, Sotirios A., 160
Barker, Ernest, 89, 92, 114, 122, 148, 220

240 | Index

Baron, Salo Wittmayer, 115
Barth, Karl, 17
Bataille, Georges, 67
Beard, Charles, 123
Bellow, Saul, 5
Benardete, Seth, 149, 151, 160
Benjamin, Walter, 15, 37, 66, 73, 82, 93, 197
Bentham, Jeremy, 152
Bergbohm, Carl, 70
Berlin, Isaiah, 171, 187
Berns, Laurence, 152, 158, 160, 196, 223
Berns, Walter, 152, 160, 223
Bernsohn, Miriam, 66
Bible, 22, 33–34, 45, 49, 51, 125, 136, 179, 200, 216
Biblical Science, 33–36, 44–45, 49–52, 68, 70, 136, 187–188
Bismarck, Otto von, 27
Blackstone, William, 152
Blanckenhagen, Peter Heinrich von, 149, 151
Blanton, Ted A., 196, 235
Bloch, Ernst, 86
Bloom, Allan, 5, 151–152, 160, 223
Blumenfeld, Kurt, 164, 222
Bolotin, David, 160
Borkenau, Franz, 97
Borodianski, Haim, 43, 216
Boschwitz, Friedemann Philipp, 86
Bourgeois Morality and Society, 6, 12–14, 39–40, 58–62, 101–106, 129–130, 176, 180
Bradley, Philips, 125
Brett, Gordon, 219
Brockdorff, Cay von, 97
Bruell, Christopher, 160
Brunner, Emil, 86
Bruno, Giordano, 49
Buber, Martin, 15, 21, 23, 29, 31–32, 81, 86, 92, 149–150, 154, 197, 215

Buchanan, Scott, 115
Bultmann, Rudolf, 81, 86
Burger, Ronna, 220–221
Burke, Edmund, 95, 125, 152, 155, 172, 180
Burnam, Jeffrey, 160
Burnyeat, Myles F., 221
Bush, George W., Jr., 157
Butterworth, Charles, 160

Caillois, Roger, 67
Calvin, John (Jean Calvin), 44, 50
Caplan, Jerrold R., 196
Cassel, David, 41
Cassirer, Ernst, 15–16, 65–66, 86, 97
Catlin, George Edward, 219
Cavendish, William, 90–91
Cephalus, 211
Cicero (Marcus Tullius Cicero), 13, 101, 155, 172
Claremont Men's College (California), 187, 195
Clinias, 210–211
Cobban, Alfred, 147
Cohen, Hermann, 12, 15, 19, 29–36, 40–41, 44, 47, 52, 73–75, 94–95, 119, 196, 216
Cohen, Hymen Ezra, 219
Collingwood, Robin George, 155, 171
Columbus, Christopher (Cristoforo Colombo), 180
Common Sense, 18, 72, 78, 134, 143, 168, 174, 183, 206–207
Comte, Auguste, 155
Contemplative Life, 3, 38, 50, 77–78, 111–112, 118, 167, 201–202, 212–214
Corbin, Henry, 67
Costa, Uriel da, 44, 49, 68
Cox, Richard, 160
Crito, 206–207
Critobulus, 202

Cropsey, Joseph, 124, 151–152, 157, 160, 187, 195, 197, 208, 223
Cunow, Heinrich, 97
Cyrus II of Persia (Cyrus the Great), 205

Dannhauser, Werner, 152, 156, 159, 160, 223
David, Jennie, 11
Decisionism, 38, 58–62, 94, 108
Democracy, 5, 13, 15, 27, 34–35, 69, 194
Democritus, 49
Demosthenes, 101
Descartes, René, 74, 77, 93–95, 125, 152, 168
Deutsch, Kenneth L., 160, 196, 221, 223
Dewey, John, 123
Diamond, Martin, 152
Dilthey, Wilhelm, 71, 97
Dionysodorus, 206–207
Discourses on the First Decade of Titus Livius (Machiavelli), 6, 155, 157, 159, 177–179, 205
Divine Law, 73–80, 111–112, 140–141, 173–174, 208–214
Donoso Cortés, Juan, 62
Dostoevsky, Fyodor, 85
Drury, Shadia B., 221

Ebbinghaus, Julius, 18, 56–57, 65, 97, 217
Ehrenberg, Hans Philipp, 86
Eidelberg, Paul, 160
Eisner, Kurt, 12
Elbogen, Ismar, 45, 216
Eliade, Mircea, 149
Emancipation, 15, 23–24, 27–36, 41–42, 45–46, 132
Enlightenment, 5, 15–23, 32–35, 42–51, 71–78, 93–98

Epicure, 44, 49, 68
Euclid, 98
Euripides, 101
Euthydemus, 206–207
Euthydemus (Plato), 195, 205–206
Exile, 2–3, 23–24, 65–66, 85–89, 113–117, 163
Existentialism, 37–40, 54, 94, 153

Feiler, Arthur, 124
Feuchtwanger, Ludwig, 220
Feuerbach, Ludwig, 49
Fraenkel, Eduard, 15
Fraenkel, Zacharias, 41
Frank, Erich, 65
Freies Jüdisches Lehrhaus, 18, 30, 37, 123
Freud, Siegmund, 47, 97, 150
Friedrich, Carl Joachim, 12, 58
Fromm, Erich, 215

Gadamer, Hans-Georg, 18, 66–67, 86, 92, 134, 151, 165–166, 220
Galileo (Galileo Galilei), 90, 98, 107
Gassendi, Pierre, 49
Geiger, Abraham, 41
George, Stefan, 97
German Bildung, 12–14
German Conservatism, 27, 54
German Humanism, 12–14
German-Jewish Culture, 15–16, 19, 27–29, 32, 36
  XVIII Century, 45–46
  XIX Century, 41–42
  XX Century, 41–43
German Culture and Philosophy, 12–14, 38, 96–97, 114, 124, 126–131, 163–164, 197
  XIX Century, 180–181
  XX Century, 15–19, 58–59, 126–130
Gersonides, 46–47, 53, 71, 73, 77, 88, 109, 217

Gierke, Otto von, 97
Gildin, Hilail, 151, 160
Gilson, Étienne, 66, 85, 89
Ginzberg, Asher, 21, 23
Glatzer, Nahum, 43
Glazer, Nathan, 162
Goethe, Johann Wolfgang von, 13, 27
Gogarten, Friedrich, 65, 84
Goitein, Fritz, 215
Goldwater, Barry, 160
Goldwin, Robert A., 195
Gordin, Jacob, 66
Gordon, Brett, 219
Gordon, Jacob, 216
Gorgias, 204
Gough, John W., 222
Gourevitch, Victor, 160
Graetz, Heinrich, 41
Green, Kenneth Hart, 136
Green, Simon J.D., 87, 125
Grene, David, 149
Groethuysen, Bernard, 66
Grotius, Hugo (Huig de Groot), 71, 155
Guide of the Perplexed (Maimonides), 6, 31, 74–76, 111, 136–138, 155, 158, 187–188, 221
Gurian, Waldemar, 182
Gurvitch, Georges, 66, 86
Guttmann, Julius, 19, 41–42, 44–46, 65–66, 73–74, 80–83, 86, 93, 119, 154, 216, 218

ha-Levi, Yehuda, 77, 109, 116, 119–120, 124, 221
Hardin, Charles M., 149
Harrington, James, 155
Hartmann, Nicolai, 15
Haskalah, 20
Havelock, Eric A., 171
Hayek, Friedrich August von, 149
Hebrew University of Jerusalem, 80, 108, 151, 154, 188, 198, 208

Hegel, Georg Wilhelm Friedrich, 13, 30, 67, 120, 128, 152, 155, 168, 180, 184
Heidegger, Martin, 18–19, 37–39, 47, 54, 56, 86, 94–95, 126, 128–129, 150, 166, 168, 172, 180–182, 197, 208
Heimann, Eduard, 124
Heine, Heinrich, 41
Heinemann, Fritz, 66, 86
Hermeneutics, 5, 44, 68, 70, 108, 110, 114, 118–119, 132–138, 165–166, 177–179, 193
Herodotus, 13, 117
Herzl, Theodor, 20–21, 25, 27, 132
Hesiod, 124
Hess, Moses, 41
Hiero, 143–146
Hiero (Xenophon), 67, 119, 143–144, 157, 183, 204
Himmelfarb, Milton, 223
Hinneberg, Paul, 65
Hirst, Aggie, 222
Historicism, 2, 6, 48, 55–58, 74, 108, 119–121, 128, 133, 143, 148, 153, 169–172, 180–182, 197
History of Philosophy, 49, 57, 68, 73–74, 83, 95, 109, 113, 132–135, 156, 171
Hitler, Adolf, 6, 27, 58, 82, 130, 164
Hobbes, Thomas, 3, 18, 44, 48–49, 54–55, 57–61, 66–72, 77, 81, 84–85, 87–108, 113, 125, 139, 150–153, 155, 158, 163, 167, 172, 175–176, 180–181, 187, 190, 208, 218–219
Hochschule für die Wissenschaft des Judentums, 19, 41, 139, 218
Holmes, Stephen, 221
Homer, 13, 101
Hooker, Robert, 125
Horace (Quintus Horatius Flaccus), 13
Horkheimer, Max, 97

Hula, Erich, 124
Hume, David, 49, 152, 168
Husik, Isaac, 172, 218
Husserl, Edmund, 17–19, 47, 122, 196
Hutchins, Robert Maynard, 125, 148–149
Hyamson, Moses, 220–221

Ibn Tibbon, Samuel, 188

Jabotinsky, Vladimir, 22
Jacobi, Friedrich Heinrich, 15–16, 46–48
Jaeger, Werner, 18–19
Jaffa, Harry V., 124, 152, 160, 195
Jaspers, Karl, 164–165, 222
Jellinek, Georg, 97
Jewish Faith, 14, 23–24, 27, 28–33, 36, 41–42, 75, 83, 114, 136, 198–199, 217
Jewish Orthodoxy, 14–15, 19–21, 26, 31–35, 43, 46–48, 51–53, 72–74, 94–95, 217
Jewish Tradition, 11–12, 20, 22–25, 28, 31–33, 40–43, 47, 83, 138, 199–200
Jhering, Rudolf von, 97
Jodl, Friedrich, 97
Johnson, Alvin, 115, 119, 123, 125
Jonas, Hans, 15, 86
Joseph, Max, 215
Jouvenel, Bertrand de, 149
Jüdischer Wanderbund Blau-Weiss, 20
Jünger, Ernst, 126, 128–129

Kallen, Horace, 124
Kant, Immanuel, 13, 15, 33–34, 68, 83, 155, 168, 171, 180
Kartell Jüdischer Verbindungen, 19, 21
Kass, Leon, 196
Kaufmann, Felix, 124
Kelsen, Hans, 70–71, 108, 174
Kendall, Willmoore, 131, 153–154, 161, 223
Kern, Hélène, 222
Kerwin, Jerome G., 149–150

Klein, Jacob, 15, 21, 37, 53, 67, 80–81, 86, 88–92, 115–118, 120, 130, 136, 149, 151, 153, 155, 164–165, 195–197, 217–218
Kleinias, 213
Kleist, Heinrich von, 13
Klibansky, Raymond, 86
Köhler, Lotte, 222
Kojève, Alexandre, 67–68, 85–90, 92, 98–99, 120, 151, 165, 182–186, 218–219, 222
Koyré, Alexandre, 66–67, 86, 92, 120, 125, 218
Kraemer, Joel, 222
Kraus, Paul, 47, 66, 93, 109, 117
Krüger, Gerhard, 2, 38, 45–47, 56, 65, 67–68, 70, 81, 85–86, 88, 91–92, 130, 165, 187, 217–218
Kuhn, Helmut, 167
Kultur/Zivilisation Debate, 54, 71, 97, 126–129

Lacan, Jacques, 67
Lagarde, Paul de, 24
Laird, John, 85, 89
Landsberg, Paul Ludwig, 86
Lange, Friedrich Albert, 97
Laski, Harold, 89, 115
Laws (Plato), 75, 88, 109–111, 118, 125, 142, 155, 189, 196–197, 207–211, 213–214
Leiris, Michel, 67
Léon, Paul, 219
Leoni, Bruno, 149
Lerner, Ralph, 152, 158, 160, 188, 223
Lessing, Gotthold Ephraim, 3, 13, 46, 116, 118, 124
Lévi, Sylvain, 66
Levy, Israel, 41
Liberalism, 20, 27–29, 32, 39, 68, 100–105
    Ancient Liberalism, 193–194

244 | Index

Liberalism *(continued)*
  Critique of Liberalism, 5, 12–14, 20, 22, 57–63, 148, 220
  Modern Liberalism, 27–32, 68–69, 100–101, 104–105, 170–171, 193–194
Lichtheim, George, 1
Livy (Titus Livius), 13, 101, 178–179, 204–205
Locke, John, 70, 95, 125, 152–153, 155, 172, 180–181
Lomnitz, Johanna, 117
Lowenthal, David, 124, 151, 160
Löwenthal, Leo, 215
Löwith, Karl, 13, 15, 18, 26, 66–67, 73, 86–88, 91–92, 120–121, 130, 165, 184, 187, 197, 217
Lubienski, Zbigniew, 68, 89, 218
Lucretius (Titus Lucretius Carus), 151, 187
Lukács, György, 97
Luther, Martin, 13, 152
Lycurgus, 118

Machiavelli, Niccolò, 1, 3, 6, 9, 44, 49, 95, 122, 150, 152, 155, 157–158, 163, 176–180, 190, 196, 203–205, 208
Macpherson, Crawford B., 187, 222
Magid, Henry M., 124, 152, 160
Mahdi, Muhsin, 151–152, 160
Maimonides, Moses, 2–3, 5–6, 19, 41, 44, 46–48, 50, 53, 57, 66, 71–80, 82–84, 88, 92–95, 98, 108–111, 113, 115–116, 118–119, 135–139, 149–150, 152, 155, 163, 167, 187–188, 208, 220–222
Mannheim, Karl, 56
Mansfield, Harvey Jr., 152
Maritain, Jacques, 66
Marjolin, Robert, 120
Marschak, Jacob, 124

Marsilius of Padua (Marsilio da Padova), 152, 155
Marx, Karl, 39, 49, 152, 155, 180, 191
Mass Culture, 6, 123–124, 161–162
Massignon, Louis, 66, 149
Masters, Roger, 160
Mayer, Carl, 124
McKeon, Richard, 115, 126, 153
Medieval Islamic Philosophy, 52–54, 71–78, 92–95, 108–112, 139–142
Medieval Jewish Philosophy, 31, 46–47, 52–54, 71–78, 80–84, 92–95, 172
Megillos, 210, 213
Meier, Heinrich, 217
Meinecke, Friedrich, 97
Mendelssohn, Moses, 3, 15, 31, 40–42, 45–46, 48, 73–74, 81, 83, 94, 150, 187, 216–217, 226
Merleau-Ponty, Maurice, 67
Merriam, Charles, 126, 147
Messianism, 22, 24, 28, 33, 185, 192
Michaelis, Erich, 215
Minos, 209
Mintz, Samuel I., 187, 222
Mittwoch, Eugen, 45, 216
Modern Rationalism, 12, 14, 16–17, 36–39, 52–54, 74, 93–96
Modern State, 106–108, 121–122
Modernity, 92–96, 167–168
  Crisis of Modernity, 16–18, 20, 38–39
  Critique of Modernity, 14, 49–52, 55–57, 106–108
  Foundation of Modernity, 59–60, 68–69, 176–177, 179–181
Moeller van den Bruck, Arthur, 126
Momigliano, Arnaldo, 110, 149
Montesquieu (Charles-Louis de Secondat), 151, 155
More, Thomas, 155
Morgenthau, Hans, 148

Moses, 33, 51, 150
Moses, Walter, 215
Motzkin, Aryeh L., 160
Munk, Solomon, 41
Murley, John A., 160, 196, 221, 223
Myers, David N., 216

Nagy, Imre, 191
Natorp, Paul, 15, 166
Natural Law, 99–102, 108, 125, 181, 187, 211
Natural Right, 34, 54, 61, 70–71, 97–103, 108, 117, 119, 125, 150, 155, 167–169, 172–175, 180–181, 205
Nazism, 114, 124, 126, 128–129, 147, 164
Nef, John Ulrich, 114, 125, 148, 219–220
Neoconservatism, 157–158
Neo-Kantian Philosophy, 15–16, 34–35, 43–44, 80–84, 94
New School for Social Research (New York), 4, 114–117, 120, 123, 125, 130, 142, 147, 152, 176, 199, 220
Nietzsche, Friedrich, 3, 12–14, 22, 27, 38–39, 47, 54, 93–97, 128, 152, 155, 168, 181, 185, 196, 208
Nihilism, 13, 53–54, 73, 84, 93–97, 124–130, 168, 174–175, 208
Nordau, Max, 21
Nordmann, Ingeborg, 222
Norton, Anne, 221

Oakeshott, Michael, 92, 148, 219
Osgood, Robert, 160
Otto, Rudolf, 16–17

Paine, Thomas, 152
Pangle, Thomas L., 160
Pantheismusstreit, 16, 46, 116
Passerin d'Entrèves, Alessandro, 147–148

Pekarsky, Maurice, 150, 199
Pekelis, Alexander, 125
Persecution, 5, 8, 118, 124, 133–135, 142, 172, 203
Petry, Thomas, 66
Petry, Walther, 66
Peyrère, Isaac de la, 44, 49, 68
Pilling, Iris, 222
Pines, Shlomo, 66, 93, 154–155, 187–188, 219
Plato, 1–2, 5, 12–13, 38, 48, 55–57, 66–69, 71, 75–76, 79–80, 88, 94–95, 100, 109–111, 115, 118–122, 124–125, 135, 137, 139–142, 150–152, 155, 158, 172, 175, 187, 189–192, 195–197, 201–202, 205, 207–208, 223
Pocock, John G.A., 221
Political Conservatism, 3–4, 5–9, 21–23, 85–86, 123–124, 163, 189, 192–193
Political Philosophy, 6–9, 62–63, 68–79, 97–112, 125–126, 142–146, 152, 167–193, 198–214
  Ancient Greek, 142–146, 190–194, 205–214
  Islamic and Jewish Medieval Philosophy, 71–80, 108–112, 135–142
  Early Modernity, 175–179, 201–205
  XVII Century, 68–71, 97–108
  XVIII and XIX Centuries, 15, 30–36, 45–47, 73–74
  XX Century, 19–26, 57–63, 70–71, 96–97, 126–132, 182–186
Political Realism, 21, 192
Popper, Karl, 149
Positivism, 48, 108, 153–154, 169–170
  Legal Positivism, 70, 108, 174–175
  Social Positivism, 4–5, 119, 121, 169–172
Prince (Machiavelli), 6, 155

Index | 245

Pritchett, Charles Herman, 149, 163
Progress, 13, 38–39, 56–59, 71, 83, 94–99, 184–186
Protagoras, 204

Queneau, Raymond, 67, 120, 183
Querelle des anciens et des modernes, 54, 71, 80, 98, 120, 122, 148

Rawidowicz, Simon, 43, 45, 81, 86, 93, 154, 216
Read, Conyers, 114
Reinhardt, Karl, 15, 149
Relativism, 38, 53, 56, 74, 84, 94–95, 109, 166, 170–171, 175
Republic (Plato), 75, 111, 125, 139, 150, 155, 157, 159, 189, 191–193, 209, 211, 213–214
Return, 2, 55, 71–74
  to Classical Philosophy, 37–38, 98, 143, 190–192
  to Judaism, 14–16, 19–20, 28–32, 36, 43, 47–48, 52, 94
Rey, Abel, 66, 86
Reynolds, Noel B., 219
Ricoeur, Paul, 149
Riezler, Kurt, 123–125
Rockefeller Foundation, 58, 65, 68, 85, 87–89, 218
Rosen, Stanley, 152, 160
Rosenzweig, Franz, 15, 17–18, 29–32, 37, 40–41, 44–45, 47, 52, 57, 74, 84, 86, 94, 119, 216
Rotenstreich, Nathan, 83
Rousseau, Jean-Jacques, 70, 95, 119, 121, 124, 150, 155, 172, 180–181, 190

Saadia, Gaon, 19, 47
Salomon, Albert, 124–125
Saner, Hans, 222
Saxonhouse, Arlene W., 219

Schaefer, David L., 223
Scheler, Max, 16
Schelsky, Helmut, 97
Schiller, Friedrich, 12–13
Schleiermacher, Friedrich, 83, 118
Schmitt, Carl, 45, 52, 55, 58–63, 65–66, 68–69, 83, 94–95, 97, 100, 108, 126, 128–129, 217–218
Schocken, Salman, 92
Scholem, Gershom, 1–2, 15, 19, 25, 37, 43, 66, 73, 80–83, 87–88, 92, 134, 151, 154, 165, 187–188, 192, 196–198, 200, 215, 222–223
Schopenhauer, Arthur, 12
Schrock, Thomas S., 160
Schultz, Theodore, 148
Schütz, Alfred, 125
Sée, Henri, 87
Seneca (Lucius Annaeus Seneca), 101
Shakespeare, William, 9, 151
Sheppard, Eugene R., 115
Shils, Edward S., 147–149, 221
Sidney Sussex College (Cambridge), 87
Siegfried, André, 67
Simon, Ernst, 21, 92, 215
Simon, Yves R., 149, 222
Simonides, 143–146
Sinclair, Elsa M., 92
Smith, Adam, 180
Smith, J. Winfree, 196, 124
Socialism, 12–13, 35–36, 180–181
Socrates, 55, 66, 116, 118, 135, 139–141, 151, 180, 182, 187, 189–190, 195–196, 202–203, 205–207, 209–211
Sombart, Werner, 97
Sophistry, 74–76, 93, 205–207
Sophocles, 13, 151
Sovereignty, 107–108
Spanier, Arthur, 216
Speier, Hans, 121, 151
Spengler, Oswald, 20, 38–39, 47, 86, 97, 126, 128–129, 191

Spinoza, Baruch, 3, 19, 27, 32–36, 41, 44–46, 48–51, 53–55, 57, 66, 68, 70–72, 74, 77, 80, 84, 88, 92–95, 97–98, 103, 109, 116, 119, 124–125, 132, 136, 139, 155, 167, 176, 180, 187, 217–218
Staples, Brent, 221
Stein, Lorenz von, 97
Steinschneider, Moritz, 41
Steinthal, Hermann, 41
Stenzel, Julius, 86
Stern, Josef, 222
Stern, Selma, 216
St. John's College (Annapolis), 115, 118–119, 151, 195–197
Storing, Herbert J., 152, 157, 160
Strauss, Abraham, 12
Strauss, Bettina, 47, 117
Strauss, Bruno, 43, 216
Strauss, David, 11
Strauss, Hugo, 11
Strauss, Meyer, 11
Strauss, Thomas, 89, 116
Strauss Clay, Jenny, 117
Stuart Mill, John, 151
Swift, Jonathan, 151

Tacitus (Publius Cornelius Tacitus or Gaius Cornelius Tacitus), 13, 101
Tarcov, Nathan, 195
Taubes, Jacob, 222
Täubler, Eugen, 41–42
Tawney, Richard H., 87, 89, 92, 114–115, 125, 148, 219–221
Thackeray, William Makepeace, 85
Theological-Political Problem, 19, 58, 61–63, 72–80, 84, 94, 116, 136–138, 199–201, 208–214
Thomas Aquinas (Tommaso d'Aquino), 125, 169, 172, 200
Thrasymachus, 141

Thucydides, 13, 90, 101, 117, 155, 189–191, 196–197
Tillich, Paul, 65
Tocqueville, Alexis de, 152
Tönnies, Ferdinand, 89, 91, 96, 129
Toynbee, Arnold J., 149
Tractatus Theologico-Politicus (Spinoza), 19, 32–36, 41, 44, 48, 50, 52–53, 158
Troeltsch, Ernst, 16, 97
Tyranny, 9, 142–143
   Ancient Tyranny, 142–146
   Modern Tyranny, 121–122, 142–143, 182–186

Universal and Homogeneous State, 182–186
University of Berlin, 15, 18–19, 37, 44, 47
University of Chicago, 114, 147–151, 158, 162, 164, 187, 195, 199, 217–222
University of Freiburg, 17–18, 57, 86, 197
University of Marburg, 15, 17, 46, 67
Utopia, 183–185m 189–190, 192–193

Vajda, Georges, 93, 154, 219
Veblen, Thorstein, 123
Vico, Giambattista, 155
Virgil (Publius Vergilius Maro), 13
Voegelin, Eric, 88, 97, 121–122, 153, 182–183, 220, 222
Voltaire (François-Marie Arouet), 49, 71, 77, 94

Waelhens, Alphonse de, 219
Weber, Max, 16–18, 38, 47, 61, 97, 104, 129, 155, 169–172, 181, 187
Weil, Eric, 120
Weimar Republic, 3, 5–6, 20, 27, 38–39, 73, 127, 187

Weinberg, Hans, 25–26, 215
Weltsch, Robert, 21
White, Howard B., 124, 152, 160, 224
White, Leonard D., 126, 148
Wild, John, 120
Winiarski, Warren, 152
Winograd, Richard, 150
Wisdom, 3, 6–8, 118, 137–138, 142, 144–145, 167–168, 184–185, 189–194, 199–201, 207–214
　Love of Wisdom, 2–3, 71–76, 95–96, 108–112, 134–135, 138–142, 201–214
　Search for Wisdom, 2–3, 7, 50–51, 55–57, 62–63, 72, 79–80, 93–96, 110–112, 115–116, 132–133, 136–137, 167–168, 172–173, 190–194, 200, 207–214
Wissenschaft des Judentums, 3, 15, 19–20, 30, 41–43, 45–46, 70, 74, 80, 139, 216, 218
Wolin, Sheldon, 187

Wood, Gordon S., 221

Xenophon, 3, 5, 13, 66–67, 95, 117–120, 124, 143–145, 148, 155, 157–158, 182–184, 187, 189–190, 196, 201–205, 220
Xenos, Nicholas, 221

Young-Bruehl, Elisabeth, 222

Zeus, 209–210
Zionism, 2–3, 12–16, 19–32, 35–37, 43, 47–48, 52–53, 55, 57, 74, 81, 87, 113–114, 131–132, 215
　Cultural Zionism, 19–29, 32–36, 47–48, 51–53
　Political Zionism, 13–14, 16, 19–29, 37, 40, 47–48, 53, 57, 74, 81, 131–132
　Religious Zionism, 14–16, 19–29
Zunz, Leopold, 41

CPSIA information can be obtained
at www.ICGtesting.com
Printed in the USA
BVHW081857090223
658229BV00003B/62